GCSE Business

Revising for GCSE Business can feel like a full-time job, and the Grade 9-1 course is tougher than ever. Luckily, CGP is here to help...

This amazing all-in-one book is packed with revision notes and questions, along with business examples to really get you in the zone.

What's more, we've also included plenty of worked exam-style questions, so you can pitch yourself perfectly in the exams.

How to access your free Online Edition

This book includes a free Online Edition to read on your PC, Mac or tablet. You'll just need to go to **cgpbooks.co.uk/extras** and enter this code:

3054 3516 6248 6497

By the way, this code only works for one person. If somebody else has used this book before you, they might have already claimed the Online Edition.

Complete
Revision & Practice

Everything you need to pass the exams!

Contents

What to Expect in The Exams

Section 1 — Business in the Real World

Section 2 — Influences on Business

Section 3 — Business Operations

Section 4 — Human Resources

Section 5 — Marketing

Section 6 — Finance

Practice Exams

Published by CGP
Based on the classic CGP style created by Richard Parsons

Editors: Charlotte Burrows, Emily Howe, Ciara McGlade and Rachael Rogers

Contributor: Colin Harber-Stuart

ISBN: 978 1 78294 691 5

With thanks to Victoria Skelton and Karen Wells for the proofreading.

With thanks to Ana Pungartnik for the copyright research.

Printed by Bell & Bain Ltd, Glasgow.
Clipart from Corel®

The Exams

Before you start with your Business revision, it's worth getting to grips with what the exams will be like. The next few pages are all about what the examiners will look for, and the types of questions you might have to answer.

Make Sure You Know the **Structure** of Your **Exams**

To help you prepare for sitting your exams, try to find out the answers to the following questions:

1) How many exam papers do you need to sit?
2) What sections of your course will be tested in each paper?
3) How much time do you get to complete each paper?
4) How many marks is each paper worth?
5) What percentage of your total Business GCSE is each paper worth?

The Examiners are Looking for **Three Types of Skills**

There are basically three types of skill and knowledge that you need to show to get marks in the exams:

Demonstrate knowledge and understanding

- This skill is all about recalling, selecting and communicating.
- You need to show that you've got a really good understanding of the facts, and that you can use appropriate business terms, e.g. sole trader, marketing mix, supply chain.

Apply knowledge and understanding

- This skill is all about applying what you know to different situations.
- Make sure your answer is relevant to the situation that's been described.
- For example, an exam question might tell you about a sole trader who wants to buy a new piece of equipment, and ask you to suggest how they could raise the necessary finance. Here, you wouldn't want to suggest that the company issue more shares (since only a limited company can have shares and sole traders are unlimited).

Analyse and evaluate to demonstrate understanding, make judgements and draw conclusions

- This skill is all about using evidence to make judgements and reach conclusions.
- For example, if you recommend that a business raises money using a mortgage rather than an overdraft, you need to explain why, using what you know about finance.
- Your ideas need to be structured in a logical way so that your arguments make sense.
- Often, these questions won't have a right answer. The important thing is using evidence from the question to support the conclusion you've come to.

You get marks for showing different skills in the exams...

Preparing for your exams involves more than just learning the material. Finding out what sections of the course are tested in each paper you'll sit means you can revise the right material for each exam.

Answering Questions

Doing well in Business is made a whole lot easier if you know how to answer the questions...

Make Sure you **Read the Question**

1) Command words are just the bit of the question that tell you what to do.
2) Here's a summary of the most common command words you're likely to come across and an idea of what you'll be expected to do for each one:

Command word	What to do
State, Give or Identify	These words ask for a statement — you don't need to back it up with evidence. You may have to interpret data shown on a graph or in a table to get your answer.
Define	You need to write down what a term means.
Calculate	Some questions ask for a bit of maths. Remember to show your working.
Complete	You need to fill in the missing parts of some information you've been given (e.g. complete a table).
Explain or Outline	This means you need to give reasons for things. You need to show that you understand how business issues can impact other areas of a business.
Discuss	You should give a long answer, which describes and explains a business issue.
Analyse	This means "Examine in detail." You should talk about the main features of the thing you're analysing. Then explain how these features collectively affect the business.
Recommend or Justify	You're likely to be given some information about a business and asked to say whether the business should do something, or to choose between two options for what the business could do.
Evaluate	You should discuss and analyse both sides of an issue. You should finish your answer with a conclusion giving an overall judgement.
Give reasons for your answer	This means you need to include lots of points and explain why they're relevant to your answer. Link your ideas together to build a balanced argument.
Use evidence to support your answer	This means you need to pick out specific information from a case study or piece of data that you've been given, in order to back up your answer.

3) In general, you'll need to spend more time and write more for questions that are worth more marks.
4) For questions worth lots of marks, it might help to write a quick plan to make sure you don't miss anything, and to make sure you show all the skills from the previous page.

Command words tell you how to answer a question...

For each question in the exam, look at the command word and the number of marks it's worth. Use these to work out what the question is asking for and roughly how long you should take to answer it.

Answering Questions

Some questions are quite straightforward when it comes to answering them. Others will need you to think a bit more about how to answer them and what you should be writing to get as many marks as you can.

You'll have to Answer Questions About **Case Studies**

1) For questions that are based on case study information or on data, make sure you use evidence from the case study or data set as well as your knowledge of Business in your answer.

2) For questions that use command words such as 'recommend' or 'evaluate', there may be advantages and disadvantages of a situation to think about — to get all the marks, you'll need to give both sides of the argument before coming to a conclusion.

You'll often have to consider how different parts of a business work together when answering case study questions.

3) Before you get started on your answer, read the case study and any data all the way through. Then read the whole question carefully and make sure you've understood what you're being asked to do.

You'll be Tested on Your **Maths Skills**

1) Maths is everywhere, and your GCSE Business exams are no exception.

2) You might be asked do some calculations using financial data, or interpret a graph.

3) If you're doing a calculation question, make sure you show your working — even if your final answer's wrong, you could still get some marks if your method was correct.

4) And don't forget to take a calculator to the exams.

Read all the information before you start your answer...

Questions that are worth lots of marks in the exams are likely to be testing your judgement as well as your knowledge of business. For these questions, make sure you support your ideas with evidence — either from your own knowledge, or from information that's been given to you.

Why Businesses Exist

There are lots of different reasons why someone might come up with a new idea for a business. In the end, the purpose of most businesses can be boiled down to one of two things — either to provide goods or services.

Businesses Supply **Goods** or **Services**

1) Businesses sell products to customers who are willing to pay for them.
2) The products a business sells should satisfy the needs of the customers they hope to sell to. These needs may include the price or quality of the product, the choice of products or the convenience of buying and using the product (see p.5).
3) Products can be goods or services:

- Goods are physical items like books or furniture.
- Services are actions performed by other people to aid the customer, e.g. barbers and plumbers provide services.

4) Some businesses provide goods or services that are 'needs' — things that you can't live without (like water and food).
5) Others provide goods or services that are 'wants' — things you would like to have, but can survive without (like holidays and jewellery).

New Business Ideas Come About for a **Variety** of Reasons

1) The world we live in is always changing, and so businesses must be dynamic and adapt to these changes.
2) This often results in people coming up with new business ideas.

- Many new business ideas come about from changes in technology. For example, the invention of tablets meant lots of people came up with ideas for apps that could be used on these devices.
- Some business ideas come about because of changes in what customers want. For example, these days people are much more concerned about the environment, so many businesses have started up that offer more environmentally friendly products.
- Sometimes, a good or service becomes obsolete — this means it's no longer used, usually because it has become out-dated and has been replaced by something else. Business owners have to come up with new ideas so that their business survives. E.g. as video tapes became obsolete, video rental stores started stocking dvds in order to survive.

3) New business ideas will either be completely original (there hasn't been anything like it before) or an adaptation of an existing product or idea (but the business will have found a way to improve it or make it more relevant to customers at the time).

BUSINESS EXAMPLE

In the 1970s, James Dyson came up with the idea of a vacuum cleaner that didn't need dust bags. Customers wanted to buy the vacuum cleaner, as it meant they no longer had to buy replacement bags and the new vacuum cleaner didn't lose suction.

A business needs to sell things that people want to buy...

You need to know the definitions of lots of business terms to pass your Business GCSE. As you're revising, you could make a list of business terms you come across and their meanings (e.g. goods and services). Then you could check you're confident you know each entry on your list before exam time.

Enterprise

Enterprise is all about turning business ideas into reality. To make a business a success, the owners must have a clear idea of the purpose of their business activity.

Businesses **Wouldn't Exist** Without **Enterprise**

1) Business enterprise is the process of identifying new business opportunities, and then taking advantage of them. It can involve thinking of a new idea, and then developing it into a new business, or helping an existing business to expand by coming up with new ideas.
2) All business activity needs to have at least one purpose. A purpose could be to:

- Provide people with a good or a service (see previous page).

- Meet customer needs — this means providing goods and services that people will want to buy. Customer needs often change so firms may need to change the products they sell to keep up.

- Add value to an existing product — this means a business finds a way to improve a product, so customers are willing to pay more for it compared to competitors' products. There are several ways a business can add value to a product. For example, it could:
    - make a product more convenient for customers to get or use (e.g. a mobile hairdresser might be more convenient for customers than having to visit a hairdresser's salon).
    - build a good brand image for a product (see p.118) — customers will be more willing to spend money on the product as they'll recognise the brand and know that it's trustworthy and desirable.
    - improve the product's design or quality.
    - give the product a unique selling point (USP). This is some feature that makes it different from its competitors, which makes it an original product.

  A firm's brand image is the impression that customers have of the firm or its products.

- Distribute goods — e.g. a business might buy products from a manufacturer and then sell them on to other businesses or to individual customers.

- Benefit other people — this could be by making goods or providing a service. For example, there are businesses that organise volunteers to go into schools and help children learn how to read. Many of these businesses are not-for-profit organisations (see p.12).

- Fulfill a business opportunity — this is an investment in e.g. equipment, which will allow an individual (or a group of people) to start a business. For example, a person may buy rights to a franchise. This is where they start their own business under the name of another company (see p.13). They may do this if they notice that branches of the company aren't available in their local area.

3) An entrepreneur is someone who takes on the risks of enterprise activity.
4) Entrepreneurs are really important — without them, we'd never have any new businesses.

To have enterprise, people need to both spot and take opportunities...

Entrepreneurs need to have a really good vision of the business they want to create and what the main purposes of its activity will be. There's much more about entrepreneurs coming up on the next page.

Enterprise

Entrepreneurs are people who take on the risks of business enterprise (see the previous page).
It's time for some more about why they might do this and the personal qualities they're likely to have.

Entrepreneurs Have Different Objectives

There are lots of possible reasons why someone might decide to become an entrepreneur. For example...

1) There might be financial reasons — if the business is successful and makes a profit, the entrepreneur could earn more money than they did before. This could give them a better quality of life.
2) Some people start a business when they identify a gap in the market — i.e. they think of a useful good or service that no other business is providing.
3) Some people might want the independence of being their own boss. This means they can decide what they do each day, and make the decisions about how the business will be run. They might also enjoy more flexible working hours, meaning it's easier to fit work around other commitments, like childcare.
4) Some people want to follow an interest. E.g. a history-lover might set up a tour company for a historical site. Being interested in what they do can a give a person a lot of job satisfaction.
5) Some people are simply dissatisfied with their current job. Starting up a new business can help them to feel happier and more motivated to go to work.
6) For many people, running a business is a challenge that they enjoy.
7) Some people start a business because they want to benefit others. This could be done by starting a charity, or by having social objectives for their business.

Entrepreneurs Need Particular Qualities

A successful entrepreneur is likely to have most of the following characteristics:

- Hardworking and determined — it takes a lot of hard work and determination to turn ideas into practice. Entrepreneurs often work long hours. To begin with, they may be working alone, so they have to do all the different tasks involved in running a business, such as accounting, business planning and sales and marketing.
- Organised — entrepreneurs have to have good organisational skills to keep on top of all the day-to-day tasks of running the business as well as planning for the future. E.g. they have to make sure they're properly prepared for meetings and that they're in control of their finances.
- Innovative and creative — to come up with new ideas and think of solutions to problems that come up.
- A willingness to take a calculated risk — there are lots of unknowns involved in running a business. An entrepreneur will probably give up their current job and invest money that they could lose if the business fails. They can write a business plan to work out if the business is a good idea (see p.26), but they can't know exactly what's going to happen before they start.
- Able to make business decisions — there are lots of decisions that need to be made when running a business, and not all of them are easy to make. For example, an entrepreneur needs to be able to decide on the business's aims, its structure, who to employ, how to grow and what to do if things start going wrong.
- Confident — an entrepreneur needs to be confident that their business idea is a good one, and able to persuade other people that it is as well.

It takes a certain type of person to be an entrepreneur...

Entrepreneurs may have different reasons for starting their business, but they're likely to have lots of similar qualities. Make sure you know what these qualities are, and why they're important for running a business.

Sectors of the Economy

The types of things that businesses do can be broken down into three main categories — making raw materials, manufacturing goods or providing services. These three categories are the three sectors of the economy.

The **Sector** a Business is in Tells You **What** it **Provides**

There are three sectors of the economy:

Primary Sector

1) The primary sector produces raw materials — any natural resources which are used to make goods or services.
2) They can be extracted from the ground. The mining industry provides coal, oil, gas, and metals like iron. The quarrying industry provides stone.
3) They can be grown. E.g. the farming industry grows food (both animals and crops are natural resources).
4) They can be collected. The fishing industry "collects" fish from the sea.

Secondary Sector

1) The secondary sector manufactures goods. They turn raw materials into finished goods. For example, a chocolate factory turns raw materials such as cocoa and milk into chocolate.
2) The building and construction industries are also in the secondary sector.

Tertiary Sector

1) The tertiary sector provides services.
2) Some firms provide services for other businesses — like warehousing and advertising.
3) Some firms provide services for consumers — like hairdressers, shops and restaurants.
4) Financial services like banking and insurance are used by both businesses and consumers.

Many businesses are part of more than one sector.

- Cumbrian Cow is a café that sells ice cream. So it's part of the tertiary sector.
- The owners of Cumbrian Cow manufacture the ice cream themselves, so they're part of the secondary sector as well.
- The owners also own a dairy farm which produces the milk they use to make the ice cream. The farm is part of the primary sector.
- So the owners have businesses in all three sectors of the economy.

All three sectors are important...

Each sector of the economy needs each of the others. For example, the secondary sector manufactures products. Without the primary sector, it wouldn't be able to get the raw materials needed to produce these products. Without the tertiary sector, it wouldn't be able to distribute the products once they've been made.

Factors of Production

Businesses couldn't operate without resources. Unfortunately, there are only limited amounts of most resources.

There are Four Factors of Production

Resources are needed to make products. Resources can be divided into four factors of production. These factors are: land, labour, capital and enterprise.

1 Land

As well as actual 'territory', land includes all the Earth's natural resources:

- Non-renewable resources, such as natural gas, oil and coal.
- Renewable resources like wind or tidal power, or wood from trees.
- Materials extracted by mining (e.g. diamonds and gold).
- Water.
- Animals found in an area.

Nearly all things that fall under the category of 'land' are scarce — there aren't enough natural resources to satisfy the demands of everyone.

2 Labour

1) Labour is the work done by the people who contribute to the production process.
2) Different people have different levels of education, experience or training. These factors can make some people more 'valuable' or productive in the workplace than others.

Individuals and firms are rewarded for providing these factors, e.g. with wages, rent, interest or profit.

3 Capital

1) Capital is the equipment, factories and schools that help to produce goods or services.
2) Capital is different from land because capital has to be made first.

4 Enterprise

Enterprise refers to the people (entrepreneurs) who take risks and create things from the other three factors of production (see page 6).

Opportunity Costs Help People Choose How to Use Resources

1) Most factors of production are limited. To work out the best way to use them, managers will often look at the opportunity cost of a decision.
2) Opportunity cost is the benefit that's given up in order to do something else — it's the cost of the choice that's made. It's the idea that money or time spent doing one thing is likely to mean missing out on doing something else.
3) So it puts a value on the product or business decision in terms of what the business had to give up to make it.
4) Businesses must choose where to use their limited resources. Managers compare opportunity costs when making decisions.

BUSINESS EXAMPLE

- Go-Kart Village have £10 000 to invest in their business.
- They could spend the money on some new go-karts or on redecorating their building.
- If they choose to redecorate, the opportunity cost is the new go-karts and the extra money they could have made from people using them.

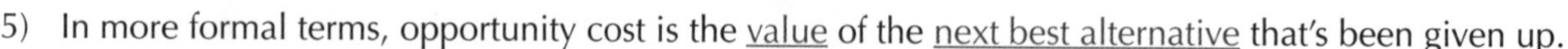

5) In more formal terms, opportunity cost is the value of the next best alternative that's been given up.

Many resources are limited, so businesses should avoid wasting them...

Managers need to know what resources they have and then they need to find the best way to use them.

Business Ownership Structures

There are a few types of business legal structure you need to know about, covered here and on the next two pages. You should know what they are, the differences between them and the advantages and disadvantages of each.

Sole Traders — the Easiest Business to Start

Sole trader businesses have just one owner (though the owner may employ other people to work for them). Most small businesses are sole traders. You don't need to do much except start trading. Examples include plumbers, hairdressers, newsagents and fishmongers.

Sole traders — advantages

1) They're easy to set up, which means they're great for start-up businesses.
2) You get to be your own boss.
3) You alone decide what happens to any profit.

Sole traders — disadvantages

1) You might have to work long hours and may not get many holidays.
2) You have unlimited liability. This means that if the business goes bust owing £10 million, you are liable (legally responsible) for paying back all of the debt — which might mean you have to sell everything you own.
3) You're unincorporated. This means the business doesn't have its own legal identity. So if anyone sues the business, they'll sue you personally.
4) It can be hard to raise money. Banks see sole traders as risky, so it may be hard to get a loan. You often have to rely on your own savings, or family and friends.

Some companies have limited liability — which means the amount of debt the owners have to pay back is limited to the amount they invested (see next page).

For more about finding finance for a business, see p.128-130.

Partnerships are Like Two or More Sole Traders

You get partnerships in businesses like accountancy firms, solicitors and doctors' surgeries. Partnerships generally have between two and twenty partners. Each partner has an equal say in making decisions and an equal share of the profits — unless they have an agreement called a deed of partnership that says different.

Partnerships — advantages

1) More owners means more ideas, and a greater range of skills and expertise — e.g. one partner might be great at sales, while another is good at planning.
2) It also means more people to share the work.
3) More owners means more capital (money) can be put into the business, so it can grow faster.

Partnerships — disadvantages

1) Each partner is legally responsible for what all the other partners do.
2) Like sole traders, most partnerships have unlimited liability (see above).
3) More owners means more disagreements. You're not the only boss. If the partners disagree about which direction the business should go in and how much time to put in, it can get unpleasant.
4) The profits are shared between the partners. So if a sole trader decides to go into partnership with another person, they could end up with less money for themselves.

The owners of sole traders and partnerships are liable for all the firm's debts...

These structures are easy to set up which makes them great for small businesses. But they do come with risks.

Business Ownership Structures

As well as the unlimited companies on the previous page, there are also two types of limited structure a business might take. The first is covered here, and the second is on the next page.

Limited Companies Are Owned by Shareholders

There are two types of limited company — private and public. But both kinds have some important differences compared to sole traders and partnerships:

See the next page for more on public limited companies.

1) A limited company is incorporated — it has a separate legal identity from the owners. So any money, property, tax bills, etc. in the company's name belong to the company, not the owners.

2) Being incorporated means the owners have limited liability. If anything goes wrong (e.g. somebody sues the company or it goes bust) it's the company that's liable, not the owners. The owners only risk losing the money that they have invested.

3) It is owned by shareholders. The more shares you own, the more control you get.

Private Limited Companies — Ownership Is Restricted

1) 'Private' means that shares can only be sold if all the shareholders agree. The shareholders are often all members of the same family.
2) Private limited companies have Ltd. after their name.

Ltd. — advantages

1) The big advantage over sole traders and partnerships is limited liability — you can't lose more than you invest.
2) Being incorporated, the company can continue trading after a shareholder dies — unlike partnerships.
3) It's easier for a Ltd. company to get a loan or mortgage than it is for a sole trader or partnership.
4) For someone to buy shares, all the other shareholders have to agree. So the owners keep a lot of control over how the business is managed and how many people get to share the profits.

It's hard for someone to take over a Ltd. company — to do so, all the shareholders of the Ltd. company would have to agree to sell shares.

Ltd. — disadvantages

1) They're more expensive to set up than partnerships because of all the legal paperwork you have to do.
2) Unlike sole traders or partnerships, the company is legally obliged to publish its accounts every year (although they don't have to be made public).

Limited liability means there's less financial risk for the owners...

Many of the shops and businesses you see on the high street will be private limited companies. Even CGP is in on the act — have a hunt at the front of the book to see if you can find a little 'Ltd.' after our name.

Business Ownership Structures

The second type of limited companies are public limited companies. Like private limited companies, they're incorporated and have limited liability, but the big difference is that the owners can't control who buys shares.

Public Limited Companies — Anyone Can Buy Shares

1) 'Public' means that the company shares are traded on a stock exchange, and can be bought and sold by anyone.
2) Firms often become public limited companies when they want to expand.
3) Public limited companies have 'PLC' after their name.

PLC — advantages

1) Much more capital can be raised by a PLC than by any other kind of business.
2) That helps the company to expand and diversify.
3) Like private limited companies, they also have the benefits of having limited liability, and being incorporated.

PLC — disadvantages

1) It can be hard to get lots of shareholders to agree on how the business is run. Each shareholder has very little say (unless they own a lot of shares).
2) It's easy for someone to buy enough shares to take over the company — if they can convince shareholders to sell.
3) The accounts have to be made public — so everyone (including competitors) can see if a business is struggling.
4) More shareholders means there's more people wanting a share of the profits.

A Business has to Choose its Legal Structure

1) When you start a new business, you need to decide whether to have limited or unlimited liability.
2) Smaller businesses (sole traders and partnerships) tend to have unlimited liability, while larger businesses have limited liability (they'll be 'Ltds' or 'PLCs').
3) The other thing to decide is the amount of control you want over how the business is run. Sole traders and private limited companies (Ltds) tend to give an entrepreneur more control than partnerships or PLCs.
4) Businesses don't have to keep the structure they start off with — the structure can change over time.
5) For example, a sole trader might form a partnership if someone they know (e.g. an employee or family member) wants to invest money into the business in return for a share of the profits.
6) Often, as a business grows, a sole trader or partnership will decide to incorporate the business and may also decide to make shares public. Most very large businesses are public limited companies.

1) The supermarket chain Morrisons started when the sole trader William Morrison started trading from a market stall in Bradford. The business did well, and he started to open stores in the Bradford area.
2) In 1940, the company was incorporated — this would have protected William Morrison's investments, and would have made it easier to raise money so the company could grow more.
3) The company continued to expand. In 1967, the company became a public limited company to help raise the funds so it could expand further.

Depending on the firm, some legal structures are better than others...

If you get asked about the best legal structure for a business, have a look at all the information you've been given before making your decision. You should think about things like the size of the business, how much money it has, how much money it needs, and how much control the owners want.

Not-For-Profit Organisations

Not-for-profit organisations aren't aiming to make a profit for their owners. Like 'for-profit' businesses, there's a huge variety of different not-for-profit organisations, and all of them need to choose the best structure.

Not-for-Profit Businesses Need to Generate Income

1) 'Not-for-profit' businesses don't try to make a profit (at least, not for their owners).

2) They need to generate enough income to cover their costs, but any surplus is put back into the business or used to fund projects that help the community.

3) There are lots of not-for-profit organisations, and their size and aims can be very different. E.g. a local amateur dramatics society might have 50 members and aim to put on a yearly show, while a larger not-for-profit firm might work in ten different countries and aim to banish world poverty.

4) Many not-for-profit organisations have charitable status. This means they get some tax relief and they're able to apply for certain grants. But they can be hard to set up as there are lots of rules they have to follow. Also, many charities are funded mainly by donations and grants — which means they may not have a stable income.

5) Social enterprises are another type of not-for-profit organisation. These make money by selling products — they are similar to 'for-profit' businesses but their aims are always centred around using their profits to benefit society in some way. As they make their own profit through what they sell, they don't rely as heavily on donations and grants as many charities.

Charities and social enterprises are types of organisation — they are not legal structures.

6) Not-for-profit firms can be hard to manage, particularly if there's always uncertainty about how much finance they'll have available, and if they rely on volunteers rather than permanent members of staff.

Not-for-Profit Businesses Must Choose a Legal Structure

1) As not-for-profit organisations can be so varied, there are many different legal structures they can have.
2) They can choose to be an 'unincorporated association'. These are easy to set up but the people who manage the organisation have unlimited liability.
3) Bigger organisations tend to be incorporated so that the people who run them have limited liability. They are often 'limited by guarantee', meaning that some of its members guarantee that they'll pay a fixed amount of money on behalf of the business if it goes bust.

Not-for-profit organisations still need to cover their costs...

Don't be put off by the fact these organisations aren't trying to make a profit. When choosing between limited and unlimited liability, the benefits and drawbacks are just the same as for other businesses.

Franchises

Now on to a slightly different type of business. Franchises use the name or products of another firm, even though they're a separate business. They can be a quick and easy way for an entrepreneur to start running a business.

Franchising Uses the Brand Name or Product of Another Firm

1) Some people will start up a business as a franchise of another company.
2) This is where they sell the products or use the trademarks of another firm. They then give the firm they're franchising from a fee or a percentage of their profits.
3) The product manufacturers are known as franchisors and the firms selling their products are franchisees.
4) Some franchises trade under the name of the franchisee but advertise that they sell a particular manufacturer's products. Car dealerships are an example of this type of franchise.
5) Branded franchises go one stage further. The franchisee buys the right to trade under the name of the franchisor. Most of the big firms in the fast-food industry are this type of franchise.

Franchising Has Benefits and Drawbacks for the Franchisee...

Franchising — advantages

- Customers will already recognise the franchisor's brand so are more likely to buy from the franchisee. This means there's less risk of the business failing.
- As franchises are less risky than starting a business from scratch, it can be easier to get a bank loan to start up.
- The franchisor might provide the franchisee with training, or help with things like management and accounting.

Franchising — disadvantages

- The franchisor might have strict rules about what the business can sell and how it can operate, so the franchisee's freedom is limited.
- The franchisee usually has to pay a lot of money to start the franchise and then make regular payments to the franchisor. These costs may mean they end up with less money than if they started a business from scratch.

...and Also for the Franchisor

1) Franchising increases a franchisor's income (as it gets money from the franchisee), and it increases the market share (see p.16) and brand awareness of products. It also means the firm doesn't have the usual risks and costs of running a new outlet — the franchisee is responsible for these.
2) However, if a franchisee has poor standards the franchisor's brand could get a bad reputation.

Allowing other people to set up franchises is one way a business can expand — it's a type of organic growth (see p.29).

A franchise is a separate business from the franchisor...

Use the internet to search for 'franchise opportunities' and read the details of two different franchises that are available to buy. Write an evaluation of which franchise you would choose to run. Think about things such as the initial investment required and the benefits each franchisor offers.

Worked Exam Questions

Understanding how to answer questions will help you to pick up marks in the exams. So have a look at the examples below to get an idea of the types of questions you might face and how to answer them.

1 Look at **Item A** below.

Item A — Special Day Bouquet:
Dirk owns Special Day Bouquet, a florist shop that provides unique bouquets for events and weddings. Dirk is the only person in the business who is able to make these bouquets. One weekend he is offered two contracts. The first is to provide bouquets and table decorations for a photo shoot for a wedding magazine. For this he would receive £600 and have his business's name printed in the magazine. The second is to provide flowers for a local stately home that is holding an art festival, for which he would receive £1000. Dirk doesn't have enough time to prepare flowers for both events, so decides to accept the offer from the stately home.

Outline which factor of production is limiting Dirk's ability to take on both contracts.

[2]

You should give one factor of production, and briefly explain why it is limited.

Sample answer:

Dirk has limited labour, as he is the only person who is able to make the bouquets and he doesn't have time to complete both orders.

Use information from the item to explain your answer.

2 Explain **one** benefit to shareholders if a business has limited liability.

[3]

Sample answer:

Having limited liability means the shareholders aren't liable for the debts of the business if it goes bust, so their financial risk is reduced as if the business fails they will only lose the money they have invested.

You should explain what limited liability means for the shareholders.

You get a mark for stating a benefit.

Make sure you explain the overall impact on the shareholders.

Exam Questions

1 Which of the following is a purpose of business activity?
Put a cross (X) in **one** correct box.

A To employ entrepreneurs. ☐
B To provide goods. ☐
C To be sustainable. ☑
D To train employees. ☐

[Total 1 mark]

2 Look at **Item A** below.

Item A — Harte & Sole:
In 2013, Bushra Ahmed realised there weren't any companies that produced fashionable, vegan-friendly and ethically produced shoes, and that people would be willing to buy them. So she quit a high-pressure job as a journalist to set up her ethical shoe company, Harte & Sole. After visiting many trade shows, she found a manufacturer who could provide her with the shoes she needed, in small quantities so she never needed to hold much stock at her small office.
In 2014, Bushra was invited to pitch her shoes to a nationwide retail chain. In the two weeks before her presentation, Bushra worked every day to prepare herself. The pitch was a success and the retail chain gave Bushra a contract to supply them with her shoes.

Analyse how Bushra has shown that she has the qualities needed to be a successful entrepreneur.

Bushra has identified a gap in the market and come up with a completely unique item that has never been seen before. ~~Most successful entrepreneurs start like this.~~ She then found a manufacturer who ~~that can~~ could supply her with the shoes. She got the shoes in small quantities because she had a small office. After slowly growing her business, she was invited to pitch her shoes to a nationwide retailer. She worked every day to prepare herself and in the end got a contract.

[Total 6 marks]

Business Aims and Objectives

Businesses need to have aims — overall goals that they want to achieve. They also need objectives, which are like mini aims (see page 17). Aims and objectives can be financial (see below) or non-financial (see next page).

Financial Aims Can be Measured in Terms of Money

Survival

Around 60% of new firms close within five years of starting, so just surviving is the main and most important short-term aim of all new businesses. This means the business needs to have enough money to stay open, e.g. to buy stock and pay staff.

Maximise Profit

The vast majority of firms will aim to maximise profits. However, it may take a few years for a new firm to make any profit at all.

Growth

Many firms will aim to grow, but growth can mean different things. E.g. it might mean increasing the number of employees, increasing the number of products sold, or increasing income from sales.

Some firms want to grow domestically (in the country where they were set up). Others want to grow internationally (expand into other countries).

Increase Shareholder Value

Limited companies have shareholders. Shareholders get a share of the firm's profits and can sell their shares to make money (the better the firm is doing, the more each share is worth). Many firms aim to increase shareholder value (make their shareholders more wealthy) by increasing the value of the firm, e.g. by making more profit or by growing.

Increase Market Share

Market share tells you what percentage of a market's total sales a particular product or company has made. When a business first starts up it has zero market share... so one of its first aims is to capture a part of the market and establish itself. It can then aim to increase its market share by taking sales away from competition, or by persuading new customers to enter the market and buy its products.

Beijing Palace has a big market share already, but New Noodles might want to try and increase its share of the market.

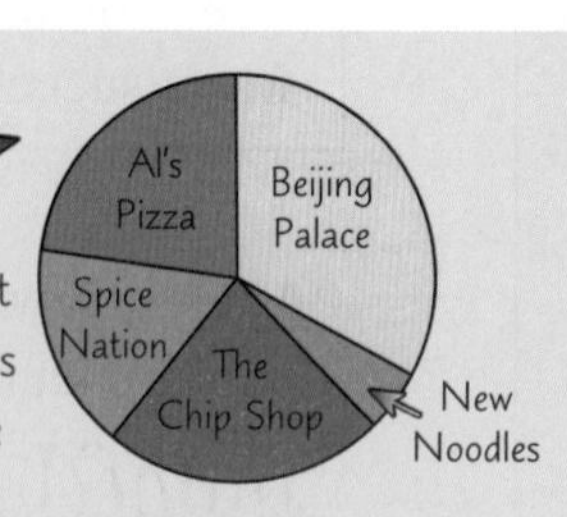

Maximise Sales

Increasing sales is a good way for a business to grow its market share. The business can monitor sales in terms of how many of a particular product it sells, or by how much money it takes in from selling its products. This is not the same as maximising profit. For example, a business might reduce prices in order to increase sales, but selling products more cheaply means it won't make as much profit (see page 25).

Achieve Financial Security

Many businesses will depend on external sources of finance such as loans or the business owners' personal savings when they first start. So an aim for a new business is likely to be achieving a point where it can depend on its own revenue to fund its activities (i.e. its sales go beyond its break-even point — see p.131).

There are many different financial aims a business can set...

Having aims is important for a firm. Managers use aims to make decisions about how the firm should be run. And having aims means anyone interested in the firm can easily work out what the business is all about.

Business Aims and Objectives

On the previous page you met some financial aims businesses may have. Not all aims are about money, though. Coming up are some non-financial aims, and a bit on how businesses use objectives to achieve their aims.

A Business May have **Non-Financial Aims**

Do What's Right Socially and Ethically

Some firms want to make sure they are acting in ways that are best for society and that society believes are morally right (e.g. many consumers think that it's wrong to test cosmetics on animals). They may also want to make sure their activities don't cause unnecessary harm to the environment. Other firms are set up to provide a service that benefits others.

Achieve Customer Satisfaction

Customer satisfaction measures how happy consumers are with the products provided by the firm. The firm can measure this by carrying out customer opinion surveys, a type of market research (see p.100).

Personal Reasons

There may be personal reasons why an entrepreneur decides to start a business (see p.6).
For example, they may want the personal challenge of running a business or want the satisfaction of owning their own business. Some entrepreneurs want the independence and control of being their own boss.

Objectives Help Businesses **Achieve** Their **Aims** and **Monitor Success**

1) Once a firm has established its aims, it needs to set business objectives.
2) Just like with aims, there are different types of objectives. They can be related to the same things as aims, such as survival, profit, growth, or customer satisfaction.
3) Objectives are more specific than aims — they're measurable steps on the way to the aim. E.g. if a firm's aim is to grow, an objective might be to increase income from sales by 30% over two years.
4) Once objectives have been set they act as clear targets for firms to work towards.
5) A business can check back after a period of time to see whether its objectives have been achieved. This is a way of measuring success.
6) A common objective to look at is profit — e.g. if the firm met a yearly profit target it's a sign of success.
7) There are loads of ways other than profit to measure success, depending on the firm's objectives. For example, a firm could count the number of employees it has to see if it's met its growth objectives, or look at the value of its shares on the stock market to see if it's met its shareholder value objectives.

Objectives break aims down into smaller steps...

It's no good having aims if you don't know how to achieve them and can't tell for certain when they've been accomplished. So setting objectives to act as stepping stones to achieve the aims is really important for firms.

Changes in Business Aims and Objectives

The aims and objectives a business sets depends on the business, e.g. its size and the market it's selling to. But aims and objectives aren't set in stone — they may be changed as the business and the world around it changes.

Not All Companies Have the **Same Objectives**

There are different factors that affect the objectives of a business:

- The size of the business — many small, local businesses depend on word of mouth to survive, so a major objective for them might be customer satisfaction. They may be more concerned with survival and growth rather than increasing market share. Larger businesses get more attention from the public, so they might set objectives about acting ethically and protecting the environment to try to avoid bad publicity. Larger businesses may also be PLCs, so they might focus on increasing shareholder value.
- The level of competition the business faces — if a business is in a highly competitive market, it might focus on customer satisfaction so that it can win customers from its rivals. Increasing or holding on to its market share might be more important than maximising profits. If a firm doesn't face much competition, its objectives may be focused more on growth and maximising profits.
- The type of business — e.g. not-for-profit businesses (see p.12) are more likely to focus on social or ethical objectives, rather than growth or profit.

A Company's **Aims** and **Objectives** Can **Change** in **Different Ways**

As a business evolves, its aims and objectives are likely to change. For example, it might want to...

Change whether it aims to survive or grow

A new, start-up business's aims are likely to be focused on survival. However, once it is stable, aims might be centred around growth and maximising profits for reinvestment. If it becomes a large, established business, it might aim to have the largest market share. But if the economy takes a downturn, the business might start struggling, and its aims could once more become focused on survival.

Change the size of its workforce

For example, if a business is expanding, it might aim to recruit more staff. If a business has recently taken over another firm, it might aim to reduce the size of its workforce so it doesn't have multiple people carrying out the same role.

Enter or exit new markets

A business could aim to enter a new market, e.g. by targeting a different group of people in the same place, or by starting to sell products in a new location (e.g. in other countries). This could be because the business is growing, but may also be because their existing markets are shrinking and they need to find new places to sell their items. If a product isn't selling well in a particular market, the business's aims are likely to change so that they exit that market.

Change the size of its product range

For example, if a business has a product that's selling really well, it might aim to bring out more products in the same range with different features. If it has products in a range that don't sell well, it might aim to decrease the product range and concentrate on promoting and growing its best-selling products.

Different businesses will aim to achieve different things...

Think about two different businesses. Write down the main features of each business (e.g. what goods or services they provide), and then think of how their aims might be different and why this might be.

Changes in Business Aims and Objectives

Time for more detail on why a firm's aims and objectives might change. It could be to do with things going on outside the business that it can't control, or things going on inside the business that it has more control over.

The **Business Environment** can Affect a Company's Objectives

The business environment is dynamic (ever-changing) — the law, the economy, market conditions, technology or the expectations of customers may all change. Firms need to be able to keep up with these changes. They can do this by changing their objectives. E.g.

- New legislation — companies may need to adjust their aims and objectives when new laws are introduced. E.g. in 2016, a new living wage was introduced. This affected many companies' profit aims and objectives, as they had to pay higher wages.

- Changes in the economy — e.g. if there's a recession, a company's growth objectives might be put on hold while it concentrates on survival.

- Changes in market conditions — if a market grows, a company may alter its aims to focus on growing sales. However, if a market shrinks, a company might be more focused on survival or targeting new markets. If a market gets more competitive, a company might focus more on maintaining its market share or maximising sales, rather than maximising profits or growing its market share.

- Changes in technology — companies need to keep up to date with new technology, especially if their competitors are using it. They may need to alter their aims and objectives so they spend more money on getting new equipment and training staff rather than investing in growth.

- Environmental expectations — recently people have become more concerned about the impact a business has on the environment — objectives related to environmental impact have become more important for many companies to avoid losing customers.

Factors **Within** a Company can Affect its **Aims** and **Objectives**

- Performance — if a company performs better or worse than expected, aims and objectives may be changed. For example, if it sells more than expected one month, future sales objectives might be increased to match this.

- Internal changes — changes within the company can affect what its aims and objectives are. For example, if the management changes, then the new managers might have different priorities for the business, which will cause its aims and objectives to be changed.

Businesses need to respond to the world around them...

The business environment is always changing. Firms need to adapt to these changes or they may have problems.

Stakeholders

A stakeholder is anyone who's affected by a business. Even small businesses may have lots of stakeholders.

Different Stakeholders Have Different Ideas of Success

Different stakeholders are affected by the business in different ways. This means they have different opinions about what makes a firm successful and what its objectives should be.

Internal Stakeholders are Involved in the Operations of the Business

The owners are the most important stakeholders. They make a profit if the business is successful and decide what happens to the business. In a limited company, the shareholders are the owners (see p.10). Shareholders usually want high dividends, and a high share price.

Dividends are payments that the shareholders get if the company makes a profit. The more shares a shareholder owns, the higher their dividend will be.

Managers and other employees are interested in their job security and promotion prospects. These are improved if the firm is profitable and growing. Employees also want a decent wage and good working conditions. So they may benefit most when objectives are based on profitability, growth and ethics.

External Stakeholders are Groups Outside the Business

A firm buys its raw materials from suppliers. If the firm is profitable and grows they'll need more materials and the supplier will get more business. So suppliers benefit most when the firm sets objectives based on profitability and growth.

The local community where the business is based will suffer if the firm causes noise and pollution. They may gain if the firm provides good jobs and sponsors local activities. If the business employs local people, these employees will then have money to spend in local shops, which is good for the local economy. So the local community may benefit when objectives are based on minimising environmental impacts, ethical considerations, profitability and growth.

The government will receive taxes if the firm makes a profit. They may benefit most when objectives are based on profitability, growth, or job creation.

Customers want high quality products at low prices. They benefit when objectives are based on customer satisfaction.

A pressure group is an organisation that tries to influence what people think about a certain subject. They can influence the decisions a firm makes by creating bad publicity for the firm if they don't agree with the firm's actions. E.g. in 2015, farming pressure groups such as Farmers For Action, held nationwide protests about the low prices some supermarkets paid for milk. Many pressure groups are satisfied when businesses set objectives based on ethical considerations or minimising environmental impacts.

A business's actions might affect stakeholders in different ways...

Don't just learn who the different stakeholders of a business are. Make sure you understand why these groups are stakeholders, and how they might be affected by the different things a business does.

More on Stakeholders

Different stakeholders have different opinions about what a firm should be doing. A firm can't always please all of its stakeholders, so it will have to prioritise the opinions of the stakeholders it sees as being most important.

Stakeholders Influence Objectives to Varying Degrees

1) The owners make the decisions in a firm, so they're they most influential stakeholders.

2) However, they need to consider the interests of other stakeholders when they're setting their objectives.

3) Often, stakeholders will have conflicting opinions about the firm's objectives and its activities.

4) The firm may decide to ignore the opinions of some stakeholders, but they'll need to take others into account if they want to survive as a firm. For example:
   - No business can ignore its customers. If it can't sell its products it won't survive.
   - A business may want to hold onto its money for as long as possible, but suppliers will become unhappy if they're not paid on time.
   - If a business doesn't have happy workers it may become unproductive.
   - But a company may not mind being unpopular in the local community if it sells most of its products somewhere else.

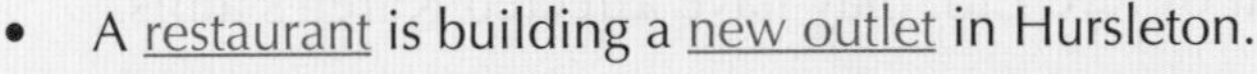

- A restaurant is building a new outlet in Hursleton.
- The owners want the restaurant opened as soon as possible so it can start making an income. However, this would mean working at night, which is noisy and could disturb local residents. The company wants to keep the residents happy, so that they become customers.
- So the company has to balance the interests of both stakeholders (the owners and the local community) to make sure the restaurant is built in a quick, but non-disruptive way.

A business may have to make compromises for different stakeholders...

Businesses need to try to please their stakeholders as much as they can — it could affect things such as their sales, their funding or their productivity if they don't. But there are times when different stakeholder groups have completely different opinions. In these situations, the business will have to decide which group is most important for their success, or try to make a decision that is a compromise for both groups.

Worked Exam Questions

Like it or not, you'll have to answer real exam questions at some point. Having a good look at these worked examples will help you to prepare for the real thing — and the more prepared you are, the less stressed you'll be.

1 Look at **Item A** below.

Item A — Karen's Sarnies:
Karen Booth is opening Karen's Sarnies, a small sandwich shop in Nantwich, Cheshire. In her first year, Karen's main aim is to survive. For the years after that, Karen has other aims, such as to maximise profit.

a) Identify **two** aims a small business might have, other than survival and maximising profit. *[2]*

Your answer should be suitable for a small business. So, for example, 'achieving market domination' wouldn't be an acceptable answer.

Sample answer:

To increase income from sales and to have high customer satisfaction.

You might also have said to increase the number of employees, to increase market share or to achieve financial security.

Item B — Karen's Sarnies:
Three years after Karen's Sarnies opened, Rye Ltd., a large, national sandwich retailer, opened a branch on the same street.

b) Explain **one** way in which the arrival of Rye Ltd. may have affected Karen's aims. *[4]*

There are 4 marks, so as well as clearly describing one way in which Karen's aims might have changed, you also need to give a detailed explanation of why the arrival of Rye Ltd. would have had this effect.

Sample answer:

Karen may have had to change her aims to focus more on maintaining her market share. This is because Rye Ltd. is a direct competitor of Karen's Sarnies. It is a large, national company meaning it is likely to have a well established brand, so is likely to take lots of customers from Karen.

You should have picked up that Rye Ltd. is a competitor to Karen's Sarnies, and also that it is a much larger, more established business. You should think about the impact these things might have on Karen's Sarnies when writing your answer.

Exam Questions

1 Explain how business aims are different to business objectives.

....

....

....

[Total 3 marks]

2 Look at **Item A** below.

Item A — Better Energy Plc.:
Better Energy Plc. are a company that own power plants. They are planning to expand by building a new wind farm near the town of Madingborough. As part of the project, Better Energy Plc. will also invest in improving the roads around Madingborough. Madingborough is in an Area of Outstanding Natural Beauty. Many of the local residents are employed in the local tourism industry.
The residents have protested about the proposed wind farm, claiming that it will spoil the views of the area. Better Energy Plc. had considered a second site for the wind farm that was offshore. However, this option would have cost double the price of the Madingborough site and would have taken a year longer to build.

a) Outline **one** benefit to the local residents of the wind farm being built near Madingborough.

....

....

[2]

b) Explain **one** conflict between stakeholders Better Energy Plc. may have considered when choosing where to build their wind farm.

....

....

....

....

....

....

....

[4]

[Total 6 marks]

Revenue and Costs

All businesses need to know how much money they have coming in, and how much they're spending.

Revenue is the Income Earned by a Business

1) Businesses earn most of their income from selling their products to customers.
2) Revenue can be calculated by multiplying sales (the number of units sold) by the price (the amount the customer pays).

revenue = sales × price

Sales can also be called the 'quantity sold' or the 'sales volume'.

If Light Up Sport Ltd. sell 20 000 tennis balls at £2 each — their sales revenue will be £40 000.

Costs are the Expenses Paid Out to Run the Business

Fixed and Variable Costs

- Fixed costs don't vary with output (the amount a business produces). They have to be paid even if the firm produces nothing. For example, the rent, insurance and fixed salaries for employees such as managers.
- Variable costs are costs that will increase as the firm expands output. For example, the costs of factory labour, raw materials and running machinery.

total variable cost = sales × variable cost per unit

- Fixed costs are only fixed over a short period of time — an expanding firm's fixed costs will go up.
- The total costs for a firm are the fixed and variable costs added together:

total costs = variable costs + fixed costs

Average Unit Cost

- Average unit cost is how much each product costs to make.
- To find the average unit cost, divide the total cost by output (number of products made).
- To make a profit (see next page) the firm must charge a higher price than this.
- Average unit costs usually fall as the firm grows, due to economies of scale (see p.28).

average unit cost = total cost ÷ output

Light Up Sport Ltd. has an output of 20 000 tennis balls, at a total cost of £30 000.
The average unit cost = £30 000 ÷ 20 000 = £1.50 per ball.
The selling price should be more than £1.50 per ball.

Some costs change with output, whilst others stay the same...

Make sure you learn the equations for calculations such as these, because you won't be given them in the exams. Try writing them out lots of times, until you feel confident that you really know them.

Profit

The previous page showed you how to calculate the revenue of a business and also its costs.
A business will look at the difference between these values to work out whether its making a profit or a loss.

Businesses Make a Profit if They Earn More Than They Spend

1) Profit (or loss) is the difference between revenue and costs over a period of time.

profit = revenue – costs

Light Up Sport Ltd. sells 20 000 tennis balls in a month at £2 each.
Over the same month its total costs are £30 000.
Profit = (20 000 × £2) – £30 000 = £40 000 – £30 000 = £10 000
So the business makes £10 000 profit in the month.

2) If costs are higher than revenue, the business will make a loss instead of a profit, and the answer to the calculation above will be negative.

Gross Profit and Net Profit Show Different Things

1) A business can calculate its net profit and gross profit from its financial data.
2) Gross profit is the profit a firm makes after the cost of making products (the cost of sales) is taken into account.
3) Net profit is the profit a firm makes when all expenses (that includes the operating expenses, e.g. salaries and rent, the interest paid on loans and the cost of sales) are taken into account.
4) Before calculating any kind of profit, it's important to know what the revenue is (see previous page).
5) To calculate the gross profit, take away the cost of sales from the revenue:

   gross profit = revenue – cost of sales

6) To calculate the net profit, you can use the following formula:

   net profit = gross profit – (operating expenses + interest)

Businesses need their revenue to be higher than their costs...

Whenever you get questions that involve calculations, always make sure you show your working. That way, even if your final answer isn't correct, you could still pick up some marks for your method.

The Business Plan

It's vital that a business has a clear idea of what it's going to do if it wants to be successful — this is where the business plan comes in. You need to know why businesses have them and what they should contain.

The Plan is for the **Owner** and **Financial Backers**

1) A business plan is an outline of what a business will do, and how it aims to do it.
2) Business plans are useful for people starting a business and also when an existing firm wants to make changes.
3) A business plan forces the owner to think carefully about what the business is going to do, how it will be organised and what resources it needs. This should help the owner to make decisions that will help the business to succeed. It also allows the owner to calculate how much money is needed.
4) The plan can be used to convince financial backers (e.g. banks) that the idea is a sound investment.
5) Business plans help owners to reduce their risk. If the business is a bad idea, the planning should help the owner or the financial backers realise this before they've wasted too much time and money.
6) For a new business, the business plan helps managers decide what objectives need to be set to achieve their aims once the business is up and running.

The Business Plan Describes **How** the Business will be **Run**

There's no single correct way to write a business plan — but most good 'uns for new firms include these things:

1) The business idea — this should explain what the firm is all about. It could include details of the product the firm will be selling, such as how the firm will achieve its unique selling point (USP) (p.5).
2) Business aims and objectives — aims usually say something general and obvious, e.g. "To be the market-leading sandwich shop in Kent." Objectives are more specific, e.g. "To average 160 sandwich sales per lunchtime over 4 years."
3) Target market — the plan should explain who the business is aiming to sell to. This should be backed up by market research (p.99-101) showing that the target market will be interested in buying the product.
4) Marketing mix — the plan should describe how the business will sell its products with a marketing mix using the 4 Ps (p.95).
5) Location — the plan should describe where the business will locate and why. For example, whether it wants to be near its target market, or near its suppliers (see next page).
6) Finance — the plan should explain how much money is needed to start up the business, and identify where this money will come from. There should be a cash flow forecast and forecasts of the business's costs, revenue and profits. There should also be ratios to show any backer the likely return on their investment.

All these financial bits and bobs are covered on p.24-25 and in Section 6.

Business Plans **Don't** Solve Everything

1) Business plans can have their drawbacks. For example, writing one can take lots of time and money. In the end, the benefit of writing one may not outweigh the cost.
2) Some people will be too optimistic when writing a business plan and end up with problems later on. E.g. if they don't sell as much as they predicted, they may struggle to pay their bills.
3) Managers may stick too tightly to the plan. If something unexpected happens that wasn't in the plan (e.g. a new competitor starts up), managers might be slow to change their plans, which could cause problems.

A business plan tells you what a new business will do and how it will work...

The best laid business plans might not stop a fledgling business from going under — but anyone starting a firm without one would need improbable amounts of luck to survive. In short, business plans are very important.

Location

Deciding where to locate can be a big decision for a firm. When a firm chooses its location, it often has to compromise between being where it's cheapest and being where it would generate the most income.

Location is Influenced by Different Factors

When a business is choosing where to locate, it might think about these things...

Location of the Market

- Some firms pay more to transport their finished products than their raw materials. These types of firms find it cheapest to locate near to their customers.
- Some businesses locate near to their market so people know about them and can easily get to them. It also helps them to get sales through passing trade (e.g. from people who walk past the business).
- Firms that sell products across the world may set up production sites in countries where they have a large market. This reduces transport costs and means they won't have to pay import taxes in these countries.

Location of Raw Materials

Locating close to raw materials can lower transport costs. This is especially true for firms that use bulky raw materials to produce smaller finished products.

Labour Supply

- Locating close to an area of high unemployment may help to keep a firm's wages low.
- There should also be a good selection of people to choose from, and a firm should be able to find enough workers.
- If the area is built-up, there may be colleges that can provide training for employees who need particular skills.

Cost

- The cost of labour varies in different countries. Many large firms have call centres and factories in places such as India or China where wages are lower.
- How much the firm can afford to spend on renting or buying will affect where it is — some areas are much more expensive than others. E.g. it costs a lot more to rent a shop on the high street than it does in a quieter area of town.
- Sometimes the government gives grants or tax breaks for firms who locate in areas of high unemployment, which lowers their total expenditure.

Competition

- Being near competitors can be an advantage — it can mean it's easier to find skilled labour, there are already local suppliers, and customers will know where to come.
- However, some businesses prefer to be away from competitors so they don't lose sales or don't have to reduce their prices to be more competitive.

Using the Internet

- The internet means that the location of some firms is more flexible.
- E.g. trading over the internet (e-commerce) means manufacturers can be further from their market, but closer to their raw materials. It may also mean they don't need fixed premises (e.g. a shop) to sell from.
- Documents can be accessed over the internet, so some firms don't need fixed premises for offices. Instead, employees can work from home and the firm can potentially employ people all over the world.

The nature of the business will influence what they prioritise when choosing their location. For example, a business that relies on customers visiting its site is likely to prioritise being close to the market. However, a manufacturing firm may prioritise somewhere close to its raw materials or with a good labour supply.

REVISION TASK

Location is often a compromise between different factors...

Choose three different businesses that you know. Write down three factors that you think would have been important to them when they decided where to locate. Make sure you include your reasons too.

Expanding Businesses

There are lots of different ways that firms can expand (these are covered on the next two pages). But first here's a page about one of the main benefits of being a big firm, as well as some of the drawbacks.

Larger Firms Benefit from Economies of Scale

1) Larger firms generally make more products and have more money than smaller firms.
2) Being larger means that the average unit cost of each product falls — these reductions in cost are called economies of scale.
3) Economies of scale can happen for different reasons. Here are two of them:

1 Purchasing Economies of Scale

- These happen when a large firm buys its supplies in bulk and so gets them at a cheaper unit price than a small firm.

2 Technical Economies of Scale

- These occur because a large firm can afford to buy and operate more advanced machinery than smaller firms.
- Also, the law of increased dimensions means that, for example, a factory that's ten times as big will be less than ten times as expensive.

4) As the average unit cost of making each product is lower, firms can make more profit on each item they sell.
5) Also, lower average unit costs mean larger firms can afford to charge their customers less for products than smaller firms can. This may make customers more likely to buy their products, leading to increased sales and more profit.
6) The profits can be reinvested into the business so it can expand even more.

There are also Diseconomies of Scale

It's not all good news for large firms though — growth brings with it the risks of diseconomies of scale. These are areas where growth can lead to increases in average unit costs. For example:

1) The bigger the firm, the harder and more expensive it is to manage it properly.

2) Bigger firms have more people, so it can be harder to communicate within the company. Decisions take time to reach the whole workforce, and workers at the bottom of the organisational structure feel insignificant. Workers can get demotivated, which may cause productivity to go down.

3) The production process may become more complex and more difficult to coordinate. For example, different departments may end up working on very similar projects without knowing.

Average unit costs can increase or decrease as a business grows...

If you're feeling hazy about average unit costs, have a look back at page 24. The important thing here is that the average cost of producing each item may change as a business grows. Make sure you understand why.

Internal Expansion

There are two main types of expansion — internal and external. First up, it's internal expansion.

Internal Expansion is Low Risk but can be Slow

1) Internal expansion (organic growth) is when a firm grows by reinvesting its profits to expand its own activities.
2) Internal expansion is good as it's relatively inexpensive. Also, it generally means the firm expands by doing more of what it's already good at — making its existing products (increasing its output). So it's fairly low risk.
3) The firm grows slowly, so it's easier to make sure quality doesn't suffer and new staff are trained well.
4) The problem is that it can take a long time to achieve growth — some owners don't want to wait this long to start making more money.
5) Here are some methods of internal expansion:

Franchising (see p.13) can be classed as organic growth. It's different to the methods of growth on this page, as it involves new companies being formed.

Targeting new markets

- This is when a business aims to sell its products to people who it hasn't tried to sell to before.
- Firms can use new technology to target new markets. For example, they could use e-commerce:

1) E-commerce is where a firm sells products via the internet.
2) The firm has access to a larger market because they can sell to people who aren't near a shop.
3) It's cheaper than setting up and running a new store — the firm doesn't have to pay for rent and won't have to hire as many staff.
4) But technology for e-commerce (e.g. websites or apps) has to be regularly updated. And any technical problems can cause customers to become unsatisfied.

- Technology may also mean items are cheaper to produce, so a firm might be able to lower its prices and target a lower income market.
- A firm could also set up branches in other countries so they can sell directly in markets abroad.
- They could change the marketing mix (p.95) of the product (e.g. the price) so it appeals to a new market.

Developing new products

- Selling a brand new product will increase sales for a business, allowing it to grow.
- The business may increase its market share as they'll be the only firm selling that product to start with.
- To sell a new product, firms need innovation — this is when someone comes up with a new product or way of doing things. Often, innovation comes about as a result of research and development.

Opening new stores

- This is fairly low risk. If the new store operates in a similar way to the existing stores, it should be a success, and so the business can increase its sales.
- However, opening a store means lots of extra costs, e.g. rent and staff pay. The company needs to make sure it can afford these new costs.

Outsourcing

- A business could pay another firm to carry out tasks it could do itself — this is outsourcing.
- The outsourcing firm might be able to do tasks more quickly, cheaply or to a higher standard than the business can do itself.
- But outsourcing means the business loses some control over parts of its operations. And the firm they've outsourced to might not prioritise their work if they've also got other customers.
- The business could also get a bad reputation if the firm it outsources to has poor standards.

There are lots of ways to grow internally...

Whichever method of growth a company chooses, the end result should be that its revenue increases.

External Expansion

External expansion (or inorganic growth) means expanding by working with other businesses. External expansion is faster than internal expansion (see previous page), but it can be difficult for all the businesses involved.

Mergers and Takeovers are Two Ways to Expand Externally

1) A merger is when two firms join together to form a new (but larger) firm.
2) A takeover is when an existing firm expands by buying more than half the shares in another firm.
3) External expansion means that the business grows much more quickly than with internal expansion.
4) There are various ways a firm can merge with or take over other firms. Each way falls into one of three types:

VERTICAL EXPANSION is when two firms at different points in the supply chain join together. For example:

- A firm could take over a customer, e.g. a soft drinks company takes over a chain of juice bars.
- This gives the firm greater access to customers. Owning its own retail outlets will make it easier to sell its products.

- A firm could join with a supplier, e.g. a soft drinks company takes over a fruit farm.
- This allows a firm to control the supply, cost and quality of its raw materials.

- HORIZONTAL EXPANSION is when two competitors join together.
- For example, a soft drinks company takes over another company which makes soft drinks.
- This creates a firm with more economies of scale and a bigger market share. It will be more able to compete than before.

- DIVERSIFICATION is when two unrelated firms join together
- For example, a soft drinks company takes over a tinned food firm.
- This means the firm will expand by diversifying into new markets. This reduces the risks that come from relying on just a few products.

BUSINESS EXAMPLE

- In 2010, the confectionery firm Kraft Foods Inc. (now Mondelēz International) bought enough shares to take over its competitor Cadbury.
- By taking over Cadbury, Kraft Foods Inc. became the largest seller of chocolate and confectionery in the world.
- Buying Cadbury also meant that Kraft Foods Inc. immediately had good market shares in parts of the world where it hadn't sold much before.

Mergers and Takeovers Don't Always Go Smoothly

1) Less than half of all takeovers and mergers are successful. It's very hard to make two different businesses work as one. Management styles often differ between firms — the employees of one firm may be used to one company culture and not be motivated by the style used in the other.
2) Mergers and takeovers can also create bad feeling. Often a firm agrees to be taken over, but sometimes the takeover bid is hostile and unpopular.
3) Mergers and takeovers often lead to cost-cutting. This may mean making lots of people redundant, so they can lead to tension and uncertainty among workers.

External expansion involves two companies becoming one...

External expansion means that a firm can quickly increase its market share by combining with another company. But not all firms operate in the same way, and this can cause problems that may impact costs and productivity.

Worked Exam Questions

Having a go at questions is a great way to revise and get you ready for the exams. The questions below will give you an idea of some of the question types you might get in the exams, and how to answer them if you do.

1 Explain **one** benefit and **one** drawback to a business of expanding by setting up a website to sell products through.

[4]

Sample answer:

Selling products via the internet means that the business has access to a much larger market, so its sales are likely to increase. However, there's a risk that the website could have technical problems, which could cause customers to become dissatisfied, and the business's sales to drop.

Make sure you clearly state one advantage and one disadvantage of selling via a website in your answer. You also need to give a clear explanation of the impact that each of these things could have on the business.

2 A new business makes scarves and sells them for £7. **Figure 1** shows the number of scarves sold by the business in three years and the total costs for each year.

Figure 1

	Year 1	Year 2	Year 3
Number of scarves sold	850	450	1200
Total revenue (£)	5950	3150	....
Total costs (£)	4700	3600	6200

a) Using the information provided, calculate the total revenue for Year 3.
Show your working.

[2]

Sample answer:

revenue = sales × price

revenue = 1200 × 7 = £8400

Show all the steps in your working — including writing down any equations you use.

total revenue = £ 8400

b) Identify the year in which the business made a loss.

[1]

You should use the information in the table to find the answer.

Sample answer:

Year 2

To find the year when the firm made a loss, you need to find the year when total costs are greater than total revenue.

Exam Questions

1 What type of expansion takes place if a company merges with one of its suppliers? Put a cross (X) in the correct box.

- **A** horizontal ☐
- **B** vertical ☐
- **C** diversification ☐
- **D** outsourcing ☐

[Total 1 mark]

2 Which of the following pieces of information would you expect to find in a business plan? Put a cross (X) in **two** correct boxes.

- **A** Laws the business will have to follow. ☐
- **B** How the business will communicate with its employees. ☐
- **C** Where the business will be located. ☐
- **D** Forecasts of bar gate stock graphs. ☐
- **E** What the business idea is. ☐

[Total 2 marks]

3 Explain **one** disadvantage to a business of locating near businesses of the same type.

....

....

....

....

[Total 3 marks]

4 Explain **one** disadvantage of expanding by internal growth.

....

....

....

....

[Total 3 marks]

Revision Summary for Section 1

It's almost the end of Business in the Real World. Just time for a few questions to test what you've learnt.

- Try these questions and tick off each one when you get it right.
- When you've done all the questions for a topic and are completely happy with it, tick off the topic.

Enterprise and Business Activity (p.4-8)

1) Define the term 'goods'.
2) Explain three reasons why new business ideas come about.
3) What is business enterprise?
4) Describe two reasons why someone might decide to become an entrepreneur.
5) Give an example of a type of business that you would find in:
   a) the primary sector, b) the secondary sector, c) the tertiary sector.
6) Name the four factors of production.

Business Ownership Structures (p.9-13)

7) True or false? A sole trader is responsible for all the debts of a business.
8) State two types of business ownership structure that have limited liability.
9) Give two disadvantages of being a public limited company rather than a private limited company.
10) What is a not-for-profit organisation?
11) What is franchising?

Business Aims and Stakeholders (p.16-21)

12) Describe two financial aims a business might have.
13) Give three examples of how a business's aims and objectives might change as it grows.
14) Explain two external influences that could affect a business's aims and objectives.
15) Describe what is meant by the term 'stakeholder'.
16) State four possible stakeholders in a business.

Finance, Business Plans and Location (p.24-27)

17) Explain the difference between fixed and variable costs.
18) State the equation that can be used to calculate average unit cost.
19) Describe the difference between gross profit and net profit.
20) Explain one reason why it is important to write a business plan when setting up a business.
21) State one disadvantage of writing a business plan.
22) List five factors that may influence the location chosen for a business.

Business Growth (p.28-30)

23) What are economies of scale?
24) State two diseconomies of scale a business might experience as it grows.
25) Explain three methods of internal expansion a business could use.
26) Describe the difference between takeovers and mergers.
27) Explain two disadvantages of external expansion.

Employment and the Law

'Employment law' describes the many different laws associated with the relationship between employers and employees. The laws are generally about pay, recruitment, discrimination and health and safety.

All Employees Have a **Contract of Employment**

1) A contract of employment is a legal agreement between an employee and an employer. As soon as an employee accepts a job offer, they enter into a verbal contract with their employer.
2) An employer must give employees a written statement of employment within two months of starting work. This document explains the details of the contract between the employer and the employee. It will contain:

- the job title (or a brief job description)
- the starting date of the employment
- the hours of work, the starting pay and the regular date of payment
- where the employee will be working
- the holiday the employee's entitled to (see below)
- details of sickness pay and any company pension
- information about disciplinary procedures
- the length of notice the employee has to give if they want to leave

3) Having a contract written down helps an employee avoid being taken advantage of as it records their rights.
4) The contract an employee is given should match any information about the job that they were told during the recruitment process. For example, a business can't pay an employee a lower salary than they offered to them during recruitment. So businesses need to make sure jobs they advertise match the details of the contract.
5) If a firm doesn't provide an employee with a written statement of their contract, they may be fined.

Employees are Entitled to **Paid Holiday**

1) Employers must give their employees a certain amount of paid holiday each year — e.g. a full time worker is entitled to at least 28 days of paid holiday each year — which can include bank holidays.
2) This means businesses need to make sure they employ enough people to cover employees who are away — sometimes this might mean taking on extra workers for short periods of time.
3) For most businesses, it's illegal for employees to work more than an average of 48 hours per week. So they need to make sure they employ enough people to get all the work done.

Businesses Have to **Pay** Staff a **Minimum Amount**

1) There are laws about the minimum amount employers have to pay their staff.
2) Workers aged 24 and under but of school leaving age have to be paid the National Minimum Wage (NMW) — the exact amount depends on the age of the worker and the type of work. Workers aged 25 and over have to be paid the National Living Wage (NLW) — this is slightly more than the National Minimum Wage.

- The NMW and NLW mean that companies can't cut their costs by paying workers less than the legal minimum. If they do, they're breaking the law.
- If a company doesn't pay its workers enough, it could be given large fines. It could also get bad publicity, and consumers might stop using the business.
- The NMW and NLW can increase a firm's costs. This can lead to increased prices, meaning a possible fall in sales and a reduced income for the firm. Some firms may not be able to afford to pay the NMW or NLW to all of their staff, so may have to lose some staff in order to survive.
- The NMW and NLW can have benefits for companies though — they can lead to better motivated staff and increased productivity.

The NMW and the NLW are usually increased each year.

These laws help to ensure that businesses treat their employees fairly...

Staying within the law can be expensive, and it can take lots of time to check that all the business's operations are legal. But if a firm doesn't follow the law, the consequences could be much worse.

Employment and the Law

Some important employment laws were covered on the previous page, but those aren't the only laws that businesses need to follow. Coming up are a few more laws they have to follow when dealing with employees.

There Are Laws About **Recruitment**

1) Recruitment procedures must not discriminate against anyone because of, for example, their religion, gender, race, age, sexual orientation or because of disabilities. This is covered by the Equality Act 2010.
2) Firms must also make sure that any new recruits have a legal right to work in the UK. This can involve extra work for firms as they may have to carefully check new recruits' documents (e.g. passports and visas), but employing people illegally can result in big fines and possibly even the closure of the firm.

Businesses **Can't Discriminate**

1) Apart from recruitment (see above), the other main equal opportunities issue covered by the Equality Act 2010 is pay — all employees must be paid the same if they do the same job (or work of equal value) for the same employer.
2) If a company is found to have discriminated against someone, they'll have to pay compensation.
3) If any employee in a company is accused of discrimination, the company could also be held responsible. So companies need to take reasonable steps to prevent discrimination within the workplace — such as staff training and writing company policies about equal rights.

The Workplace Needs to be **Safe**

1) Health and safety legislation helps to make sure that risks to people at work are properly controlled.

- The Health and Safety at Work Act of 1974 requires all employers and their employees to take responsibility for health and safety.
- Firms need to carry out risk assessments to identify possible dangers.
- They need to take reasonable steps to reduce the risks. For example, accident books need to be kept, and first-aiders trained. All staff must receive health and safety training. Health and safety equipment must also be provided — e.g. hard hats on building sites.

Health and safety laws protect visitors to a firm (e.g. customers) as well as the workers.

2) A safe working environment should mean fewer accidents, and so fewer injuries. And hopefully it means a more productive workforce too — since people should need less time off work to recover.
3) It could also encourage people to apply to work for a company if they know they're safe to work for.
4) Following health and safety laws can be expensive — e.g. paying for staff to go on safety courses.
5) But businesses that don't follow health and safety laws can be prosecuted, fined and even closed down.
6) They may also have to pay compensation to anyone who's injured, and could get bad publicity.

These laws can have big impacts on businesses...

The important thing here is understanding how the laws affect businesses. Make sure you understand how a business may be affected if it follows the law, and also what might happen if it breaks the law.

Consumer Law

There are laws restricting how firms sell their products — the aim is to protect the consumer. If these laws weren't in place, some businesses might be tempted to be a bit dishonest.

The **Consumer Rights Act** Sets **Conditions** for Products

The Consumer Rights Act 2015 covers how goods and services can be sold. It basically states that goods should meet three criteria:

1 The product should be fit for its purpose

The product has to do the job it was designed for — if you buy a bucket, say, it's not much use if it leaks water out of the bottom.

2 The product should match its description

- The way a business describes a product it's selling is called a 'trade description'. It's illegal for a retailer to give a false trade description.
- This includes the size or quantity of the product, the materials it's made from, and its properties.
- It's also illegal to claim that a product has been endorsed or approved by a person or an organisation unless it really has been.

3 The product should be of satisfactory quality

- This means that the product should be well made — it shouldn't fall apart after a couple of uses.
- It also means that it shouldn't cause other problems for the buyer — e.g. a fridge should keep food cold, but it shouldn't make a noise like a jet plane at the same time.
- To be of a satisfactory quality, the product also needs to be safe to use.

If products don't meet the legal requirements, customers can ask for their money back, a repair or a replacement.

Consumer Laws **Affect** Businesses

1) If a business breaks consumer law it is faced with the cost and inconvenience of having to refund the customer, or repair or replace their item.
2) The case could even end up in court if the customer is unhappy with the business's response about their item (which costs the business even more if the customer wins the case).
3) As well as being expensive, breaking consumer law can harm the reputation of the business, which could lead to a reduction in sales.
4) So businesses have to be very careful when selling products and services to their customers.
5) They need to make sure they train their staff properly, so they sell products accurately and understand what a customer's rights are if they are unhappy with a product.

Firms need to make sure they keep up to date with all legislation that they need to follow — any changes to the legislation could mean that they need to make changes to their business. For example, a change to consumer law could mean that they have to rewrite any terms and conditions they give their customers and retrain their staff.

Consumer law means firms have to provide what they've said they're selling...

Following consumer law can increase costs for a business, but it should also mean that customers are happier with the products they buy. And happy customers should mean more sales for the business in the long term.

Technology and Business

The development of new technology has meant that firms can sell products and communicate in new ways.

E-Commerce Means Buying and Selling Online

There's lots more about e-commerce on p.123-124.

1) E-commerce is using the internet to buy or sell products.
2) Many firms now have websites where customers can buy their products.
3) E-commerce means that firms can reach wider markets compared to just having traditional shops — e.g. a small business in Dorset could end up selling products to someone in New Zealand.
4) E-commerce can be really convenient for consumers — it means they can buy products from all over the world, at any time of the day and they don't have to spend ages queuing up to buy products.
5) Firms have had to adapt to e-commerce as it's become more important. For example, they've had to build websites, employ IT specialists and develop systems to distribute products to online customers.

Firms can Communicate Digitally

Firms regularly need to communicate with their stakeholders (see p.20).
There are many ways firms can use technology to do this:

- WEBSITES: Websites are a great way to communicate with customers — e.g. by posting blogs or providing customer service (such as FAQs). Websites can also be used to publish reports to shareholders.
- EMAIL: Email is a very quick way of communicating with stakeholders, either on a personal level (e.g. to respond to a customer query) or on a bigger scale (e.g. to tell all employees they can go home early).
- MOBILE APPS: These are programs used on mobile devices, such as smartphones or tablets. They are usually used by firms to communicate with customers, for example by giving information about where stores are located, the products the company sells and any special offers.
- LIVE CHATS: Live chats are an instant messaging service. They have many uses — e.g. employees can use them to talk to each other from different locations, or customers can use them to speak with a customer service advisor via the internet.
- VIDEO CALLS: Employees who work for the same business in different locations may use video calling to hold meetings, rather than travelling to meet. This can also be a good way for businesses to communicate with important shareholders, who may all live in different places.
- SOCIAL MEDIA: Social media includes websites (e.g. Facebook®, Twitter) and applications that allow people to communicate and share content online. It makes it really easy for users to share information with other users — information can be in many forms, such as written messages or articles, pictures, videos, or links to other sites. This means social media is a great way for businesses to communicate — it can be used to display lots of different types of information, it can be updated regularly and it can be seen by loads of people at once. Businesses use social media for all sorts of purposes — e.g. to provide customer service, to advertise their products, or to promote local events.

Digital Communication Has Changed How Businesses Operate

Digital communication has helped to cause globalisation — this is the process of the world becoming more connected (p.49-50).

1) Digital communication means that businesses can communicate with people all over the world. This has made it easier for businesses to operate in more than one country and so have access to markets that they may not have been able to sell to before. Companies that operate in more than one country are called multinationals (see p.49).
2) It also means that more people are able to work from home, as they're still able to access documents online, and can talk to colleagues using email or video calls — there's more on this on p.84.

New forms of digital communication have made e-commerce much easier...

Digital communication is really useful, as it means firms can instantly talk to people even if they're far away.

Technology and Business

As well as affecting communication and where products are sold, technology has also affected how firms operate.

Technology Has Made it Easier for Us to Pay for Products

1) There are now lots of different payment systems that can be used to pay for products. For example:

- Online payments — Nearly all firms allow you to pay online by entering your debit or credit card details. But there are other online payment systems (e.g. PayPal) that mean you don't have to enter your card details on every website you buy from, and offer a higher level of cyber-security (so your bank details are less likely to get stolen).
- Chip and PIN — this is where you put your debit or credit card into a terminal (a machine at a checkout) and enter your unique PIN to pay. If you lose your card, you know that someone else can't go on a spending spree with it unless they know your PIN.
- Contactless payments — this is where you pay for something just by holding your debit or credit card or smart device near a terminal. (Using a smart device for contactless payments involves downloading an app first — e.g. Apple Pay™ or Android Pay™.)

2) Having safer and easier payment systems can encourage customers to shop with the firm.
3) Faster payment methods also mean that businesses can serve more customers in any given time, so their revenue could increase.

Technology has Changed the way Businesses Operate

ICT includes loads of things, such as computers, phone networks and the internet.

1) Developments in technology, such as improvements in information and communications technology (ICT) have improved how businesses work.
2) For example, businesses can often use new technology in place of people to carry out processes. This can lead to reduced costs in the long term — e.g. because fewer man-hours are needed to carry out tasks.
3) However, adapting to new technology can be very expensive. E.g. a firm may have to buy equipment or train staff to use new computer systems. They may also need to hire staff with the skills to use the new technology.
4) As well as improving processes, firms need to adapt to changes in technology to stay competitive. E.g. if a firm's competitors are communicating with customers using apps then the firm should also consider doing this.
5) New technology can lead to increased sales for a business. For example, e-commerce may boost a firm's sales as they can reach a bigger market. Modern payment systems may lead to increased sales as it's easier and faster for people to buy products so they may buy products more often from the firm.
6) New technology can also affect a firm's marketing mix (see p.95). For example, e-commerce means that customers have more choice of firms to buy from as they can buy from firms in places all over the world, not just in their local area. This means that firms may need to change their pricing strategies or the way they promote their products to become more competitive. The growth of social media means that many firms are choosing to promote their products through this channel rather than through more traditional routes, such as newspaper adverts.

The marketing mix of business includes the products it sells, the prices it charges, the promotion it uses and the places it sells its products.

BUSINESS EXAMPLE

1) In 2015, Katie Patel bought Glisten Up Cars, a car wash firm.
2) Katie bought handheld contactless payment terminals, which meant that people could pay for their car wash from their cars, rather than having to pay in cash or go into the office. This was more convenient for customers, so sales increased.
3) Katie also set up a website to inform customers about the firm, and set up social media accounts to advertise the firm and promote its special offers. These measures also led to increased sales.

New technology may be expensive, but can reduce costs in the long term...

Technology is always changing. Keeping up with these changes can make a firm competitive and increase sales.

Ethical Considerations

Ethics are moral principles of right and wrong. Many stakeholders are concerned about firms acting ethically.

Ethical Issues Have Become Important for Businesses

1) Many firms have their own ethical policies. This means they've developed ways of working that stakeholders think are fair and honest.
2) The ways that UK firms treat employees and suppliers in other countries raises many ethical issues.

- In some countries, it's not illegal for people to work very long hours for very low pay. Some firms set up factories in these countries to reduce their labour costs — many people think this is unethical if it exploits workers from foreign countries.
- Firms can write codes of conduct for any factories they have overseas. This helps to ensure the workers are treated ethically. For example, they can put limits on the number of hours somebody can work each week so they don't get too tired. They could carry out checks to make sure the code is being followed.
- Firms that buy raw materials from developing countries can choose to buy from Fair Trade sources — this means people in developing countries who produce the goods (e.g. cocoa farmers) are paid a fair price so they can earn decent wages.

3) Businesses need to treat their employees in the UK ethically too. E.g. businesses should reward staff fairly, keep personal details about staff private and provide a comfortable working environment.
4) Treating people well isn't the only ethical issue for a business. When marketing products, firms have to follow codes of practice. For example, promotions such as adverts can't be dishonest or insult other brands (although competing products can now be compared in a fair way). Some products can't be advertised at all — e.g. cigarette adverts are banned on health grounds.
5) Firms are also under pressure to carry out product development in an ethical way — this means using non-toxic materials, paying close attention to safety, and not using animal testing.
6) Firms should also treat their customers ethically. For example, sales staff should be honest about the products they are selling to the customer, and the business should respond professionally to any complaints.

Acting Ethically can have Benefits and Drawbacks

1) Ethical policies can be costly for a firm. For example, by treating workers fairly and making sure they are all paid a fair wage, a business is likely to have higher labour costs than if they didn't work ethically.
2) Also, if a firm is committed to using ethically sourced materials (e.g. Fair Trade products) they may find it more difficult to find suppliers and have to pay a higher price for their materials.
3) These increased costs mean that a firm doesn't make as much profit on each item that it sells. It could put its prices up so that it makes more profit per item, but higher prices might lead to lower sales (so the business still ends up with less profit).
4) However, despite potentially making less profit, many firms are still keen to work ethically.
5) Firms might change their marketing to emphasise the fact that they have strong ethical policies. For example, the Co-op advertises all its chocolate as Fair Trade produced. By advertising its ethical policies, a business might gain customers and increase its profits — there are plenty of people who think that ethical practices are more important than price.
6) Acting ethically can have a positive effect on other stakeholders as well. For example, some shareholders will be more likely to invest in a firm if it has shown that it behaves ethically. Treating staff ethically can mean workers are more motivated, which should make the firm more productive. Treating customers ethically will give them better satisfaction with the business, and make them more likely to buy from it again.

There are lots of different groups a business should treat ethically...

Find a news story about a company that hasn't been treating its stakeholders ethically. Write down the stakeholders that were affected, and also what the business could have done to be more ethical.

Environmental Influences

Business operations can affect the outside world, and this can have long term effects on the environment.

Businesses Can **Reduce** Their **Impact** on the **Environment**

1) All businesses can have an impact on the environment. They produce waste, lots of which ends up in landfills. They can also cause traffic congestion in the area where they're based if staff, customers and delivery lorries are driving there. Factories, cars and lorries can also cause air, noise and water pollution.
2) Luckily, there are steps a business can take to reduce these impacts on the environment:

- Companies can reduce the amount of packaging on their products. They can also recycle things such as delivery boxes, or unwanted goods. These things mean that less waste goes to landfill.
- Companies can dispose of hazardous waste carefully so that it doesn't pollute land or water.
- Companies can encourage car share schemes so that they reduce traffic caused by their staff driving to work. They can also support cycle to work schemes, where they help employees to buy bikes.
- To help reduce air pollution, a business can buy more efficient machinery that is less polluting.
- Noise pollution can be a big problem for some firms, such as those in the construction industry. To reduce noise pollution, they can buy quieter machinery, or put up sound barriers or insulation.

Businesses can Aim to be More **Sustainable**

1) Being sustainable means working in a way that doesn't damage the Earth for future generations.
2) People are worried that the combined impact of global businesses is damaging the Earth at the moment:

Resource depletion

Many resources used by businesses are non-renewable (e.g. coal and oil). If these resources run out, there's no way we can replace them.

Climate change

Many industries release carbon dioxide (and other chemicals) into the atmosphere. Carbon dioxide is also released when power stations generate electricity. The rise of carbon dioxide (and other 'greenhouse gases') in the atmosphere is contributing to the Earth's climate becoming warmer — this is called global warming. Global warming is a type of climate change — and it causes other types of climate change, such as changes in rainfall patterns. The consequences of global warming include ice caps melting, sea levels rising, more flooding... which could have knock-on effects for plant and animal life (including us).

3) Many firms are now working hard to make sure their operations are more sustainable. For example, they're using more renewable energy resources (such as wind and solar power), vehicles and machinery that produce less carbon dioxide and electrical goods that are more energy efficient.

BUSINESS EXAMPLE

1) In 2007, Marks and Spencer launched Plan A — a business plan to reduce its environmental impact and improve its ethics.
2) They started doing things like designing buildings that wasted less energy and used more sustainable materials.
3) By 2014, Marks and Spencer's global operations were carbon neutral — this means that, overall, the business doesn't add any carbon dioxide to the atmosphere.

Businesses are becoming more concerned about their impact on the Earth...

Firms need to be careful about their operations so they don't end up damaging the Earth for future generations.

Environmental Influences

The previous page had lots of things a business can do to be more environmentally friendly. Now it's time to find out about the benefits and drawbacks of these actions.

There are **Pros** and **Cons** to Being **Environmentally Friendly**

1) As people become more aware of environmental issues, consumers are changing their buying decisions — people are now buying more "environmentally friendly" products.

2) Taking environmental issues seriously can give firms a competitive advantage — a "green image" can attract new customers and increase sales.

3) However, there can be a trade-off for a business between being sustainable and making profit. For example, buying new equipment and developing new processes in order to be more sustainable can be expensive. Firms have to weigh up the benefits against the negative effect it could have on their profits.

A Business Might **Change** its **Policies** due to **Pressure Groups**

1) Pressure groups are organisations that try to influence decisions made by the government or by businesses (see p.20).
2) If a pressure group runs a campaign against a certain firm or industry (e.g. by highlighting areas where it could be more environmentally friendly or ethical) customers might start to view the firm or industry in a bad light. This means the firms involved could lose custom if people stop buying from them.
3) To improve their image in the public eye, businesses can change their marketing mix (see p.95). For example, a business might have to change its products in response to activity from pressure groups — e.g. by making sure the materials are more ethically sourced, or have less of an impact on the environment. It might also run promotional campaigns to repair the negative publicity the pressure group has caused.

- Supermarkets have been under pressure from groups such as WRAP and Friends of the Earth to reduce the amount of food that they waste.
- As customers have become more environmentally conscious, this pressure has increased.
- Many supermarkets have now changed their policies to reduce food waste — e.g. by changing processes with suppliers so food is fresher when it reaches the store, so it's less likely to go off.
- Supermarkets are also changing the products they sell — for example, some sell vegetables that are slightly strange looking for a cheaper price, so farmers don't have to throw them away.

External stakeholders can affect how a business behaves...

If you're asked a question about how environmental policies can impact a business, make sure you remember to explain both the benefits and the drawbacks. Think about the possible costs the policies will have for the business, but also how the policies might make the firm more competitive.

Worked Exam Questions

In the exams, you'll be given questions that start by giving you some information about a business. Go through the worked example questions below to get an idea of how to deal with these sorts of questions.

1 Look at **Item A** below.

> **Item A — ForKids:**
> ForKids, a company which makes plastic children's toys, has just opened a new factory near a residential area. The factory has several pieces of machinery for making toys. Recently ForKids has received a complaint from a nearby resident about the noise from the factory.
>
> Once the toys have been made, they are packaged individually in large cardboard boxes and transported in vans to distribution centres throughout the country.

a) Explain **two** ways in which the managers of ForKids could minimise the impact of the new factory on the surrounding environment.

[4]

You get two marks for stating two things the managers could do. The other two marks are for explaining why each of these things would reduce the impact on the environment.

Sample Answer:

1. They could package products more efficiently, so that fewer van journeys are needed to transport products, leading to less pollution.

Make sure you link your answer back to the details in the item — the actions need to be things that it would be possible for the managers at ForKids to do.

2. They could use machinery that is quieter, as this would reduce noise pollution.

You could also have said that reducing the amount of packaging on products would mean that they would use fewer resources, or that they could use more efficient machinery to reduce air pollution.

b) Outline **one** advantage to ForKids of making the new factory more environmentally friendly.

[2]

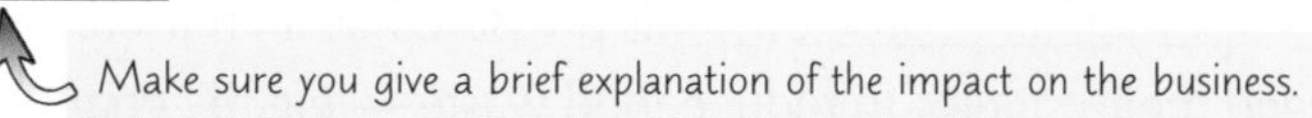

Make sure you give a brief explanation of the impact on the business.

Sample Answer:

It could improve the image of ForKids which will attract new customers.

The first mark is for stating one advantage of making the factory more environmentally friendly. The second mark is for explaining how this will benefit the business.

As well as attracting customers, you could also have said that improving its image will increase sales for ForKids.

Exam Questions

1 By law, all employers must pay their staff at least the national minimum wage.
Explain **one** advantage and **one** disadvantage that minimum wage law has for businesses.

Advantage: ....

....

Disadvantage: ....

....

[Total 4 marks]

2 Look at **Item A** below.

Item A — Beancraft Ltd.:
Beancraft Ltd. is a UK company that makes coffee. It buys coffee beans from plantations in less economically developed countries. Unlike most of its competitors in the UK, Beancraft Ltd. only uses plantations that have been certified by a Fair Trade organisation. There are more plantations worldwide that are not Fair Trade certified than those that are.

Analyse the effects of using a source of coffee beans that is Fair Trade certified on the financial success of Beancraft Ltd.

....

....

....

....

....

....

....

....

....

....

....

[Total 6 marks]

Unemployment and Government Taxes

The economic climate can have a huge effect on firms, but it's something that they can't control.
The economic climate includes many different economic conditions — first up, unemployment and taxes.

Unemployment is a **Big Problem**

People are unemployed when they're able to work but can't find a job. The level of employment (the number of people in work) changes over time, and this can have a big effect on businesses.

1) Unemployment means the economy as a whole produces less output than if everyone was employed. So everyone suffers from unemployment — in theory at least.
2) UK unemployment was very high in 2010 — around 2.5 million. In 2016, this had fallen to about 1.6 million.
3) Some firms can actually benefit from unemployment. They may be able to pay lower wages if there are lots of unemployed people desperate for a job. It can also mean they can fill jobs without any difficulty. In areas of high unemployment, the government may even give grants to businesses who open and provide jobs in the area. These factors may encourage a firm to grow when unemployment is high.
4) But there can also be big problems for businesses when there are high levels of unemployment. Less employment means lots of people have less disposable income. This can lead to a lack of demand for products from the unemployed, so sales can fall. A firm may respond by, e.g. reducing prices, reducing output or making staff redundant.
5) It may also be a problem if businesses hire people who have been unemployed for a while — people may lose skills while they're unemployed, so businesses may need to retrain them.

Disposable income is the money that people have left once they have paid tax.

Tax is Money That Goes to the **Government**

1) Both consumers and businesses have to pay tax. For example, consumers have to pay tax on money they earn (called income tax). Businesses have to pay tax on their profits. They also have to pay other taxes, such as environmental tax on activities that harm the environment, and tax on premises they own.
2) Tax rates are set by the government. Changes to tax rates can have a big impact on businesses:

- If the amount of income tax that consumers need to pay falls, they will have more disposable income. This means that consumer spending is likely to increase, leading to increased revenue for firms. The opposite is true if income tax increases — consumer spending is likely to fall.
- If the amount of tax that a business needs to pay increases, it reduces the amount of money they have available to reinvest. This can lead to slow growth for a business. If environmental tax increases, a firm may try to be more environmentally-friendly to avoid paying extra tax, e.g. by recycling more. But the tax increases may force the firm to find ways to cut costs in order to survive or meet their profit targets, e.g. by making staff redundant. They may also consider relocating the business abroad to a country where businesses pay less tax.
- If the government reduces taxes that a business has to pay, it means the business will have more money available to reinvest. This can help businesses to grow. However, lower business taxes might encourage firms from abroad to set up in the UK. This increases competition in the market and may lead to a fall in sales for UK businesses if they don't compete well.

Taxes are a cost for a business, but can change over time...

Make sure you know the ins and outs of unemployment and tax and the effects they can have on businesses.

Inflation and Consumer Income

Another two economic conditions now and it's two which are always changing — prices and incomes.

Inflation is an **Increase** in the **Price** of **Goods and Services**

In general, the price of goods and services inflates (goes up) over time. The prices of hundreds of products that an average UK household would buy is regularly tracked. The percentage increase in the price of these products over time is used to measure the rate of inflation. Inflation can have many different effects on a business. E.g.

Consumer Spending

When inflation rises, consumer spending is likely to go up in the short-term — people rush to buy more products before prices go up even more. This creates extra revenue for a business, which can lead to higher profits (depending on how much the increase in inflation has affected its costs). However, if wages don't go up at the same rate as inflation, demand for products can start to fall (there's more on this below).

Cost of Labour

With high inflation, employees can put pressure on employers to increase wages so that they can afford the higher prices being charged for the things they need. This can increase a business's costs and reduce its profits.

Global Competition

A high inflation rate makes UK exports (products sold to other counties) expensive, so UK firms become less competitive globally. This means that a firm that sells lots of exports may see its sales fall. However, when inflation is low, sales of exports are likely to increase.

When inflation is high, business growth tends to be low. Businesses find it hard to predict what is going to happen to their costs and sales. This can make them reluctant to take risks and invest in their business.

Changes in **Income** can Affect Businesses

Over time, the amount that people earn (their income) increases. However, incomes don't necessarily change at the same rate as inflation.

If inflation is rising at a faster rate than income, income is said to be going down in 'real terms'.

Income rises at a slower rate than inflation...

- People will have to spend a greater proportion of their income on things they really need — such as food.
- So they'll have less money left to spend on luxuries, such as going to the cinema, or buying new shoes — the demand for these products will go down.
- Businesses that provide luxuries will suffer — their sales are likely to go down, leading to lower profits. They could lower their prices or spend more on advertising to increase demand again, but this is still likely to lead to lower profits.
- Some businesses benefit if people's incomes are relatively low. Stores selling goods at discount prices are likely to see sales go up as more customers will be making an effort to buy things as cheaply as they can.

Income rises at a faster rate than inflation...

- People will be spending a smaller proportion of their income on things they need. This means they'll have more money to spend on luxuries, and the demand for these goods and services will go up.
- Businesses providing luxuries will see an increase in sales and their profits are likely to increase.
- Stores selling goods at discount prices may see their sales and profit go down as people start worrying less about getting things for the cheapest possible price.

The inflation rate is how fast prices are increasing...

You might find inflation a bit tricky to understand, so have another read before you go on. Make sure you understand how changes in inflation and income can together affect consumer spending. You should also understand the effect of inflation on costs for businesses and competition in other parts of the world.

Interest Rates

On to another economic condition now — interest rates. Many businesses and consumers will borrow money at some point. The amount of money they have to pay back depends on the interest rate.

Interest is Added to Loans and Savings

1) When you borrow money, you usually have to pay it back with interest — this means that you pay back more than you borrowed.
2) If you save money, you earn interest — the amount of money in your savings account will increase over time.

- The amount of interest you pay or earn depends on the interest rate — it's usually given as a percentage. The higher the interest rate, the more you pay or earn.
- In the UK, the Bank of England sets the base rate of interest — most other interest rates are linked to this. The base rate fluctuates (goes up and down) depending on how good the economy is.

Calculating the interest on a loan

1) Interest can be written as a percentage of the original amount borrowed. To find the amount of interest that a business has paid on a loan just use the following equation:

$$\text{interest (on loans)} = \frac{\text{total repayment} - \text{borrowed amount}}{\text{borrowed amount}} \times 100$$

2) So if a company takes out a loan of £10 000 and pays it off with interest to a total of £10 800,

$$\text{the interest} = \frac{10\,800 - 10\,000}{10\,000} \times 100 = (800 \div 10\,000) \times 100 = 8\%$$

Low Interest Rates Lead to Increased Spending

1) When the interest rate is cut, it's cheaper to borrow money. But you get less interest when you save money at a bank.
2) When rates are low, firms and consumers borrow more and save less.
3) Consumers have more money to spend, so demand for goods and services goes up. This means that firms are likely to make more profit and may need to increase output.
4) Firms that borrow money to finance their spending (e.g. by using overdrafts and loans) will have smaller interest repayments, so they have more money available to spend on other parts of the business. They may also choose to borrow more while interest rates are low, e.g. if they want to grow the business.

High Interest Rates Lead to Decreased Spending

1) Increases in interest rates have the opposite effect to cuts — borrowing money becomes more expensive, but savers get better returns on their investments.
2) Firms and consumers will have less money available to spend — they'll be paying higher rates on money they've borrowed. They're also likely to be trying to save more, in order to take advantage of higher returns.
3) This reduces demand for products, so firms often sell less and their profits may go down.
4) It may also mean that firms can't afford to pay everyone who works for them — so some people may be made redundant, and unemployment may go up.

Interest rates affect whether people save or spend...

Interest rates are like a see-saw — if interest rates go down, spending goes up. If interest rates go up, spending goes down. Have another read to make sure you know why this happens.

Competition

Most firms have rivals selling similar products. So firms work hard to attract customers away from their rivals.

A **Market** can be a **Place**, a **Product** or a Group of **People**

The word market can mean three slightly different things:

1) A place where goods are traded between customers and suppliers. A village market square seems pretty different from an internet shopping website — but they're both examples of markets.
2) Trade in a particular type of product, e.g. the oil market.
3) The potential customers for a product, e.g. the age 18–25 market.

Competitors are the different businesses that sell the same products in the same market. They compete with each other over sales to customers.

Competition Affects How Businesses **Make Decisions**

1) Most businesses face competition. A competitive market is one where there are a large number of producers selling to a large number of consumers.
2) To stand out in a competitive environment, businesses need to make decisions that will persuade customers to buy from them, rather than their competitors.
3) When making these decisions, the business might look at the strengths and weaknesses of its competitors in the following areas:

- Price — Customers will often want to pay less for a given product. If all the products in the market are the same, then price becomes one of the most important factors affecting which products customers will buy. Therefore firms may decide to charge lower prices than they would like, to stop customers from buying elsewhere. However, this will mean that a firm may not make much profit per product sold.
- Customer service — Offering customer service can attract customers and may mean that customers will be willing to pay more money for a product (and having a reputation for poor customer service might put customers off). So to stand out from the competition, a business might decide to train its staff in good customer service, or provide extra services (such as user training) when the customer buys the product.
- Quality — Offering better quality products may mean that customers are more satisfied. This may mean that the business will be more competitive, even if its products are more expensive. In order to convince customers that their products are better than their rivals', businesses may decide to spend money on developing high quality products or on promotional material that emphasises quality. However, this will be costly for the firm.
- Product range — Having a large range of products may make a business more attractive to customers. E.g. a greengrocer's may be able to compete with a convenience store if it sells more types of fruit and vegetables, since customers will have a better selection in one place. A business may also try to fill any gap in the market (supply a previously unmet consumer need) by developing new products. There won't be any competition for the new products and the firm may appear more innovative than its competitors and so be more attractive to customers. However, developing products will increase a business's costs.
- Location — Customers may be more likely to buy from a business if it sells products in a convenient place as they won't have the inconvenience of travelling or waiting for the product. Therefore businesses may decide to open stores in particular locations or to sell items online in order to offer the greatest convenience to customers as possible.

Businesses need to stand out from their competition...

Next time you're on your local high street, have a look and find two shops that are competitors. Then work out which shop is stronger in terms of price and which is stronger in terms of quality.

Competition

Not all businesses face competition. There are certain reasons why a business may have very few competitors, or even none at all. This could be due to the products a business sells, or the market it is in.

Some Businesses Face **Very Little** or **No** Competition

There are a number of reasons why a business might not face much competition. For example...

1 A product is new

- When a business creates a brand new product, initially it won't have any competition.
- Anyone who wants the product will have to buy it from this business.
- This will continue until other businesses start selling similar products.

When a business creates a new product, it may take out a patent. This means other businesses can't copy their idea for a set period of time, and keeps competition low.

2 The market is small

- Some businesses sell very specialist products that not many people want to buy.
- There probably won't be much competition as the market won't be big enough for many businesses to survive.
- For example, not many people have houses with thatched roofs.
- So there aren't many qualified thatchers, and the competition between them is low.

3 It's difficult to enter the market

- Some markets are hard to start a business in because the cost of setting up a new business is too high.
- This could be because the equipment needed is expensive, or because the employees require specialist skills meaning they may need lots of training and expect high wages.
- Not many businesses will be set up to sell to these markets, and there'll be low competition.

BUSINESS EXAMPLE

1) There's very little competition in the commercial planes market — Boeing and Airbus are the two main competitors.
2) It would be very difficult for a new company to start making planes. They'd need lots of space and the equipment and materials needed to build a plane would cost a lot. Employees also need to be carefully trained to make sure the plane is built safely.

Some markets have more competition than others...

Having no competition is a big advantage for businesses. The fewer competitors there are, the more likely customers are to buy from the business. So the business should have better sales. A business has little control over its market, so many businesses focus on developing new products to make themselves unique.

Globalisation

Better technology makes it easier to communicate and travel round the world. Which causes globalisation...

Globalisation Means the World is More Interconnected

1) Globalisation is the process by which businesses and countries around the world become more connected. It has resulted in single businesses operating in lots of countries. They can be based anywhere, and can buy from and sell to any country.
2) Globalisation means there's a much larger market that UK businesses can trade with — they're trading with people all over the world, not just people in their own town or country.
3) However, having a global market means there can be lots more competition. So businesses (both in the UK and worldwide) need to be able to stand out from the competition. Here are a few ways they do that:

- Many UK companies invest lots of money in design. This means they can compete in a global market by designing new products or processes.
- The UK has a reputation for producing higher quality goods and services than many other countries. By maintaining quality and taking measures to keep prices lower than overseas competitors (e.g. being more efficient or taking advantage of economies of scale — see p.28), UK firms can compete globally.
- Firms all over the world can use e-commerce to sell products via the internet. So they can compete overseas without having to set up stores and infrastructure in other countries, which keeps costs down.
- A firm might develop an international brand — an overall message that is recognised in many countries. The firm may have to adapt its brand for different countries (e.g. a firm with a brand that portrays family values will need to research what family values means in each of the countries it's selling to) but the overall message should be the same.
- Firms may change their marketing mix (p.95) in different countries. E.g. they can change prices to make sure they're competitive, or target products and promotion at the country's culture.

A firm's brand is the impression it portrays to its customers (p.118).

Globalisation Affects the Way Businesses Operate

1) Globalisation means that it has become easier and more common for businesses to import products (buy them from abroad), and export products (sell products to other countries).
2) The effects of globalisation can have many different impacts on businesses:

- IMPORTS — firms have a larger market to buy from, so they may be able to buy supplies more cheaply, which reduces costs and can increase profits. However, more imports means there's more competition in a country. Firms may be forced to reduce their prices to stay competitive.

- EXPORTS — being able to export goods easily means firms have a larger market to sell to. This can lead to increased sales and higher profits.

- BUSINESS LOCATION — globalisation has made it easier for businesses to locate parts of their business abroad (e.g. to set up stores, factories or offices overseas). This may allow them to reduce their costs so they can make more profit, e.g. if they start producing goods closer to where they get their raw materials from, their transport costs will fall. Some firms may also set up in countries where labour is cheaper, which helps to keep their costs down.

- MULTINATIONALS — single businesses operating in more than one country are known as multinationals. When a big, multinational business enters a new country, firms already in that country may need to change the way they operate in order to compete successfully.

Globalisation

You saw on the previous page that globalisation has many advantages for businesses, but it's not always a good thing. Globalisation means there's more competition, and this can cause some businesses to suffer.

Globalisation has **Drawbacks** for Businesses

1) Higher wages in the UK means some UK industries can't compete with firms from other countries. E.g. steel from China is much cheaper than from the UK, partly because the average wage in China is lower than in the UK. So some UK industries such as steel manufacture have suffered from globalisation.

2) Other countries have different currencies to the UK. So if a business is buying or selling products in other countries, its profits are likely to be affected by changes in the exchange rate (see next page).

3) UK businesses that set up factories abroad to benefit from cheaper labour costs may get bad publicity if they're seen to be exploiting or endangering workers in these countries.

BUSINESS EXAMPLE

1) In 2012, a fire in a clothes factory in Bangladesh killed at least 117 people and injured over 200.
2) Many workers were unable to escape, partly because there weren't enough emergency exits.
3) UK businesses who outsourced their clothing manufacture to factories in Bangladesh came under scrutiny to make sure the factories they were using had a good level of fire safety and to give money to these factories to help them to improve their working conditions.

Firms Face **Barriers** to **International Trade**

Firms can't just buy and sell products across the world as much as they want — governments have set up tariffs and trade blocs as a way of trying to control international trade:

- Tariffs — these are taxes on goods that are being imported or exported. They make products imported into a country more expensive than those that are produced domestically (in the home country). This helps domestic firms stay competitive.

- Trade blocs — these are groups of countries that have few or no trade barriers between them, e.g. they can trade with each other without having to pay tariffs. Firms from countries outside the trade bloc will find it hard to compete with those inside, as their prices will be affected by having to pay tariffs.

Some methods can help protect firms from the drawbacks of globalisation...

Tariffs and trade blocs make it harder for firms to trade in some countries. Without them, businesses in the home country could suffer. So these things try to make it easier for the firms based in the country to compete.

Exchange Rates

Exchange rates show how currencies compare. They're important for firms that buy from or sell to other countries.

Exchange Rates Convert between Currencies

1) If a company wants to import products, they'll have to pay for the product in the currency of the country it was made in. For example, if a British firm is importing goods from the US, they'll have to pay for them in dollars, rather than pounds.
2) An exchange rate is the price at which one currency can be traded for another.
3) Exchange rates are affected by the economy of the country that uses the currency, and by the global economy. This means they can change over time.

- In June 2016, the UK voted to leave the European Union.
- This created a lot of uncertainty about what would happen to the UK economy.
- As a result, the value of the pound dropped overnight.
- The day before the result was announced, £1 was worth \$1.48. After the result was announced, £1 was worth just \$1.36.

A Weak Pound is Good for Exporters, Bad for Importers

1) If the value of the pound decreases, you'll be able to buy fewer dollars (or other currency) for the same price as before.
2) Pounds are cheaper, so British exports become less expensive abroad — resulting in more sales and higher profits for British firms that export products to other countries.
3) The weak pound also makes it more expensive for foreign firms to sell their products in the UK. That's good news for British firms that compete with goods imported from abroad — they won't have to reduce their prices so much to stay competitive.
4) But it's bad news for British firms that use imported raw materials — these are now more expensive so the production costs of these firms are higher. They'll need to increase the price they sell their products for to cover their costs, which could cause their sales and profits to go down.
5) The result is that the UK will have more exports and fewer imports.

- If £1 = \$1.50, a British cricket ball that costs £5 will sell in the US for 5 × 1.50 = \$7.50. And a baseball that cost \$6 in the US can be sold for 6 ÷ 1.50 = £4 in the UK.
- If the value of the pound falls so that £1 = \$1.30 the £5 cricket ball would sell in the US for 5 × 1.30 = \$6.50. The \$6 baseball can now be sold in the UK for 6 ÷ 1.30 = £4.62.

A Strong Pound is Bad for Exporters, Good for Importers

1) An increase in the value of the pound makes exports more expensive and imports cheaper. It's just the opposite effect to the example above.
2) British firms that export products to other countries are likely to see their sales and profits go down — their products will be more expensive so fewer people will buy them. They may decide to move part of their business abroad so they can trade in the currency of the country where they sell their products, meaning they will be less affected by the exchange rate.
3) British firms that import raw materials will be able to make products more cheaply, so their profits may go up.

Changes in exchange rates can have a big effect on businesses...

The important thing here is to understand how changing exchange rates affects the cost of importing or exporting. It's all to do with whether currencies are more or less expensive compared to others.

Risks and Rewards

All businesses face risks and uncertainties — whether they're new or established, big or small. But by taking these risks, there's the possibility of gaining rewards. And there are things that can be done to reduce the risks.

There are **Lots of Risks** and **Rewards** in Running a Business

Here are some examples of the risks, uncertainties and rewards that businesses have to consider:

Risks and uncertainties

1) To start a business, an entrepreneur needs money to buy equipment and pay workers. An entrepreneur will often use their own money, but they'll probably need to raise more from banks or other investors as well (see p.129). If the business makes a financial loss, it won't be able to pay back all the money that's been borrowed (and it may struggle to survive).
2) Entrepreneurs don't have much security when they are starting a new business. They'll usually have given up another job to follow their business idea, and if things go wrong they could lose money and end up without any job, which could have a huge impact on their quality of life.
3) There's always a risk that a business will fail. So the entrepreneur risks the money, time and effort they put in to trying to make the business work.
4) The health of the economy can affect all sorts of things — including unemployment levels, interest rates and exchange rates. If these things change, they can have a big impact on a business. For example, it can affect the demand for products and how much investment there is in the business.
5) Few firms know exactly what their competitors are planning. If a competitor brings out a new product or claims more market share then a firm may struggle to survive.

Rewards

1) For many entrepreneurs, one reward is seeing their business idea become a success.
2) If the business makes lots of profit, the entrepreneur could earn more money than they did before they started the business. This could give them a better quality of life.
3) Being an entrepreneur can also be rewarding as it gives the entrepreneur the independence to choose what they do day-to-day, and what direction the business goes in (see p.6).

Businesses can do **Certain Things** to **Reduce the Risks**

There are a few things that business owners can do to help make sure that their business is a success.

Planning

1) Doing a business plan (p.26) at the start makes a new business less likely to fail.
2) Established businesses also need to make plans in order to change or grow the business.
3) However, things don't always go to plan. Firms need to have 'plan Bs' in place to prepare for different scenarios. E.g. if a firm's main supplier suddenly goes bust, the firm should already have the details of other suppliers that they can use.

Even if a business does all these things, it can still fail — sometimes success is just down to luck.

Researching

1) Businesses should carry out regular market research to make sure they've got the right marketing mix for their products (p.95) — this means they should be selling the right products to people who want to buy them in the right place and at the right price.
2) Businesses should research their competition. This means they will be more aware of any new competitors and can keep up with any new products or pricing that competitors have brought in.
3) Businesses need to make sure they're aware of any planned changes to the law or predicted changes to the economy that could affect them. This allows them to prepare for the changes and make sure they have the best plans in place for dealing with them.

Entrepreneurs have to take risks if they want the rewards...

Running a business is risky. Regular planning and researching are crucial if a firm is going to survive long-term.

Worked Exam Questions

Practising exam questions is a great way to get you prepared for the real things. This page will give you an idea of the types of questions that might come up, and how you should answer them.

1 Look at **Item A** below.

Item A — Tasty Teas:
Louise is starting a new company, Tasty Teas, which sells ready cooked meals. In order to start up Tasty Teas, Louise has taken out a loan from her bank. Unlike similar products on the market, the ingredients Louise uses to make the ready cooked meals are all ethically sourced and are very high quality. Louise also offers meal varieties that aren't available from other companies in the market.

Outline **one** risk to Louise of starting up Tasty Teas. *[2]*

You know that the business has just started up, so make sure the risk you state is something that new businesses might face.

Sample Answer:

If Tasty Teas doesn't make enough profit, then Louise might not be able to pay back the money she has borrowed from the bank, and her business may fail.

Link the potential problem that you have stated to the overall impact that it could cause for Louise for your second mark.

As well as the possibility of Louise's business failing, you could also have said that she may end up losing money.

2 **Figure 1** shows how yearly interest rates changed in a country between 1900 and 2010.

Figure 1

Yearly interest rates in country A from 1900 to 2010

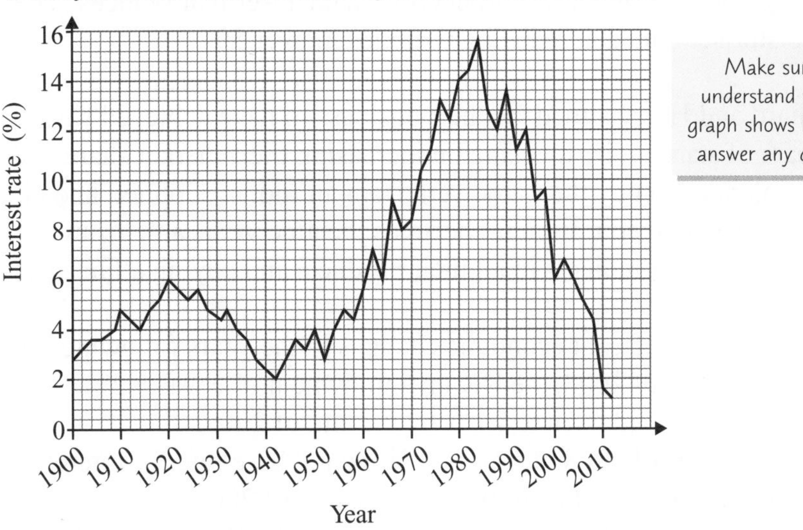

Make sure you understand what the graph shows before you answer any questions.

Outline which year was the most expensive for borrowing money. *[2]*

You need to work out how interest rates affect the cost of borrowing to find out which year would have been most expensive.

Sample Answer:

1984, because this is the year in which interest rates were at their highest.

Exam Questions

1 Discuss the possible reasons why a business might face very little competition.

....

....

....

....

....

....

....

....

....

....

[Total 6 marks]

2 Look at **Item A** below.

Item A — Clear Skin:
In 2006, Richard and Harry took out an £8000 loan to set up their partnership, Clear Skin, a business selling natural skincare products over the internet. After researching the market, they decided to launch two products — a cleanser that reduces acne, aimed at teenagers, and a moisturiser aimed at reducing wrinkles in over 50s.

Richard and Harry aimed for their business to have achieved financial security within 5 years of starting, by focusing on increasing their market share and sales during this period. They planned to buy their aloe vera from an Indian supplier, and aimed to reinvest some of their profits into education in the areas the aloe vera came from. Their other aims included using natural ingredients in all their products and paying a fair price for the ingredients.

There were significant economic changes in the years following 2007:

- At the start of 2008, the UK unemployment rate was 5.2%. This figure had risen to 7.8% by the end of 2009.
- At the start of 2008, the Bank of England base rate for interest was 5.5%. This figure had fallen to 0.5% by the end of 2009.
- At the start of 2008, the exchange rate of the British pound against the Indian currency, the rupee, was 78.2. This figure had fallen to 75.3 by the end of 2009.

Evaluate whether Clear Skin is likely to have benefited from the changing economic climate. You should use the information provided, as well as your knowledge of business.
Write your answer on a separate piece of paper.

[Total 12 marks]

Revision Summary for Section 2

That's all for Influences on Business. Time for a few questions to see what you've remembered.

- Try these questions and tick off each one when you get it right.
- When you've done all the questions for a topic and are completely happy with it, tick off the topic.

Business and the Law (p.34-36) ☐

1) Describe the difference between people who are entitled to the National Minimum Wage and people who are entitled to the National Living Wage. ☐
2) Briefly describe what the Equality Act 2010 states about recruitment in a business. ☐
3) State two possible consequences to a business of failing to follow the Health and Safety at Work Act 1974. ☐
4) Explain why breaking consumer law can be expensive for a business. ☐

Technology and Business (p.37-38) ☐

5) Explain why social media is a good method of communication for businesses. ☐
6) Give three different payment systems that can be used by businesses. ☐
7) Explain how using new technology may have a positive impact on a business's costs. ☐

Ethics and the Environment (p.39-41) ☐

8) Describe three ways in which a firm could make sure it is working ethically. ☐
9) Explain why working ethically might reduce a firm's profits. ☐
10) State two ways in which a business may damage the local environment. ☐
11) What does it mean if a business is trying to become more sustainable? ☐
12) What is meant by a pressure group? ☐

The Economy and Business (p.44-46) ☐

13) State two negative impacts that high levels of unemployment can have on a business. ☐
14) Explain how a business might be affected if the amount of tax consumers have to pay increases. ☐
15) Describe a type of business that could suffer if prices are rising at a faster rate than incomes. ☐
16) Explain what happens to consumer spending when interest rates fall. ☐
17) Explain how a firm with lots of loans will be affected by rising interest rates. ☐

Competition and Globalisation (p.47-51) ☐

18) Describe two factors about a business that can make it stand out from its competition. ☐
19) State two ways in which UK businesses make themselves competitive at an international level. ☐
20) Explain two ways in which businesses might benefit from globalisation. ☐
21) Explain two ways in which businesses might face barriers to international trade. ☐
22) What is an exchange rate? ☐

Risks and Rewards (p.52) ☐

23) Give two rewards an entrepreneur might gain by running a business. ☐
24) Describe two things a business can do to minimise the risks of failing. ☐

Supply Chain

Business operations are the activities needed for the business's day-to-day functioning. There's quite a lot of different things that businesses have to juggle to get their operations just right. First up, supply chains...

Businesses Need to Have **Dependable Supply Chains**

1) A supply chain consists of the group of firms that are involved in all the various processes required to make a finished product or service available to the customer.
2) The chain begins with the provider of raw materials (supplier) and ends with the firm that sells the finished product.
3) The members of a supply chain will vary depending on the type of product or service, but will typically include suppliers, manufacturers (firms that make products), distributors and retailers.

A distributor usually buys products from a manufacturer and sells them on to other businesses or consumers (people like me and you). A retailer sells products directly to consumers.

4) All the members of the supply chain need to be dependable. If any are unreliable, the product won't be on the shelves when it needs to be, or the quality will be poor, which reflects badly on the company selling it.
5) The more members of the supply chain there are, the longer it is. The length of the supply chain can affect the businesses within it. E.g. if the supply chain is very long, it may take a long time for a product reach the retailers. This means retailers may have to make decisions about what supplies they'll need very far in advance.
6) The customer service offered throughout a supply chain may also affect businesses. E.g. a company which sells its products through a retailer with good customer service will be likely to sell more of its products.

Companies Need to **Choose** Their **Suppliers** Carefully

It's important that a company chooses the right supplier and builds a relationship with them. To choose a supplier, the company should consider the following things:

Quality

- The quality of supplies needs to be consistent.
- Customers can be very selective about quality — the internet means it's easy for them to shop elsewhere if they're not happy with the quality of a product.
- Customers will associate poor quality with the business they buy from, not their suppliers.

Reliability and Trust

- If a supplier lets a firm down, the firm may be unable to supply its own customers.
- So firms need reliable suppliers that they can trust.
- Suppliers need to deliver high-quality products on time, or give plenty of warning if they can't.

Availability

- If a supplier is often out of stock of items, it could affect the firm's production process.
- So they need to make sure their supplier can provide stock in sufficient quantities.

Delivery

- Firms need to consider how much it will cost to get supplies delivered, and how quickly they want supplies to arrive.
- Delivery from a supplier that's near the firm is likely to be cheaper and faster than from a supplier that's further away.
- Delivery should also be reliable — if a supplier doesn't deliver stock on time or it gets damaged along the way, the business's production could be disrupted.

Price (the total cost of getting the product)

- Firms have to decide how much they want to pay for supplies and whether cost is their top priority.
- If they want to cut down the time it takes to serve customers, suppliers that offer faster delivery may rate higher than those that compete on price alone.
- Also, cheaper suppliers will often supply lower quality products. The firm needs to balance reduced costs with the quality of the product or service it wants to provide.

There are lots of factors that affect a business's choice of supplier...

If a supplier is late or supplies shoddy goods then it can have serious knock-on effects on the business.

Procurement and Logistics

Procurement is all about getting the things that a company needs. But even if a company gets its procurement right, there are still lots of things that it needs to consider to make sure things run smoothly — including logistics...

Procurement and **Logistics** are **Really Important** in a Business

1) Procurement means finding and buying things that a firm needs from suppliers outside of the firm. E.g. for a clothes manufacturer, procurement would involve finding and buying the material it needs.
2) There are several stages to procurement. First of all the firm needs to identify the goods or services that it needs to buy. Then it needs to choose what supplier to use for these goods or services and then order the right amount for the firm. Finally it needs to organise receiving the goods and services from its supplier.
3) Logistics means getting goods or services from one part of the supply chain to another. E.g. a clothes manufacturer would need to have the material it needs transported to its factory.
4) Having effective procurement and logistics systems in place improves the efficiency of a business — the business will have the supplies it needs at the right time. This means, for example, there will be no breaks in production because materials aren't available, or that materials don't have to be wasted because they didn't arrive at the right time or weren't really needed.
5) Effective procurement and logistics can reduce the overall costs of a business. If a business gets its supplies at the best price and it doesn't waste money by being inefficient it will have lower overall costs. This will reduce the unit cost — the amount it costs to make each item. So the firm can make more profit on each item or pass the savings on to the consumer by reducing prices.
6) Well-managed procurement and logistics helps to ensure a firm's products are high-quality, a reasonable price and delivered on time. This improves both customer satisfaction and the firm's reputation.

Managing a Supply Chain **Effectively** is Very Important

Companies that manage their supply chain effectively gain these benefits:

1 Good Relationship with Suppliers

A company that works closely with its suppliers can make sure that processes are being carried out in ways that are most efficient and cost-effective.

2 Finding the Best Price and Value

1) There are often many suppliers for a business to choose from.
2) Businesses that research potential suppliers can make sure they are getting the best price and value for the goods they need.

3 Reducing Waste and Unnecessary Costs

1) Companies should reduce waste wherever they can. For example, they should only buy supplies they really need. This reduces waste from having to get rid of supplies that they haven't used.
2) Companies should reduce any unnecessary costs in their supply chain. For example, if their delivery trucks are only ever half full, it might be better to get smaller vehicles that are cheaper to run.
3) Reducing waste and unnecessary costs can help to make a business more streamlined (more efficient) and have faster production times — they have the supplies they need when they need them, and spend less time dealing with waste and other things that aren't really needed.

Good supply chain management sets a business up for greatness...

Procurement and logistics often operate side by side. That means that a business will have to consider the logistics of using a particular supplier even before they choose to buy from them.

Methods of Production

Businesses need to work out how to make their products — this is called production or manufacturing. On this page you'll meet job production, then flow production and batch production are coming up on the next page.

There are Two Ultimate Reasons for Business Operations

1) Business operations generally have one of two main purposes:
   - To produce goods, such as books or cars.
   - To provide services, such as haircuts or eye tests.
2) A business that produces goods has to decide the best way to manufacture its products. There are a number of ways to do this depending on the type of product and the scale of the business operation.

Job Production is Making One Thing at a Time

1) Job production is used when a firm manufactures individual, unique products. Each product has a unique design based upon the customer's specification. Examples include the building of ships and bridges, and handmade crafts such as furniture making and made-to-measure clothes.

2) These products often require highly skilled labour and have a high labour-to-capital ratio (i.e. lots of workers are needed, but relatively little financial investment) — they can be very labour-intensive.

3) As each product is unique, they can take a long time to make. Fewer products are made in a set period of time compared to other production methods, meaning the firm's productivity will be low.

4) The business will generally have high costs, as they'll need skilled workers to produce the goods, who will have higher wages than unskilled workers. Since each product that's made is unique, the company is less able to take advantage of economies of scale, e.g. by buying materials in bulk. So their unit costs will be high.

See p.28 for more on economies of scale.

5) Higher costs mean that a company will need to give its products higher prices in order to make a profit. However, the products are unique and usually high quality, so customers may still buy the products even if the company sets its prices very high, which can lead to higher profits for a firm.

It's important for a business to use the right method of production...

Job production is generally used for products that need to be of high quality or which are made to an individual customer's wishes. See if you can think of a few different products that might be made using job production, e.g. wedding cakes, or think of businesses that might only use job production.

Methods of Production

Now onto flow production and batch production — two methods that are used to make products in larger quantities than using job production (see p.58) and a bit about why a firm might choose one method over another.

Flow Production is Making **Lots of Things Continuously**

1) This is the opposite of job production. All products are identical and the aim is to produce as many as possible along an assembly line, and make productivity as high as possible. To be efficient, production has to be continuous with no stoppages — many flow production factories operate 24 hours a day with workers rotating in shifts.

Flow production is also sometimes called mass production.

2) The aim is to gain from economies of scale and so have low average unit costs to allow competitive prices. Modern flow production techniques use robots, not people, to do most of the work. Where workers do have jobs along the assembly line they are simpler tasks than in job production. Flow production is highly capital-intensive (it needs a lot of money — to buy machinery, for example) and may also require a lot of space for product storage.

3) It is used for mass-market products. Most modern consumer goods are produced this way — chocolate bars, mobile phones, televisions... etc.

Batch Production is a **Mixture** of Job and Flow Production

1) In batch production, firms use flow production techniques to make a batch of one thing then stop, reorganise, and make a batch of something else.
2) It is suited to products that are identical to each other, but which are only produced in limited quantities — or for a limited amount of time. For example, furniture (where producers make a limited number of many different designs).
3) Batch production is faster than job production, since each product in a batch is identical. So firms that use batch production have higher productivity than firms using job production.
4) The company can also buy materials in larger quantities than job production, so can take advantage of economies of scale. This means unit costs are lower than job production, so prices can be lower and therefore more competitive.
5) However, time is needed to change between batches, so productivity is lower than for flow production.
6) Batch production is also more expensive than flow production because, for example, different machinery and tools might be needed to make different products. This means prices might not be as competitive as products made using flow production.

Batch production involves lots of stopping and starting...

Almost everything you find on supermarket shelves or in shops on the high street will have been made using flow production. It's everywhere. Batch production is what firms such as your neighbourhood bakery will do. They'll make the dough for one type of bread, bake lots of loaves, and then move on to the next thing.

Technology and Production

Technology has had huge effects on how businesses produce their goods — using technology can help to make some tasks a lot easier and faster. It's not all good news, though, there are some disadvantages too.

Technology can Affect Production

1) Advances in technology have created new ways to produce goods. For example, robots are now often used instead of human staff for tasks such as assembling products or packing products into boxes. It's usually cheaper and faster for robots to do these jobs instead of humans.

2) Technology can also be used to help design products. For example, computers can be made to design products digitally, and this information can then be fed straight into the production machine. For example, 3D printing can be used to print a prototype (a test model) of a product from a digital file. This is faster and cheaper than traditional methods of making prototypes, making the design process more efficient.

3) Using automation can be useful for a company — this is when a machine works by itself, with little or no human involvement. For example, automated greenhouses are often used in agriculture. Sensors monitor environmental conditions, such as temperature, to make sure conditions are kept at the best levels to allow the plants to grow well. Automation means processes can happen continuously with very few errors. It's faster and cheaper than using humans to do the same tasks.

4) There are advantages and disadvantages to using technology:

Advantages

- Technology can carry out processes more quickly and accurately than humans. So using technology can increase the productivity of the business and the goods that are produced should be of a more consistent quality.
- Technology means that machines can work 24/7, so production can be completely continuous.
- In the long term, it's cheaper to run machines than to pay humans to do the same thing.

Disadvantages

- Using technology can be very expensive — it can cost a lot to buy and install new machines and they may need regular maintenance and updates. Staff will also need to be trained to use the technology, which can be expensive and time-consuming.
- Some technologies might replace manual work, so staff might be worried they'll lose their jobs. This could demotivate them, causing their productivity to go down.
- Machines are often only suited to one task, which can make them inflexible. This makes it difficult if the business wants to change its production method (or the product it's making).

Whatever the type of production, technology is often used somehow...

For many firms (especially smaller ones), the costs involved in starting to use new technology can put them off doing it. However, using technology helps products to be made more cheaply, meaning firms can offer customers lower prices. So firms that don't adapt to using new technology may find themselves struggling to compete.

Production Efficiency and Managing Stock

In efficient firms there's no messing about when it comes to production — they get products made and out of the door as efficiently as they can. This will be affected by the strategies used to manage their stock. 'Just-in-time' is one way of managing stock, and there's another coming up on the next page.

Lean Production Increases Efficiency of Production

1) Lean production is a strategy businesses can use to make production more efficient.
2) In lean production, the business aims to use as few resources as possible and to have as little waste as possible.
3) Workers can also be encouraged to think about ways to improve their productivity (how much they can produce in a given time).

Products can be Made 'Just-in-Time'

1) Just-in-time (JIT) is a form of lean production.
2) JIT aims to keep stock levels to the bare minimum — preferably zero.
3) Ideally, all raw materials come in one door, are made into products and go straight out another door — all 'just in time' for delivery to customers.
4) Computer systems are usually used to calculate stock levels and automatically order more when more supplies are needed.
5) There are both advantages and disadvantages of using 'just-in-time' stock management for a business. For example:

Advantages

1) The main benefit of JIT is that it reduces the cost of having to keep stock (you need less warehouse space, fewer warehouse workers, and so on).
2) It also means stock is less likely to go out of date as it shouldn't be stored for very long.
3) JIT helps cash flow, as there won't be much delay between buying supplies and selling the product.

Disadvantages

1) The main problem is that it requires a lot of coordination between the firm and its suppliers. The firm needs to take lots of frequent deliveries of stock — if any of these deliveries don't arrive on time or there are mistakes with the order, the firm could run out of stock.
2) A JIT method also means that firms buy small quantities of stock at a time, rather than buying in bulk. This means they lose out on purchasing economies of scale (see page 28).

'Just-in-time' means that stock is ordered... well... just in time...

'Lean' means that there's not much of something, which is how lean production gets its name. It's all about making quality products with as little as possible. Make sure you understand how 'just-in-time' is a form of lean production and some of its advantages and disadvantages.

Managing Stock

As well as the 'just-in-time' stock management on the previous page, companies can use another method of stock management called 'just-in-case'. Firms that use this form of stock management can use a certain type of graph (called a bar gate stock graph) to help them keep on top of when to order stock.

'Just-in-Case' Stock Control Means That There is Always Spare Stock

1) JIC is a method of operating a production and distribution system with buffer stocks (extra stocks) of items at every stage of the process — from raw materials to finished products — just in case there is a supply shortage or customer demand increases unexpectedly.
2) The idea is that even if there's a problem with deliveries of any raw materials, the buffer stocks will mean there is still enough to satisfy demand so production can continue.
3) The main problem is that firms can be left with big stockpiles of items, which can be costly to store.

Bar Gate Stock Graphs Show a Company when to Order Materials

1) To help prevent large stockpiles of items from building up, a business can use bar gate stock graphs to help keep on top of when to order stock.
2) These graphs monitor how much stock the business has, and show when a business should order more stock so that by the time the new stock has arrived, the business hasn't needed to use its buffer. They also show the maximum amount of stock a business can hold, so that it doesn't order too much.

BUSINESS EXAMPLE

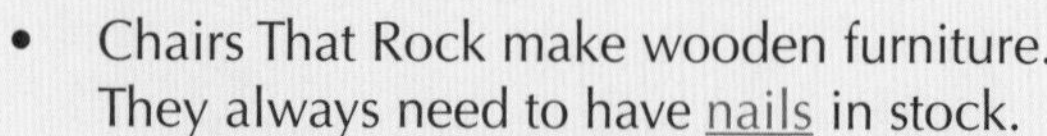

- Chairs That Rock make wooden furniture. They always need to have nails in stock.
- When stocks of nails fall to 800, they reorder more.
- The hope is that by the time the new stock arrives the stock level won't have fallen below 250 nails. 250 nails is the minimum level of nails the firm always wants to keep — it is their buffer stock level.
- You can use the bar gate stock graph to identify when an order of new nails arrived — it's where the graph is vertical.
- The height of the vertical line shows how many nails were ordered. E.g. on day 12, stock arrives. The stock level rose from 350 nails to 1150 nails. So it ordered 1150 – 350 = 800 nails.
- The amount of time it takes stock to be delivered is the difference between the time where stock is at the reorder level and the time when stock arrives. Here, the first time stock hit the reorder level was on day 6. The stock arrived on day 12, so the delivery time was 12 – 6 = 6 days.

Bar gate stock graphs help ensure stockpiles don't get out of control...

If you get a bar gate stock graph to interpret in the exam, take your time. If you need to read a figure off the graph, use a ruler to draw a line from the graph down or across to the axis you need to read from. And double check you've read the scale on the axis properly before you write your answer.

Worked Exam Question

Long answer questions might seem daunting, but they'll definitely come up in the exams so you need to learn how to answer them. By working through the example below you'll see the kind of things you need to write.

1 Look at **Item A** below.

Item A — Shake it Up:
Shake it Up is a company that makes milkshakes and delivers them to cafés across the UK. Shake it Up buys the milk for its milkshakes from a local farm. The factory manager can confirm how much milk he would like for the following day up to 6pm the day before. The farm always ensures that the order is ready for collection by Shake it Up's driver the next morning. The produce from the farm is of a high standard, so Shake it Up has been buying from the farm for many years. Recently, the farm has started to offer Shake it Up a discount on orders over £4000. Shake it Up buys enough to use this discount approximately once a week.

The directors of Shake it Up have decided to grow the business by making ice cream as well as milkshakes. As the product is new, they aren't sure what the demand will be. They are considering whether to use the same arrangement for buying and collecting cream from the farm as for milk, or whether to use Ribblethwaites, a larger farming corporation that they have not used before. Buying cream from Ribblethwaites would be cheaper than the local farm, but would mean Shake it Up had to order cream a week in advance. The cream would then be delivered to Shake it Up's factory free of charge.

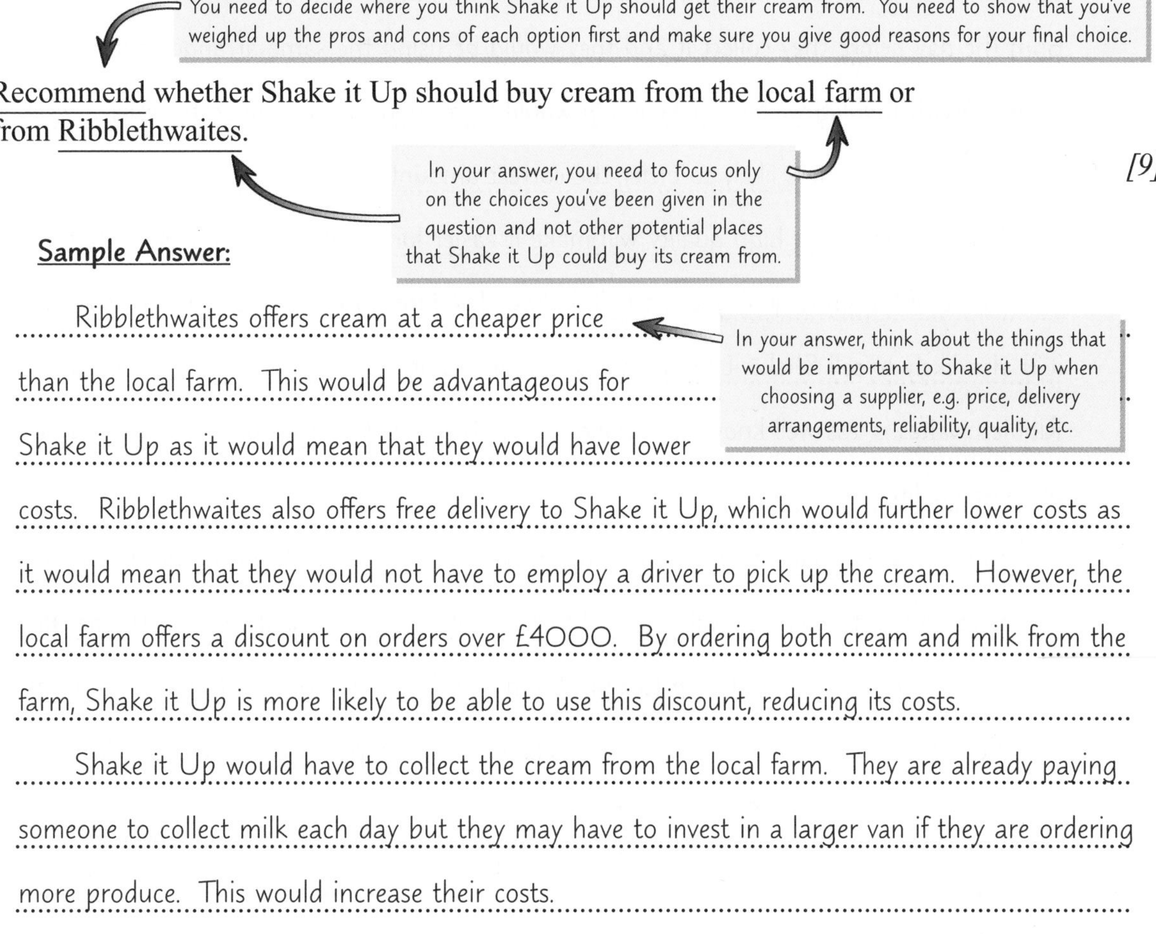

You need to decide where you think Shake it Up should get their cream from. You need to show that you've weighed up the pros and cons of each option first and make sure you give good reasons for your final choice.

Recommend whether Shake it Up should buy cream from the local farm or from Ribblethwaites. *[9]*

In your answer, you need to focus only on the choices you've been given in the question and not other potential places that Shake it Up could buy its cream from.

Sample Answer:

In your answer, think about the things that would be important to Shake it Up when choosing a supplier, e.g. price, delivery arrangements, reliability, quality, etc.

Ribblethwaites offers cream at a cheaper price than the local farm. This would be advantageous for Shake it Up as it would mean that they would have lower costs. Ribblethwaites also offers free delivery to Shake it Up, which would further lower costs as it would mean that they would not have to employ a driver to pick up the cream. However, the local farm offers a discount on orders over £4000. By ordering both cream and milk from the farm, Shake it Up is more likely to be able to use this discount, reducing its costs.

Shake it Up would have to collect the cream from the local farm. They are already paying someone to collect milk each day but they may have to invest in a larger van if they are ordering more produce. This would increase their costs.

Worked Exam Question

Shake it Up don't know how reliable Ribblethwaites is. They do know that the local farm is reliable since it ensures that milk is ready for collection the morning after it has been ordered. Since the local farm has been reliable in the past, it is likely to be reliable in supplying cream as well.

Use evidence from the information you're given in your answer. For example, the information in Item A says that the farm 'always ensures that the order is ready for collection...', which suggests the farm is reliable.

Shake it Up are unlikely to know how much cream to order because they don't know what the demand for ice cream will be. If the company orders too little cream then they may not be able to make enough ice cream to complete all of their orders, which could reduce customer satisfaction. If Shake it Up orders too much cream then some of it may go to waste, resulting in an increase in the company's costs. Having a more flexible arrangement for ordering cream would be beneficial for Shake it Up as they would be more likely to order the correct amount and therefore avoid having a surplus or shortage of cream. The arrangement with the farm is much more flexible than it would be with Ribblethwaites — Shake it Up is able to change their order for milk from the local farm up to 6pm the day before they collect it and they would be using the same arrangement for ordering cream. With Ribblethwaites, Shake it Up would have to know how much to order a week in advance, so they are less likely to order the correct amount of cream.

Make sure you explain each of the points you make.

Having cream of a high quality will make it easier for Shake it Up to ensure that its ice creams are of the same quality as its milkshakes. The farm's milk is of a high quality, therefore it is also likely to sell Shake it Up cream of a high quality, whereas the quality of produce from Ribblethwaites is less well known to Shake it Up. The fact that it is cheaper may mean that it is of lower quality.

In conclusion, Shake it Up should buy cream from the farm. Even though it will be more expensive, this cost difference will be less if they are able to use their discount. The flexibility of being able to change the order up to 6pm the day before collection is a big advantage, as is the fact they know that the farm has reliable availability and supplies high quality produce.

Don't forget to give an overall conclusion recommending which supplier Shake it Up should use. Summarise the main reasons why you think this is the best choice.

Exam Questions

1 Explain **one** advantage of a firm using batch production, rather than job production.

....

....

....

[Total 3 marks]

2 Look at **Item A** below.

Item A — The Reading Shelf:
The Reading Shelf is a firm that supplies books to bookshops around the UK. Orders from bookshops can vary a lot. It manages stock by keeping buffer levels of each book at all times and orders books in bulk from a supplier once a week. Occasionally, deliveries can be delayed. The supplier offers discounts on orders over 2000 units. The supplier has a fixed delivery charge, no matter how large the order is. The Reading Shelf stores books in a large warehouse which costs £1,500 per month to rent. So that there is space in the warehouse to store new titles of books, any copies of titles that are no longer selling are discarded at the end of each month.

The Reading Shelf is considering changing its method of stock control to just-in-time (JIT). Analyse the impact on The Reading Shelf of changing to just-in-time stock control.

....

....

....

....

....

....

....

....

....

....

....

[Total 6 marks]

Quality

Even the most productive business in the world won't get far if its products aren't up to scratch.

Customers Expect **Quality** from **All Parts** of a Business

1) Products should be good quality, of course. The quality can depend on different factors such as the materials the product is made from and the production method used to assemble the product. At the very least, customers expect products to work properly, and not fall apart straight away.
2) For businesses that provide a service, the service needs to be good quality. For example, a bus company needs to make sure its buses are clean, well-maintained and arrive when they're supposed to.
3) Monitoring quality helps a firm to control its costs. By making sure products are high quality, the firm should waste less from making products that it can't sell. It should also reduce the number of product returns it gets — this is when customers return items, often because they are poor quality. The firm has to compensate these customers (either by giving their money back or a replacement item) so it increases the firm's costs. Monitoring quality should also reduce the cost of customer service, as there should be fewer complaints.
4) If a firm is known for producing good quality items it will improve the firm's brand image. This may give the firm a competitive advantage as customers will be more likely to choose them over competitors. This means the firm may be able to charge more for its items and so could make more profit.

Firms Need to **Measure Quality**

Before firms can determine whether their products are good quality, they need to clarify what good quality means to them and find ways to measure it. There are different ways a firm can measure quality. E.g.

1) They can specify the physical properties of a product, e.g. its exact size, colour, ingredients, etc., and then test a random sample to check they meet these specifications (see below).
2) They can monitor how many products get returned and how many customer complaints they get. The firm can decide what level of returns or complaints it is comfortable with.
3) They can carry out customer surveys to assess how satisfied customers are with quality.

Firms need to have good systems in place to make sure their products are high quality — quality control (below) and quality assurance (next page) are two systems they can use.

Quality Control Involves Checking For **Faults**

1) Checking products as they're being made helps to find faults before a product reaches the customer. Products are usually checked by trained quality inspectors at three different stages:

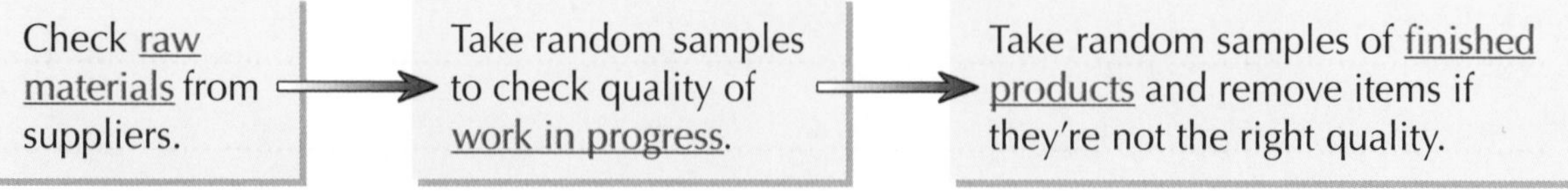

Check raw materials from suppliers.
Take random samples to check quality of work in progress.
Take random samples of finished products and remove items if they're not the right quality.

2) Defects may be spotted before they have finished making the products, reducing waste.
3) The process can be expensive (sometimes whole batches of goods might need to be scrapped). But the cost to the business would be greater if dissatisfied customers returned their products or stopped buying their products.
4) Quality control can also be carried out for businesses that provide services, even though there isn't a physical product to check. For example, many shops will employ 'secret shoppers' who visit the stores pretending to be customers, and check that the staff are providing the right quality of service. Staff in stores which have poor quality can then have training to improve their service.

Quality

Quality assurance is another method firms can use to maintain high quality standards. But whatever method of quality management a firm uses, it's easy for standards to slip if the firm grows quickly.

Quality Assurance is about Making Sure Things Don't Go Wrong

1) Quality assurance means checking that quality is being maintained throughout each process involved in making the product. It aims to stop errors from being made in the first place, rather than needing to get rid of faulty goods once they've been made.
2) For example, at each stage of a production line employees should check that the work they pass on to the next stage is good quality.
3) A firm can have its quality assessed by an external body. It may be awarded a rating or certificate that it can display to assure customers that the business provides high quality products.

BUSINESS EXAMPLE

1) VisitEngland is a company that recommends holiday ideas in the UK.
2) Among other things, VisitEngland assess visitor attractions and awards them a star rating based on the quality of the whole experience — from promotional material to the visit itself.
3) The attraction can use its VisitEngland star rating to attract customers, e.g. by displaying it on its website, leaflets, etc. This encourages the attraction to have high quality in all parts of the firm.

Total Quality Management (TQM) — a Culture of Quality

1) The TQM strategy aims to make quality the responsibility of every employee in a firm, in order to make sure that quality remains consistent. Employees are encouraged to think about the needs of the customer. The focus is on getting things right first time — this reduces costs by cutting down on waste.
2) There is an emphasis on the quality of after-sales service as well as on the quality of production, both of which will increase customer satisfaction.
3) A downside of TQM is that it takes a long time to introduce. Workers need training so that they see quality as their responsibility — employees can get demotivated as it may seem like a lot of extra work.

Rapid Growth Makes it Hard to Maintain High Quality

For businesses, growth is good — but success can bring its own problems.
When a business starts to grow very quickly, its output of products will need to increase quickly too.
Making sure quality standards stay high can become more difficult.

1) It may become expensive to carry out all the necessary quality inspections.
2) A business can also be overwhelmed by orders and cut corners to make products quicker.
3) One solution is to take on more employees — but it takes time to train new workers. Businesses have to be careful that standards don't fall in the meantime.
4) The business might become a franchisor (see p.13) — ensuring high quality standards are maintained across the franchises can involve a lot of staff training and regular inspections.
5) The business might outsource some tasks (pay another firm to do them). It can be expensive to outsource to a firm that delivers high quality (but using a cheaper firm can lead to a fall in quality).

Maintaining quality — it's more than just making an attractive product...

Make sure you understand the difference between the terms 'quality control' and 'quality assurance'. Quality control involves looking at the products at each stage to spot faults. Quality assurance is about managing processes involved in making the products, to prevent faults from happening at all.

Quality

Maintaining quality can have a few drawbacks for a firm, but in the long run it's usually beneficial. Here are some examples of the benefits and costs of maintaining quality, as well as the dangers of not maintaining it.

There Are **Benefits** and **Costs** Involved in **Maintaining Quality**

Benefits

1) HIGHER PRICE — Customers are often prepared to pay a higher price for better quality products — as long as they're still good value for money.
2) INCREASED SALES — When customers are pleased with the quality a business provides, they're likely to make repeat purchases (buy from the business again). This increases the business's sales.
3) BETTER REPUTATION AND IMAGE — Businesses that provide higher quality products are likely to have a better reputation and image than those that don't. This means new customers are more likely to choose them and existing customers will be encouraged to use them again.

Costs

1) STAFF TRAINING — To produce quality products, staff need to be doing their job properly — it's important that businesses spend money and time on training their staff well.
2) INSPECTION — Products need to be inspected to check the quality is good enough (see p.66). The inspection process costs both time and money.

Failing to Maintain Quality can Also Be **Costly**

1) DISRUPTED PROVISION OF SERVICES — if quality standards are not maintained, it may disrupt the services that a business can offer to its customers, meaning that it loses potential sales. E.g. if a cafe kitchen is found to be unhygienic, the cafe may close temporarily while it is cleaned.
2) PRODUCT RECALLS — Products need to be safe for the customer to use. If any product is found to be unsafe, products that have already been sold might have to be recalled (sent back to the manufacturer or distributor). The firms would have to offer the customers a refund or a replacement too. This can be very costly for the firms involved and can negatively affect their reputation and image.

BUSINESS EXAMPLE

1) In August 2016, Samsung launched its Galaxy Note7 smartphone.
2) After just weeks on the market, there were several reports of the phones overheating and in some cases catching fire.
3) As the products were thought to be unsafe, Samsung recalled 2.5 million of the phones.
4) Customers were offered a different phone or a refund, which was very costly for the firm.

There's a price to pay for quality — but it's worth it...

You might not think you're very fussy about what you buy, but I bet you soon notice when quality falls below what you're expecting, e.g. when you get sticky notes that just fall off everything or rubbers that make smudges on a page. If quality isn't up to scratch, sometimes businesses might even be breaking consumer laws (see p.36).

The Sales Process

At the end of the day, almost every business out there needs to sell a product, so knowing how to sell products is kind of important. So important in fact that there are two pages all about sales coming up...

Customers Want **Good Service** Throughout the **Sales Process**

There are lots of different ways of selling a product or service. E.g. products may be sold face-to-face, using telesales (over the phone) or using e-commerce (over the internet). A sales process might involve these steps:

1) Finding potential new customers — e.g. a company selling jet skis could have a stand at a boat show. They could ask people to leave contact details if they'd be interested in knowing more about jet skis.
2) Approaching potential customers — e.g. calling people who left their contact details at the boat show and inviting them into the showroom.
3) Assessing the customer's needs — e.g. finding out what sort of jet ski the person might want.
4) Presenting — e.g. showing a customer a suitable jet ski in the showroom, telling them all about it and persuading them to buy one.
5) Closing — e.g. getting the customer to formally agree to buying a jet ski (i.e. hand over their cash).
6) Follow-up — e.g. calling the customer after the sale to check they are happy with their new jet ski.

Firms should provide great customer service throughout the sales process. Ways of doing this include:

1) Having Excellent **Product Knowledge**

1) Anyone in a firm involved in the sales process should know the firm's products inside out.
2) This is important for several reasons. For example:
   - Any questions customers have can be answered quickly and accurately.
   - Staff can make sure the customer is getting the product most suited to their needs, and may be able to sell them additional products to go with their initial purchase.
   - The customer feels more confident buying from the firm — if staff seem like they don't really know what they're talking about, the customer may be wary about buying from them.

2) **Engaging** Well with the **Customer**

1) Firms should ensure that any experience customers have with them is as positive as possible.
2) This involves staff being polite and friendly with customers and making them feel important and valued. Customers shouldn't feel like they're being pushed into making a purchase, nor should they feel like sales staff aren't listening to what they want in a product.
3) Firms often think of extra ways to make the experience for the customer more positive, such as offering free refreshments or next-day delivery.

3) Having **Quick** and **Efficient** Service

1) The sales process should be quick and easy for a customer.
2) For example, the company should quickly answer any questions the customer has.
3) The sales process should also be efficient — this can be achieved by cutting down the number of steps it takes for a customer to get in touch with a company or to buy a product.
4) For example, sales people might be given authority to offer discounts to customers without needing to approve them with a manager first (which would take time).

Getting the whole sales process right is important, not just a few bits...

Try to think about how each of the points here and on the next page on providing great customer service fit into the different parts of the sales process. It could help you to remember them.

The Sales Process and Customer Service

Now for a couple more ways in which a company can make their customers happy and why this is so important.

4) Offering **Post-Sales Service**

Providing good customer service doesn't end when the sale is complete.
The firm needs to be available for their customers afterwards as well.

- The firm may offer user training — teaching the customer how to use the product they've bought.
- Some businesses have a specific after-sales helpline — customers can contact this to help resolve any issues they have with the product, e.g. if it's not working as they expected.
- Some products, like cars and boilers, might need to be serviced throughout their lifespan — firms can often do this for their customers.

5) Responding to **Customer Feedback**

1) Customers might give feedback to a business if they've had a particularly good or bad experience. This could be private feedback, e.g. an e-mail, or public feedback, such as an online review. The business may even ask the customer for feedback about their experience, e.g. to ask why the customer didn't buy from the business, or to ask how their experience could have been improved.
2) To make a customer feel their views are valued, companies should reply to the feedback. Their responses should be polite — even if the company disagrees with what the customer has said. They should also respond specifically to the comments, rather than giving a generic response. They might even offer a gift in thanks for the feedback, such as a discount on their next purchase.
3) This is particularly important for public feedback, as other potential customers might be influenced by how a business responds.
4) The business can use customer feedback to make changes to the business in order to improve the sales process for future customers.

Providing **Good Customer Service** is **Really Important**

Benefits of Good Customer Service

1) Good customer service leads to high levels of customer satisfaction.
2) Satisfied customers are more likely to remain loyal to the company and make repeat purchases from them in the future. They may also convince other individuals to buy from the company, leading to new customers.
3) Customers may be persuaded to spend more with a company that provides them with good customer service.

Dangers of Poor Customer Service

1) If a company provides poor customer service they're likely to have dissatisfied customers.
2) People like to tell others about poor customer service they have had, so the tale of poor customer service may quickly spread by word of mouth. The business ends up with a poor brand image so customers will be less loyal, and may buy from other companies. This leads to a lower market share and lower sales.

Good customer service costs money — e.g. the wages of extra staff, and costs of providing after-sales care. But customer service is crucial — most firms recognise that the benefits of customer service outweigh the costs, and ultimately increase profitability.

Happy customers are the key to a successful business...

Providing good customer service is really important. For example, a coffee shop might serve the best cup of coffee in the whole world, but if the staff are rude or service is very slow, you might not go back.

Technology and Customer Service

Advances in technology are just great — for one thing they've allowed firms to develop their customer service.

Customer Services are Developing via...

1) As the internet continues to grow and people can access it more and more easily (e.g. via tablets and smartphones), more customers are going online to buy products, find out information and communicate.
2) This is changing the ways in which firms interact with their customers and so provide customer service.

1) Websites and E-commerce

1) Companies may buy and sell their goods online — this is called e-commerce (see pages 123-124) and can be done via a website. However, companies that provide a service also have websites.
2) A website can be a really good way to provide good customer service, for example:

- Many firms include 24-hour ordering on their websites, so it's easier for customers to buy.
- Many sites provide answers to frequently asked questions (FAQs) so that customers can look up answers to queries. They also usually have contact details and provide online forms that customers can use to make enquiries or complain. Some even have a 'live chat' feature, so messages can be sent back and forth between a customer and an employee straight away.
- Some firms let customers set up online accounts so they can access services on the web (e.g. they can pay bills, top up their mobile phone credit, etc.).

2) Social Media

1) Social media includes websites (e.g. Facebook®, Twitter) and applications that allow people to communicate and share content online.

2) Firms can use these to communicate with customers, e.g. to show them how to use a product, or to let them know about offers or any changes to store opening hours.

3) It's also a quick and easy way for customers to contact a business, e.g. if they have a query or complaint. However, comments on social media may be seen by thousands of other people within minutes, so it's really important that businesses respond quickly and politely to any questions or complaints. This helps to give the firm a positive image, and is a good way to provide good customer service.

Technology can make customer service easier and cheaper for businesses...

It's important for firms to keep up to date with new technology that comes out. Customers are starting to expect more than just a good website — for example, they like dependable, user-friendly apps and live chats too.

Worked Exam Question

There's no better way for preparing for the exams than by practicing exam questions. On this page the question has already been done for you, but on the next page it's over to you to do the answers.

1 Look at **Item A** below.

Item A — SB Vans:
Saif runs SB Vans, a courier company that delivers furniture from factories to customers' homes. Saif guarantees delivery within 48 hours of the customer ordering their furniture. He will also set up the furniture for no extra cost.

Recently, SB Vans bought another courier company. This meant that there were many more new employees for the company. **Figure 1** shows how long it took for furniture to be delivered to customers in the month before and the month after the business began employing the new employees.

Figure 1

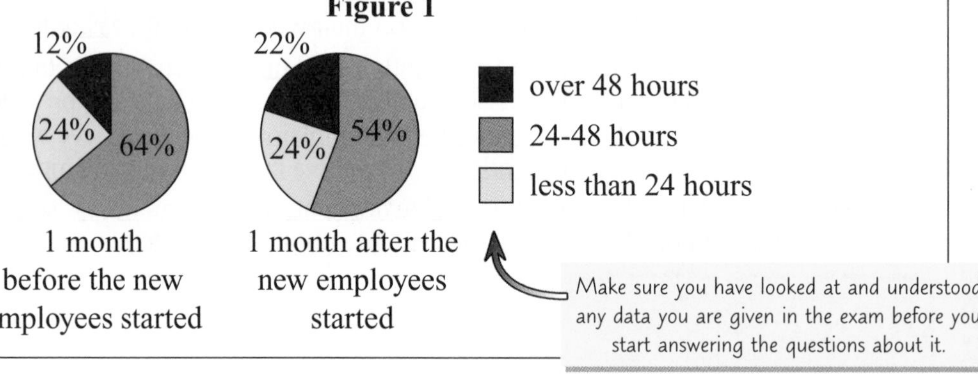

Make sure you have looked at and understood any data you are given in the exam before you start answering the questions about it.

Analyse how the effect the new employees have had on quality may impact SB Vans.

[6]

You need to know what quality means in the context of a service. SB Vans are a courier firm, so the quality of their service depends on how quickly they can deliver things.

Sample Answer:

Since the new employees started, the proportion of deliveries that have been delivered within Saif's target of 48 hours has fallen from 88% (24% + 64%) to 78% (24% + 54%). This fall in the quality of the service provided by SB Vans may lead to customer complaints, as Saif guarantees delivery within 48 hours. It may also cause SB Vans to develop a poor reputation, so it could lose its competitive advantage.

It's a good idea to use data from the context to back up your answer. If you have to do any calculations, make sure you show your working out, so that the examiner can see how you came up with the figures that you use in your answer.

Customer complaints and a poor reputation may lead to factories deciding not to use SB Vans as their courier service anymore, which would cause the business's sales to fall. Customers could also ask for compensation for the late deliveries, which may cause SB Vans' costs to go up, and so cause their profits to decrease.

Make sure you clearly explain how a fall in quality standards could affect the business. Think particularly about how and why it could affect sales and profit.

Exam Questions

1 Explain **one** way in which quality assurance can help a firm to control its costs.

....

....

....

....

[Total 3 marks]

2 Explain how an increase in a firm's spending on customer services can lead to an increase in profits.

....

....

....

....

[Total 3 marks]

3 Look at **Item A** below.

> **Item A — Bee's Travel:**
> Bee's Travel is a company that sells luggage over the phone and via its website. When new telesales staff are hired, they are given training in the products that Bee's Travel sells.
> At the end of their training period, they are given a short test about the products, and given further training if they don't score over 75%. Bee's Travel aims to answer all enquiries via the website within 24 hours of receiving them, and employs two members of staff whose job is to answer website enquiries.

a) State **one** thing Bee's Travel does to ensure its sales process is efficient.

....

[1]

b) Outline **one** impact on Bee's Travel of training its staff to have excellent product knowledge.

....

....

....

[2]

[Total 3 marks]

Revision Summary for Section 3

You've had a bit of exam practice but now it's time to test your knowledge on the whole section, get ready...

- Try these questions and tick off each one when you get it right.
- When you've done all the questions for a topic and are completely happy with it, tick off the topic.

Supply Chains (p.56-57) ☐

1) What is a supply chain? ☐
2) List four types of business that are usually part of a supply chain. ☐
3) Give three important factors that a business should consider when choosing a supplier. ☐
4) What does procurement mean? ☐
5) What does logistics mean? ☐
6) Explain how effective procurement and logistics can improve the efficiency of a business. ☐
7) Why is it important that a firm reduces waste and unnecessary costs in its supply chain? ☐

Methods of Production and Technology in Production (p.58-60) ☐

8) a) What is meant by 'job production'?
   b) Give an example of a product made by job production. ☐
9) a) What is meant by 'flow production'?
   b) Give an example of a product made by flow production. ☐
10) What is meant by 'batch production'? ☐
11) Explain one way using technology in the production process can improve productivity. ☐

Managing Stock (p.61-62) ☐

12) What does lean production mean? ☐
13) Give one advantage of using JIT stock control. ☐
14) Explain why a business may prefer to use a just-in-case (JIC) approach rather than JIT. ☐
15) Explain how a business can use a bar gate stock graph to manage its supplies. ☐

Maintaining Quality (p.66-68) ☐

16) Explain why each of the following may make it difficult for a growing business to maintain high quality standards:
   a) They franchise the business.
   b) They outsource some tasks. ☐
17) Describe the difference between quality control and quality assurance. ☐
18) Give one advantage of Total Quality Management. ☐
19) Give two costs associated with maintaining quality standards. ☐

The Sales Process, Technology and Customer Service (p.69-71) ☐

20) Briefly describe the steps in a sales process. ☐
21) Give one way in which sales staff could make sure they engage positively with their customers. ☐
22) Give three examples of post-sales services that a business might offer their customers. ☐
23) Explain why a business should always respond to customer feedback. ☐
24) Explain why providing good customer service is important for customer loyalty. ☐
Explain how the growth in social media has allowed businesses to develop their customer service. ☐

Internal Organisational Structures

Human resources is all to do with making sure a firm's employees are working as effectively as possible. There could be thousands of employees, so an internal organisational structure keeps track of how they're organised.

Human Resources Means the People Within a Firm

1) All businesses need people to run them. These people are known as the business's 'human resources'.
2) Human resources are really important — the people within a business should have all the skills and abilities needed to make the business a success.
3) As a business develops, managers might identify areas where they need more people in the business. This means they need to recruit people into these roles.
4) Many businesses have a human resources department that looks after people working in all the different areas of the firm. The department is usually involved in things such as the hiring and firing of staff, sorting out employee disputes, organising training and development and helping staff to feel motivated at work.

See pages 85-86 for how businesses recruit staff.

Organisational Structures Organise People

1) A business's internal organisational structure is how all of the people working for the business are organised.
2) It's important that a firm has a clear internal organisational structure. This makes it easy for everybody in the business to know who is responsible for what, and helps the company to make sure that it has people in every job role to deal with each of its activities.

The number of people on each layer generally increases as you go down the organisational structure.

3) Most firms have layers in their organisational structure.
4) There are four basic roles of staff, with different responsibilities, that make up the layers:

- DIRECTORS are responsible for the business's strategy (its overall direction). The directors decide on strategy and targets at regular board meetings.
- SENIOR MANAGERS organise the carrying out of the directors' strategy. A large firm may have middle and junior managers ranked below the senior managers.
- SUPERVISORS or TEAM LEADERS are ranked below managers. They usually look after specific projects or small teams of operational or support staff.
- OPERATIONAL and SUPPORT STAFF are workers who aren't responsible for other staff. They're often given specific tasks to perform by managers, supervisors or team leaders.

5) The directors are on the top layer of an organisational structure, and operational and support staff are on the lowest layer.
6) The chain connecting directors to operational and support staff is called the chain of command.
7) People at each level have authority (power) over people in the level below. People in the level below are 'subordinates' of those above them.
8) At each level, a certain amount of responsibility is delegated (passed on) to people in the level below.
9) The span of control is the number of workers who report to one manager.

Each staff member has a place in the organisational structure...

If you get a tricky business term in an exam question (e.g. span of control or chain of command), you might find it helpful to scribble down a rough note of what the term means. This could help you to get your head around what the question is asking before you start writing your answer.

Internal Organisational Structures

There are different types of organisational structure that a firm can have. Each type of structure has an impact on management and communication, so managers need to choose a structure that will suit their firm best.

An Organisational Structure can be **Tall** or **Flat**

Tall Organisational Structures

- There is a long chain of command with more layers of management.
- In a tall structure each manager only has a narrow span of control. This can make a firm more effective as managers can monitor the employees they are responsible for more closely.

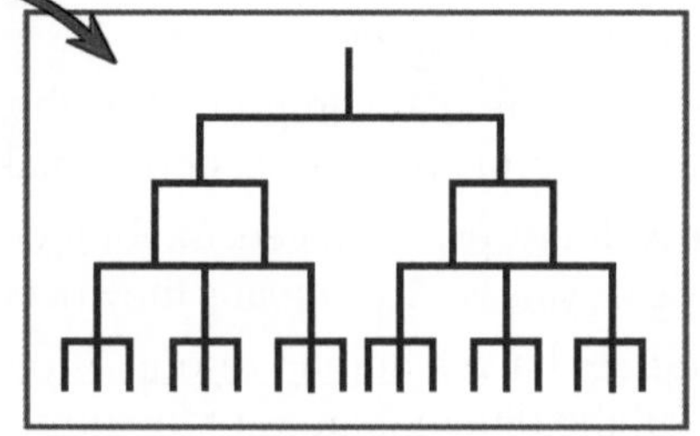

Tall organisational structures can also be called 'hierarchical' structures.

Flat Organisational Structures

- There is a short chain of command.
- Each manager has a wide span of control. This means that each manager has to manage a lot of employees at once — it can be difficult to manage a lot of employees effectively.

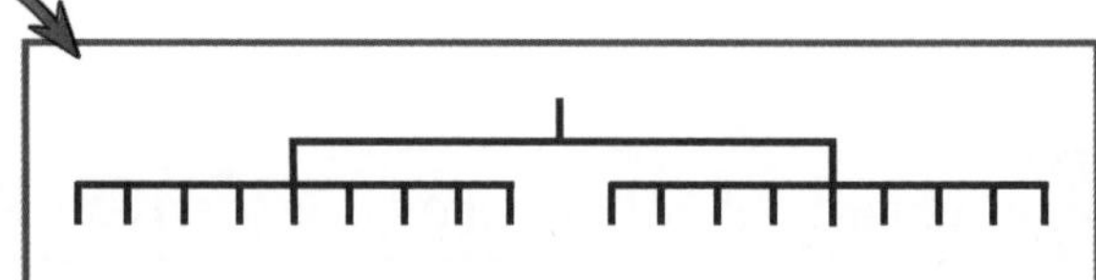

A Firm's Organisational Structure Affects **Communication**

1) The organisational structure that a business has can affect how the people within it communicate. It also depends on who is talking to who, and what they are talking about.

There's more on communication coming up on pages 79-80.

2) In a tall organisational structure, communication up and down the hierarchy can be difficult and slow as more people need to pass on the message. It can also be hard to use verbal communication (talking face-to-face or on the telephone) if lots of managers need to be involved in a conversation. Sometimes emails can be used to make communication faster, but they're not great when a discussion is needed, e.g. when making decisions. In this case meetings need to be set up in advance.

3) Communication up and down a flat organisational structure can be much faster because there are fewer layers of management. But verbal communication can still be tricky if a manager's span of control is very wide and they need to talk to each of their workers individually. However, if the manager needs to pass on the same message to each of their workers they can use emails or group meetings instead.

Tall structures have more layers of management than flat structures...

A business needs to have a good balance between its span of control and chain of command — if the span is too wide, or the chain is too long, communication within the business could really start to suffer.

More on Internal Organisational Structures

Firms need to decide how much authority to delegate at each layer of their organisational structures. This will depend on whether the bosses want a centralised or decentralised structure.

Centralised Structures Can Have **Very Powerful People** at the **Top**

1) In a centralised organisation, all major decisions are made by one person or a few senior managers at the top of the structure.
2) Advantages are that these senior managers tend to have plenty of experience, and can get an overview of the whole business. Policies will be uniform throughout the business.
3) On the downside, if all decisions need to be made by one or two people, it can slow down decision-making and communication of decisions can take a long time to filter through to employees. This means that the organisation reacts slowly to change.
4) Senior managers at the top of the organisational structure can become very powerful. But depending too heavily on a few people at the top can cause problems if those people lack specialist knowledge or if they 'lose their touch' and start making poor decisions.

In **Decentralised Structures More People** Make **Big Decisions**

1) In a decentralised organisation, the authority to make most decisions is shared out — for example, power might be delegated to regional managers or to more junior employees in individual branches of a business.
2) Advantages are that employees can use expert knowledge of their sector to make decisions. They don't always need to communicate these decisions with managers above them for approval, so changes can be made more quickly. This is really important in competitive environments, where a firm needs to respond to changes or opportunities in the market more quickly than its competitors.
3) Another advantage is that senior managers at the top of the organisational structure are not responsible for making as many decisions. This means there's less need for a central office where decisions are made (a headquarters), which can decrease a firm's fixed costs (see p.24).
4) The disadvantages are that inconsistencies may develop between departments or regions. Also, the decision-makers might not be able to see the overall needs of the business.

BUSINESS EXAMPLE

1) Supermarket chains (e.g. Tesco, Asda) have a decentralised structure.
2) Big decisions on things such as branding and marketing campaigns are made by directors at the top of the organisational structure.
3) But each store usually has its own manager who makes important decisions about the running of their store, e.g. decisions about recruiting and training staff, and controlling stock levels.

Senior managers make fewer decisions in a decentralised structure...

Firms need to choose the most appropriate structure to suit their needs (see next page for more). Often, firms start with a centralised structure, but decentralise as they get too big to make all the decisions at the top.

More on Internal Organisational Structures

Firms need to choose the most appropriate structure so that they can effectively organise the authority of people within the firm. They may also need to think about how to organise the different areas of their business.

Businesses Need to Choose the **Most Appropriate** Structure

1) The type of organisational structure a business has depends on many things, e.g. the business's size.
2) A small business is likely to have a flat structure — it's often managed just by the owner. As the business grows and gets more staff, managers might be needed to help organise and control things, so the structure gets taller.
3) The bigger the business, the greater the number of managers needed (and the greater the costs).
4) Over time, the business may delayer its structure to avoid becoming too tall — layers of management are removed (usually from the middle of the organisational structure). A business may also decentralise and encourage groups of workers to take more responsibility for their own self-management.
5) The ways in which people within the firm work may also affect its structure. E.g. if a firm has lots of temporary staff (see p.83) there may be less need for training and development, meaning fewer managers are needed.

A Business Can be Organised by **Function, Product** or **Region**

Functional Organisation

1) You get this a lot in limited companies (see p.10).
2) Each functional area does one part of the work of the business. Examples of functional areas are sales, marketing, customer service, operations, finance, human resources... and so on.
3) The main advantage is that specialists can concentrate on their particular job.
4) The main disadvantage is that the different departments may not work well together.

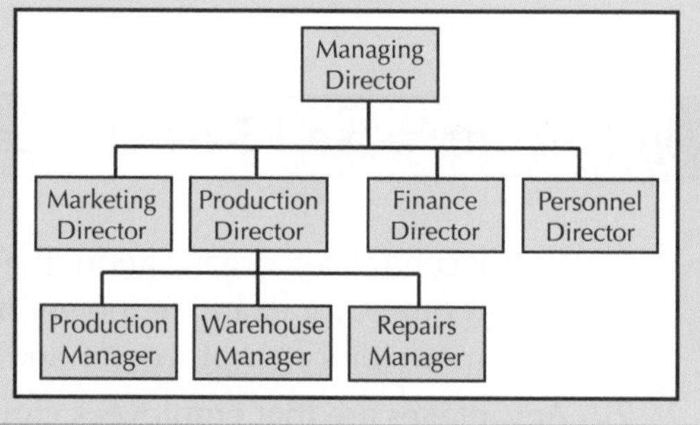

Product Organisation

1) This is common with large manufacturers who make lots of different products.
2) A product-based structure splits the organisation into different sectors. For example, One Shop plc has three sectors — home furnishings, toys and clothing.
3) The main advantage is that managers can make decisions that are relevant to each product sector.
4) A disadvantage is that there can be a wasteful duplication of resources between sectors.

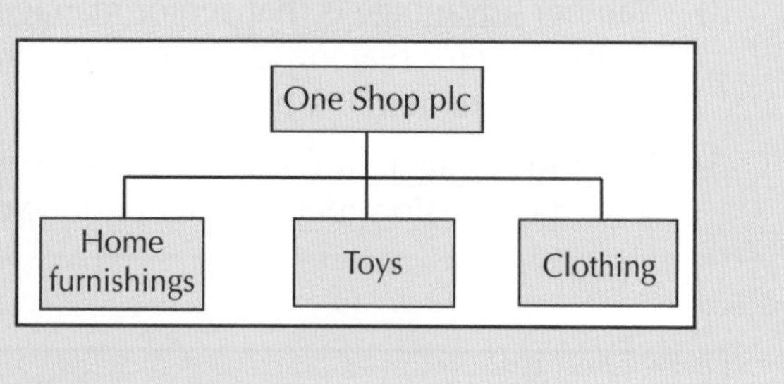

Regional Organisation

1) This is normal for a multinational business.
2) The divisions may be regional or national.
3) The main advantage is that spreading management between regions makes day-to-day control easier.
4) A disadvantage is that there can be a wasteful duplication of resources between regions.

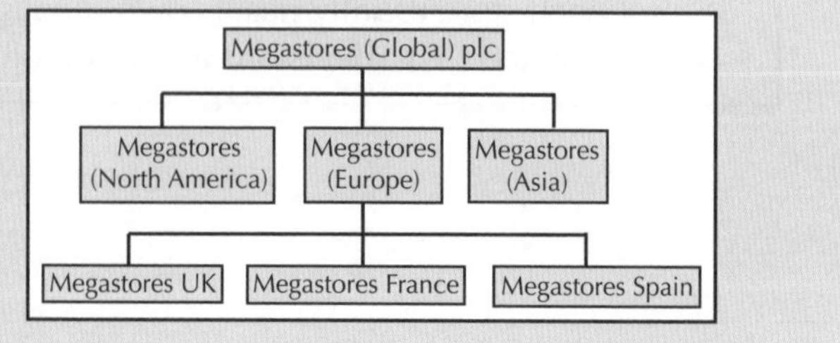

No single structure is right for every business...

Make sure you understand why some organisational structures might be suited to some businesses but not others.

Communication

A successful business needs its people to work together. This involves passing on information and sharing ideas with each other — so effective communication is a big deal in business.

There Are Lots of **Different Methods** of Communication

1) Effective communication in a business is really important — it means that different areas of the business work well together, and that everyone in the business knows what they should be doing and why. It can improve staff motivation as staff will know what's going on in the firm and are likely to feel more confident that they're doing their job properly.
2) In order to communicate effectively, messages need to reach the people that need to receive them without unnecessary delay and without being misinterpreted.
3) There are many different methods people within a business can use to communicate, and they need to choose the most effective method, depending on the situation. For example:

- Websites, emails and social media — these are all methods of digital communication and are popular ways to communicate. There's more about these methods on page 37.
- Text messages — these are another form of digital communication. They can be sent and received very quickly. They're great for passing on short, informal messages but not much use when sending detailed or sensitive information.
- Letters — businesses often use these to communicate with people outside the firm. An advantage is that both the sender and receiver can keep the letter and use it for future reference. This can be helpful if the information is important or complicated. However, posted letters take at least a day to be delivered, there's a risk letters can get lost in the post and the sender gets no immediate feedback from the reader.
- Phone calls — telephone conversations allow instant feedback. Mobile phones allow people to be contacted even when they're not in the office, which is great for people who travel a lot as part of their job (as long as they can get a signal). But there's no written record of the communication, so there's a risk that the details of what was said in the conversation may be forgotten.
- Meetings and presentations — these usually involve a group of people getting together in the same place to talk about business. These methods are good for when a message needs to be passed on to several people at once or for when a subject needs discussing (e.g. when it's useful to pass ideas back and forth between people before a decision is made). A drawback is that they can be quite time consuming and need to be arranged in advance.

Meetings and presentations allow people to communicate face-to-face. This is one of the most effective ways to communicate — body language can help express the message and it's easy to confirm the message has been properly received and understood.

There are **Barriers** to **Communication**

Firms need to overcome barriers to communication in order to communicate effectively. These include:

- Noise — it's difficult to hold a conversation in a noisy environment, such as a busy factory.
- Personalities — some employees may feel uncomfortable communicating with other people in the firm because, e.g. they don't get on personally or feel they are unapproachable.
- Distance — many businesses operate across different sites, sometimes many miles apart, so it can be difficult to speak to people face-to-face.
- Jargon — technical language used in one department may not be understood by people in other departments.

Different methods of communication are used in different situations...

Over the next week, see how many different methods of communication you can spot being used in your school or another organisation you're part of. For each method, consider why that method was chosen to pass on a message and whether another method might have been more appropriate.

Communication

Businesses need to get the balance right between having insufficient (not enough) and excessive (too much) communication. Getting the communication balance wrong can cause inefficiency and demotivated staff.

Insufficient Communication Can Cause Problems

1) Insufficient communication can lead to inefficiency. People may be slow to receive important messages about what they should be doing, meaning time and money is wasted on them doing things incorrectly. It may also mean that information isn't passed on between different departments or teams — this may mean that some tasks end up getting done more than once, or are not done in ways that are best for the business as a whole.

2) Insufficient communication can demotivate staff. They may feel frustrated if a lack of communication is stopping them from doing their job properly. Also, they may not feel valued if they're not told about things that are going on in the firm.

There's more on why it's important to keep staff motivated on page 89.

Excessive Communication Can Also Cause Issues

1) Excessive communication can lead to inefficiency. It takes time to pass on and receive messages — if people are frequently involved in communication about things that don't directly affect them it can waste valuable time. People may also start to take less notice of messages, and miss out ones that are important to them.

2) Excessive communication may mean many people are trying to pass on the same message — employees may get conflicting information from different sources and there may be confusion over which information is correct. This can lead to time being wasted while the workers find out the correct information, or mistakes being made while workers follow the wrong information. Both of these things reduce efficiency and productivity, which can reduce output.

3) Staff may feel demotivated by excessive communication — they may feel overwhelmed with all the information they are receiving and annoyed if it's affecting their ability to do their job well.

Getting the level of communication right is really important...

It's easy to think that lots of communication in a firm would be good as more people would know what's going on, but that's not always the case. Communication has to be controlled so that people quickly get the information they need, without having to filter out information they don't need or be confused by mixed messages.

Worked Exam Questions

Have a look at these worked exam questions to help you prepare for the exams. Try reading the questions and thinking about how you would answer them before you read through the sample answers.

1 Which of these statements describes the role of operational staff in a firm? Put a cross (X) in **one** correct box. *[1]*

Sample Answer:

A They are responsible for the business's strategy. ☐

B They usually look after small teams of other staff. ☐

C They manage team leaders. ☐

D They are often given specific tasks to perform by team leaders. ☒

Read all the options properly before deciding on your answer.

Make sure you mark your answer clearly. Pay attention to any instructions you're given before a set of multiple choice questions — they might tell you how to mark your answer and what to do if you want to change it.

2 Explain **one** disadvantage to a firm of having a centralised structure. *[3]*

Sample Answer:

Having a centralised structure can slow down decision-making because all major decisions are made by one person or a few senior managers at the top of the structure, meaning the firm reacts slowly to change.

You get one mark for stating a disadvantage of a centralised structure...

...and another two marks for explaining how centralisation causes this disadvantage and the overall effect on the firm.

3 Explain **one** advantage to a firm of having a tall structure rather than a flat structure. *[3]*

This is another explain question, so you need to clearly state an advantage and then talk about why it's beneficial and the overall effect it has on the firm.

Sample Answer:

Each manager will have a narrow span of control, so they can monitor the employees they are responsible for more closely and so the firm may be more effective.

Make sure you use business terms in your answers where you can.

Exam Questions

1 Explain **one** reason why effective communication in a business is important.

....

....

....

....

[Total 3 marks]

2 Look at **Item A** below.

Item A — Houghton & Son Ltd.:
Houghton & Son Ltd. make light fittings for homes.
When the business started it had one small store in the owners' home town and a flat organisational structure. Now the business has a head office and a chain of stores across the country.
Part of the firm's organisational structure is shown in **Figure 1**.

Houghton & Son Ltd.

Claire Wilkinson
UK Sales Director
↓
Andrew Gibson
Regional Sales Manager
↓
Anjali Bhat
District Sales Manager
↓
James Lake
Branch Sales Manager
↓
Liam McNulty
Branch Sales Supervisor
↓
Omar Maarouf
Salesperson

Figure 1

a) State **one** responsibility that Claire Wilkinson is likely to have in her role.

....

....

[1]

b) State **one** characteristic of a flat organisational structure.

....

[1]

c) Outline **one** reason why Houghton & Son Ltd. employed more managers as the company grew.

....

....

....

[2]

[Total 4 marks]

Ways of Working

All employees have a contract of employment — a legal agreement between themselves and their employer (see p.34). The contract includes details about the way the employee works, e.g. how many hours they have to do.

Employment Can be **Full-Time** or **Part-Time**

1) Working full-time usually means around 35-40 hours a week.
   Part-time staff work 'less than a full working week' — usually between 10 and 30 hours per week.
2) Some people prefer to have a full-time job, or need to work full-time for financial reasons.
   Other people work part-time so they can spend more time with family or on other interests.
3) There are pros and cons for businesses. Full-time staff are good if there's enough work for them to do, since they are likely to have only one job and so the business will have more control over the hours they work. But employing staff part-time can make more financial sense if a business is only really busy at certain periods. Having part-time staff that can be flexible with their hours can also be good as they can fill in when other staff members are absent (e.g. due to sickness or holidays).

Staff Can Work **Flexible Hours**

1) Employees that have been with a firm for at least 26 weeks can request to work flexibly — this is when working hours and patterns are adapted to suit the employee. E.g. a full-time employee might be allowed to work their 37 hours over four days, rather than the usual five days. This can be very motivating for staff as it makes it easier to fit other commitments around their working life.

2) Some employees have zero hour contracts — this means that the employer doesn't have to offer them any work at all. Nor does the employee have to accept any work that is offered to them. The contracts are used in businesses where there can be lots of fluctuation in demand, e.g. hotels. They are a cheap form of labour for businesses — they don't waste money paying staff when they're not really needed and they don't need to pay sick pay or holiday pay.

Employees Can be **Permanent**, **Temporary** or **Freelance**

Permanent

A permanent contract of employment has no end date. The person stays at the firm unless:
(i) they choose to leave, (ii) they're dismissed for misconduct, (iii) their job is made redundant.

Temporary

A temporary contract is for a fixed period (e.g. six months, one year, etc). At the end of the period, the contract can be renewed, or the person can leave the company.

Freelance

A freelance contract is when a self-employed person is recruited by a company, usually to work on a specific project. Freelancers can usually be hired and dismissed at short notice.

Temporary and freelance contracts can make it easier for the firm to employ people with particular skills for a particular period (without the commitment of a permanent contract). This can make it easier to adjust the number of staff according to the needs of the business.

Employers often have people working for them in different ways...

Firms need to agree with each employee how they are going to work. This often depends on what will work best for the firm, as well as how the employee would like to work. There are more ways of working coming up...

Ways of Working

This page covers another two ways in which people can work. The great variety in different ways that people can work nowadays is largely due to advancements in technology, such as the use of computers and the internet.

One Job Can be Shared Between Two People

1) Some employees job share — they share the work and pay of one full-time job with another person.
2) This is good for employees who only want to work part-time hours.
3) It can be good for employers because the two people might have different strengths that they bring to the job. It also means that if one person is absent (e.g. off sick), the other person might be able to work extra hours so the full job is still being done.
4) But for a job share to work, the responsibilities of each employee need to be very clear and the employees need to be able to communicate well with each other.

Some People are Self-Employed

1) Someone is self-employed if they run their own business, taking their income out of the profits of the firm.
2) Many people enjoy being self-employed as they get more control over the work they do and the hours they work.
3) However, they don't get the benefits of working for an employer, such as holiday pay and sick pay. Also, they may not get a regular income — as their income is taken from the profits of the firm, it may vary depending on how well the firm is doing.

Self-employed people are usually sole traders or part of partnerships (see page 9).

Technology Has Had an Impact on the Ways Employees Work

1) Advances in technology have made processes more efficient — e.g. many repetitive tasks can be done much faster and more accurately by computers than by staff. Working with technology is now a much bigger part of people's jobs, which has changed the way many people work.
2) Technology has made it easier for employees to share information and communicate with each other. E.g. documents can be put onto a firm's intranet so they can be accessed by employees in any location at any time (as long as they have an internet connection), employees can communicate via emails and video calls, and mobile devices allow people to communicate from many different locations.
3) This has impacted on the ways that people work. For example, it's easier for employees to work remotely — this means in locations away from their employers' offices, such as at home or while they're mobile (e.g. travelling on a train).

- Doubledot Media are a company that help people to start their own online firms.
- They have an office in New Zealand where the company is based.
- However, most of their staff work remotely from 27 different cities around the world.

There are lots of different ways that people can work...

The last two pages have covered lots of different ways of working. See if you can write a mini-essay on the topic, including some of the pros and cons of each method for businesses and employees.

Recruitment

Recruitment is the process of finding that special someone — that is, the best person to do a job. Businesses need to recruit people to increase their size, to gain new people with new expertise or to replace staff that have left.

Businesses Need to Be **Clear** About the Job on Offer

There are several steps involved in recruitment — job analysis, advertisement and selection.

1) Job analysis is where a firm thinks in depth about every little detail of the job in question.
2) The business then advertises the job. This usually includes a job description and a person specification, which are produced from the job analysis.
   - Job description — includes the formal title of the job, the main purpose of the job, the main duties plus any occasional duties. It will also state who the job holder will report to, and whether they will be responsible for any other staff.
   - Person specification — lists the qualifications, experience, skills and attitudes needed for the job.
3) Then the business has to go through the candidates that apply and select the best one (see next page).

A Firm can Recruit People **Internally** or **Externally**

The purpose of a job advert is to get as many suitable people as possible to apply for the job.
Firms can use job adverts to recruit internally or externally:

- INTERNAL RECRUITMENT involves recruiting current employees into new roles. The job position is advertised within the company.
- The advantages are that it's much cheaper, the post can be filled more quickly, the candidates will already know a lot about the firm, and bosses may already know the candidate well.
- On the downside, there will be no 'new blood' or new ideas, and the employee's move will leave a vacancy to fill.

- EXTERNAL RECRUITMENT involves recruiting from outside the business. The job can be advertised in lots of places, e.g. the local and national press, job centres, trade journals and employment websites.
- An advantage is that the job advert will be seen by more people, so it's more likely that the firm will find somebody really suited to the job.
- However, advertising externally isn't cheap — only specialist and senior jobs get advertised in the national press because it's very expensive.

It's **Really Important** That a Business Recruits the **Right People**

Getting the right people can have the following benefits for a business:

- High productivity — a person with the right skills and qualities for the job may only need minimal training and will be more productive than someone without these skills and qualities.
- High quality output — people with the best skills will make high quality products, e.g. if they already have experience making similar products.
- Good customer service — people well-suited to their role and who enjoy their job will provide better customer service.
- Staff retention (keeping staff) — firms want to hold on to staff so that they don't have to spend time and money recruiting people to replace them. They also don't want the inconvenience of new staff needing time to get to know the business and its customers properly, so firms don't want to replace people too often. If a person is recruited and finds out that the job isn't suited to them, they may leave.

A well-planned recruitment process helps to find the best people...

Often companies prefer to promote existing employees into higher roles and recruit externally to fill the gaps in the lower level roles. This way they know the people in the higher levels will be well suited to the company.

Recruitment

Businesses usually like to have a number of candidates when they're trying to fill a vacancy. The selection process then helps compare these candidates and decide which one is best for the job.

Candidates Explain Why They're **Right** for the Job

Businesses usually ask candidates to send a written application for a job.

1) A curriculum vitae (CV) is a summary of a person's personal details, skills, qualifications and interests. It's written in a standard format to give the firm the basic facts. Almost all firms ask for a CV.
2) Some firms will ask candidates to send a letter of application. This is a letter written by the candidate that describes why they think they are suitable for the job.
3) Many businesses ask candidates to fill in an application form. These forms give the firm the information it wants — and nothing else. This means they're much quicker to process and more relevant to the job than open-ended letters written by the candidates.
4) Many companies now like to use online application forms, where applicants fill in their details on the company's website. This allows the company to compare the applications using computer software.

Shortlisted candidates will usually be asked for references. These are statements about the character of the candidate written by someone who knows them — often a previous line manager. References are usually confidential — the candidate won't see what's written about them.

An **Interview** is the Traditional Selection Method

1) Once the closing date for applications has passed, managers in the business make a shortlist of the best applicants. Shortlisted candidates are invited for an interview with at least one manager.
2) Interviewers should ask the same questions to all candidates so that the process is fair. They shouldn't ask questions that are irrelevant to the job or that unfairly discriminate.
3) Interviews are used to assess a candidate's confidence, their social and verbal skills, and whether they'll be compatible with existing workers. Businesses also want to find out about the candidate's general attitude.
4) Some people think that interviews are not a good way to select — people don't behave naturally in a formal interview. The skills needed to be good at interview are often different from the skills needed to do the job.

Tests Can Also Help **Select** Who to **Employ**

1) Some businesses use tests — these are better than interviews for assessing the skills needed for the job. They can also be useful for spotting differences between similar candidates. There are four main types:
   - Skills tests or in-tray exercises test whether the candidate has the abilities to do the job.
   - Aptitude tests find out whether the candidate has the potential to learn how to do the job.
   - Personality tests are used to assess the candidate's personal qualities.
   - Group tests find out whether the candidate can work as part of a team — and whether they have good leadership and decision-making skills.
2) When all the candidates have been assessed, managers and HR staff meet to discuss how well the candidates have done. They then select the best candidates and offer them jobs.

Recruitment costs a lot of time and money...

Businesses can often get hundreds of applications for one job. Reading application forms, conducting interviews and setting tests all take time — some businesses have a whole recruitment department to deal with this stuff.

Training and Development

Training is the main way that a firm invests in its employees. This page covers three basic types of training.

There are **Different Types** of Training

1) Staff need training when they start working for a company so that they know how to do their job.
2) But even when they've been working for a company for a while, employees still need ongoing training. This could be to retrain them so they learn new processes or how to use new technology, or just to help them develop so that they're doing their job as well as possible.
3) Many firms plan the training they want their employees to have, but in some firms employees are encouraged to self-learn — this is where employees seek out their own training and development. E.g. they might be given access to online videos, apps and courses which teach different skills. They can pick and choose what they want to learn depending on where they want to take their career.

Induction Training is for **New Staff**

1) Induction training introduces the new employee to their workplace, and should help to make the new employee feel welcome.
2) It includes introducing them to their fellow workers and advising them of company rules and procedures. It may also include initial training on how to do their new job.
3) One advantage of induction training is that new employees feel confident when they start work. They are also less likely to make mistakes as they already know the basic procedures, meaning they can become productive as quickly as possible. They may also be more likely to stay in the job if they feel welcome and like a valued member of the team from the start.

Informal Training is Usually Done **'On-the-Job'**

1) In informal training, the employee may learn to do their job better by being shown how to do it and then practising — this is on-the-job training.
2) It's most suitable where practical skills are being taught, and when in a safe environment where communication is easy. For example, learning how to use a till in a shop or learning how to change a tyre in a mechanics workshop.
3) There is no strict plan to the training and it is usually given by other workers.
4) It's cost-effective for the employer because the employee works and learns at the same time.
5) A problem is that bad working practices may be passed on.

Formal Training is Often Carried Out **'Off-the-Job'**

1) Formal training often involves a set plan with learning objectives and a schedule.
2) The training can involve learning in a firm's training department or away from the workplace, e.g. at a local college. When it's done away from the workplace it can be called 'off-the-job' training.
3) Employers might use formal training so that their employees can gain academic qualifications (e.g. GCSEs, A-Levels), vocational qualifications (qualifications specific to their job) or apprenticeships.
4) Formal training is more expensive than informal training, but it's often higher quality because it's usually taught by people who are better qualified to train others.

REVISION TIP

The type of training usually depends on the skills needed...

Examiners like to see that you understand why firms make certain decisions. So as well as learning what training involves, make sure you understand why a firm may choose one method of training over another.

Training and Development

Training does much more than just make sure an employee knows how to do their job. Regular investment in staff training and development can keep staff motivated and allows a business to adapt to changes.

Performance Reviews Help Employees to **Develop**

As well as different methods of training, performance reviews can also play a part in employees' training and development — this is when firms set employees targets and then review their performance to make sure they're developing as they should. E.g.:

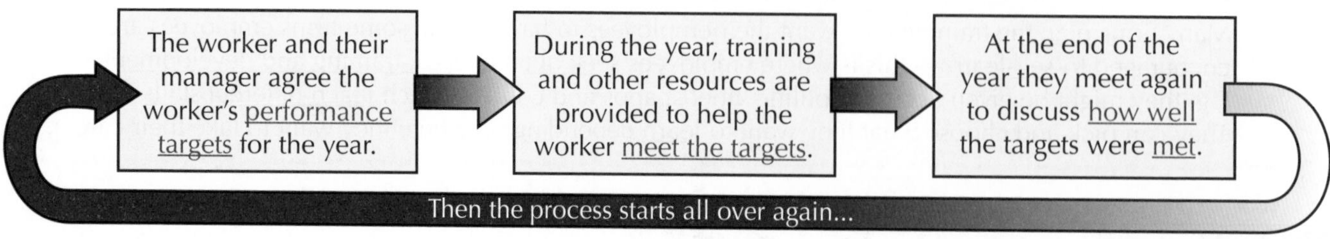

The worker and their manager agree the worker's performance targets for the year.
During the year, training and other resources are provided to help the worker meet the targets.
At the end of the year they meet again to discuss how well the targets were met.
Then the process starts all over again...

People who meet or beat their targets may be rewarded with higher pay or a promotion. If a worker doesn't meet their targets, the manager can decide what training or support they might need to help them improve.

Training and Development **Benefits** Both the **Employer** and the **Employee**

Benefits of training and development to employers

- Trained staff should be better at their jobs, which means they should be able to produce higher quality goods and provide better customer service. It should mean they're more efficient and productive too.
- Training can help staff stay up to date with changes that the business needs to go through so it can develop. For example, training can make sure staff know how to use new technology.
- Training staff can help businesses to cover skill shortages in their workforce. For example, if a manufacturing business doesn't have many people that can fix its machines, it can train existing employees to learn how to fix them rather than recruiting new staff.
- Overall, training is likely to make staff feel motivated and like they're progressing in the firm. This might increase staff retention (see p.85) which will save on recruitment costs.

Benefits of training and development to employees

- Employees with up-to-date knowledge and skills should be able to do their jobs better, which often increases job satisfaction and motivation.
- Over time, gaining new skills may mean that they can be promoted to jobs with better pay and more responsibility.

Training and development can make businesses more productive...

It makes sense for a business to make sure its employees are well-trained. Although there are costs involved in training and development, the process can make employees more motivated and more likely to stay with the firm. On top of this they'll be better at their jobs too, so you can see why firms take training very seriously.

Financial Motivation

This page covers some financial methods for motivating staff. Basically, the more money you give people, the more valued they'll feel and the happier they'll be doing their job...

Motivated Staff are More Productive

1) Motivated staff work harder, which leads to high productivity — workers want the firm to do well and so do their jobs as well as they can to help this happen.
2) Staff who are motivated and happy in their jobs are more likely to stay with the firm. Having a high level of staff retention is good for a firm as it means less time and money is spent having to recruit and train new workers, which reduces the firm's costs.
3) Having highly motivated staff may also attract new employees to the firm. This makes recruiting new staff easier because there are likely to be lots of applicants for vacancies.

Being more productive means staff can produce goods faster or using fewer resources. This reduces the unit cost of each item produced.

Financial Motivation can be Wages or a Salary

1) Most people get remuneration (payment) for the work they do for an employer (some people might not, e.g. if they're doing voluntary work).
2) Often, the more that a worker is paid, the more motivated they feel to do their job.
3) Workers can be paid with wages or with a salary.
4) Wages are commonly paid weekly or monthly — usually to manual workers. The amount paid is based on the amount of work that the employee does.
5) A salary is a fixed amount paid every month — this doesn't change even if the number of hours worked does change. It is usually paid to office staff who do not directly help to make the product. A salary of £24 000 means you are paid £2000 per month.
6) The advantage of a salary is that the firm and workers both know exactly how much the pay will be. However, it doesn't link pay directly to performance, so it doesn't encourage employees to work harder.

Employers can Give Staff Financial Extras

On top of their regular wage or salary, some firms offer staff extra financial incentives to help motivate them. E.g.:

1) Commission — this is paid to sales staff for every item they sell. It is given to them on top of a small basic salary.

2) Bonus — a lump sum added to pay, usually once a year. It's commonly paid if the worker (or the firm) has met their performance targets. Some firms give bonuses as part of a profit sharing scheme — this is, for example, where a percentage of the firm's profits is divided up between employees.

BUSINESS EXAMPLE

- John Lewis Partnership is a business that employs around 90 000 permanent staff.
- Each year, John Lewis Partnership gives a proportion of its profits to its workers as a bonus. Each employee gets a percentage of their salary. This helps to keep staff motivated.

3) Fringe benefit — any reward that is not part of a worker's main income. Examples include staff discount on the firm's products, the use of a company car, gym membership, a daily meal allowance or free health insurance. All of these perks cost money for the business, and save it for the worker.

Fringe benefits don't actually involve giving employees money, so sometimes they're seen as a non-financial method of motivation.

More money can make staff very happy...

Remember, the term 'financial motivation' can mean more than just a worker's regular income.

Non-Financial Motivation

There are more methods of motivation on this page — this time they don't involve throwing cash around..

Training Can **Boost Motivation...**

1) The main purpose of training is to help staff become better at their jobs.
2) But training can also improve motivation — being good at your job will boost your self-esteem.
3) Employees can also be trained to learn new skills. This means they can start to take on new tasks and have greater responsibility, which may stop them from becoming bored and make them more likely to want to stay with the firm.
4) They may even be told they could get a promotion once they have new skills, which may make them even more motivated. Promotion usually involves a pay rise, so it can be a form of financial motivation.

...And **Styles of Management** Can Also Have an Effect

- Authoritarian (or autocratic) managers make decisions alone, without consulting staff.
- Paternalistic managers make decisions themselves, but only after consultation with workers.
- Democratic managers allow the workforce some influence over decisions.
- Laissez-faire managers allow workers to perform tasks as they see fit, offering help if needed.

1) Generally workers feel more motivated if they're managed in a way that lets them have some input into decision-making.
2) However, no single approach is perfect for all employees and all situations. E.g. the authoritarian style can demotivate staff if they feel their views aren't valued, but it can be effective when managing crises.
3) Often a mix of different management styles is used depending on the situation.

A Good **Working Environment** can be Very Motivating

1) Employees are likely to feel happier and more motivated to go to work if they enjoy being in their work environment.
2) There are lots of things employers can do to create a positive working environment. For example, making sure all areas are kept clean and tidy, creating social areas for breaks, and encouraging a culture of friendliness and positivity (e.g. by managers taking action if anyone is being treated disrespectfully).

Staff can be Motivated by **Praise** and **Award Schemes**

1) Giving praise is a simple and cheap way to motivate employees — all it takes is for a manager to tell an employee that they are pleased with their performance when they have done a job well.
2) Praise makes workers feel appreciated and can give their self-esteem a big boost. This is likely to motivate them and make them want to continue working well so they can get praised again.
3) Some firms have award schemes to show employees that their hard work is recognised. These can be anything from awarding someone 'employee of the month', to big awards such as 'national salesperson of the year'.
4) Award schemes are motivating as the chance to win an award gives employees a reason to work hard. Employees that win awards will feel proud that their achievements have been recognised and can be seen by others in the company — this is likely to make them want to continue to work hard for the company.

Non-Financial Motivation

Here are three more methods of non-financial motivation to take you to the end of the section. These are all to do with altering the way that employees do their job.

Job Rotation Gives Workers a Change Now and Again

1) A lot of production jobs are boring and repetitive, e.g. working on a factory assembly line. Job rotation reduces this by occasionally moving workers from one job to another.
2) This motivates workers as they don't get so bored. They also learn to do different jobs, so if someone's ill, someone else will be able to cover.
3) The problem is that if one boring job is replaced by another it doesn't improve job satisfaction.

Job Enrichment Gives Workers Better Things to Do

1) Job enrichment is when a worker is given greater responsibility — for example supervising the work of new staff.
2) As a worker becomes good at their job they become more productive — they can do the same work in less time. So, giving workers more responsibility can stop them from feeling that their increased productivity is being punished by more of the same work.
3) It gives workers new challenges and so may motivate them to work harder.
4) A problem is that they may expect a pay rise as well.

Autonomy Gives Workers a Chance to Make Their Own Decisions

1) Autonomy means giving workers the freedom to make their own decisions. Workers may be told their overall goal but not told specifically how they should achieve it.
2) This responsibility motivates workers as it makes them feel trusted and like their contribution is valued.

1) Ranbir Singh owns a small chain of hotels in the North of England. Each hotel has a head chef in its restaurant.
2) Ranbir gives each head chef autonomy over the menus in their restaurant. Ranbir decides how profitable the menu should be, but leaves it up to the head chef to decide what dishes go on the menu, where the ingredients will come from, the price of each dish, etc.

Employees are motivated by much more than just money...

Don't worry if you get given information in the exam about a method of motivation that you haven't heard of before. Just remember, motivational methods all have the same, basic outcome — they make workers feel more valued, better rewarded and generally happier to go to work each day. This can make workers more productive and less likely to leave.

Worked Exam Questions

Here is another set of worked exam questions. Take time to look at them closely and make sure you understand the sample answers. You could be asked similar questions in the real exams.

1 Look at **Item A** below.

> **Item A — Chem and Co:**
> Chem and Co are a pharmaceutical company. They need to recruit a team of senior chemists to help them develop a new drug. They are planning to advertise the roles on a specialist science recruitment website.

State **two** qualities Chem and Co may look for when selecting candidates for the new roles. *[2]*

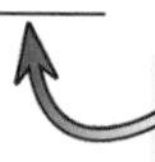

This is a 'state' question so you just need to give two answers — you don't need to explain them.

Make sure your answers are related to the specific job and company described in Item A — for example, you should have noticed that they need senior scientists and are advertising in places targeted at specialist scientists.

Sample Answer:

1. appropriate qualifications in scientific disciplines
2. previous relevant experience in laboratories

There are other answers you could have given too — e.g. the skills needed to do the job or the right attitude needed for the job.

2 Discuss how a firm can use non-financial methods to motivate its employees. *[6]*

Although the question doesn't tell you how many methods to write about, the number of marks the question is worth might give you a clue. For 6 marks, the examiners will probably be expecting you to discuss at least three methods.

Sample Answer:

A firm could use job rotation, meaning that its employees are occasionally moved from doing one job to another. This may make them feel motivated as it may stop them from becoming bored.

As this is a discuss question, make sure you give a brief description of each non-financial method and then explain how it motivates employees.

A firm could use job enrichment, meaning that its employees are given greater responsibility. This can make them feel motivated as it will give them new challenges and prevent them from feeling that once they become good at their job they are just given more of the same work to do.

A firm could give their employees autonomy, meaning that they are given the freedom to make their own decisions. This may make them feel motivated as they may feel trusted and feel like their contribution is valued.

You could have also written about other methods such as training, styles of management, the working environment, praise and award schemes.

Exam Questions

1 Look at **Item A** below.

> **Item A — Packman's Glazing:**
> Packman's Glazing is a business that sells doors and windows. They pay their junior sales staff an annual salary of £15 000. On top of their salary, sales staff also get 5% commission on each sale they make.
>
> Managers give junior sales staff the contact details of customers that have enquired about doors and windows and a monthly target of how many sales they should make. Junior sales staff who regularly meet their monthly targets are more likely to be promoted.
>
> In recent months, Packman's Glazing have lost two of their junior sales staff to a new, rival firm. One of the factors that persuaded the staff to move was the rival firm's pay scheme. They don't pay sales commission, but they pay junior sales staff an annual salary of £24 000.

a) State **one** method of financial motivation used by Packman's Glazing.

....

[1]

b) Drew is a junior salesman at Packman's Glazing.
In March his sales totalled £19 000 and his income from his salary before tax was £1250.
Calculate the total amount that Drew would have been paid in March before tax.
Show your working.

£ ....

[2]

c) The owners of Packman's Glazing are considering two options for how they pay their sales staff.

Option 1: Stay with their current pay scheme.

Option 2: Pay their staff a salary of £24 000 and remove commission.

Recommend which **one** of these two options Packman's Glazing should choose.
Give reasons for your answer.

Write your answer on a separate piece of paper.

[9]

[Total 12 marks]

Revision Summary for Section 4

Try this set of revision summary questions to find out how much you've learnt about Human Resources.

- Try these questions and tick off each one when you get it right.
- When you've done all the questions for a topic and are completely happy with it, tick off the topic.

Internal Organisational Structures and Communication (p.75-80) ☐

1) Explain why human resources are so important in a business. ☐
2) What layer of staff is usually ranked immediately below directors? ☐
3) What is meant by the span of control? ☐
4) How does the span of control differ between a tall and a flat organisational structure? ☐
5) Give one advantage of a centralised organisation. ☐
6) Give two disadvantages of a decentralised organisation. ☐
7) What is meant by the term 'delayering'? ☐
8) Give five methods of communication that might be used within firms. ☐
9) List four barriers to communication. ☐
10) Explain why insufficient communication can lead to inefficiency in a firm. ☐
11) Explain why excessive communication can demotivate staff. ☐

Ways of Working and Recruitment (p.83-86) ☐

12) What does it mean if a staff member is 'full-time'? ☐
13) Describe one way in which a firm may allow an employee to work flexible hours. ☐
14) Explain the difference between a permanent and a temporary contract of employment. ☐
15) What is a freelance contract? ☐
16) Explain why advances in technology have led to more employees working remotely. ☐
17) What is a job description? ☐
18) Give two disadvantages to a firm of filling a vacant position internally rather than externally. ☐
19) Explain why the recruitment and selection process is important for customer service. ☐
20) Why might a firm prefer candidates to fill in an application form rather than just send in their CV? ☐

Training and Motivation (p.87-91) ☐

21) What does it mean if an employee is encouraged to 'self-learn'? ☐
22) What is the purpose of induction training? ☐
23) Explain one advantage and one disadvantage of on-the-job training over off-the-job training. ☐
24) Explain how performance reviews can help staff to develop. ☐
25) Give two ways in which training benefits: a) employers b) employees. ☐
26) Explain how motivating staff affects staff retention in a business. ☐
27) Give two forms of remuneration that employees may get. ☐
28) Give three examples of fringe benefits a firm might offer its employees. ☐
29) Why might employees feel more motivated working for a democratic manager rather than an authoritarian manager? ☐
30) Explain how award schemes can help to motivate staff. ☐
31) How does job rotation help to motivate employees? ☐
32) Explain why autonomy may help to motivate workers. ☐

The Marketing Mix

Human beings have needs — essential things like water, food and shelter. Once our needs are satisfied, we start to want luxuries too, and we're prepared to pay for them. Marketing is about coming up with a product that people need or want — then making it as easy as possible for them to buy it.

There are **Four Ps** in Marketing

1) There are four elements to marketing: product, price, promotion and place — the four Ps.
2) They're the key to understanding what marketing is all about. If a firm gets them right then they should be able to inform customers about their products and make customers more likely to buy their products. This should increase the business's sales. If it gets even one of them wrong, it's in trouble.
3) Together the four Ps are called the MARKETING MIX.

1 Product

The firm must first identify customers' needs (or wants). Then it needs to come up with a product that will fulfil some (or one) of these needs. So spinach flavoured sweets, for example, probably wouldn't sell that well.

2 Price

The price must be one that the customer thinks is good value for money. This isn't the same as being cheap. You might be prepared to pay a lot of money for a brand new, 50-inch plasma-screen TV, but you'd expect an old basic 12-inch model to be much cheaper.

3 Promotion

The product must be promoted so that potential customers are aware that it exists and will want to buy it.

4 Place

Place can refer to the channel of distribution (see p.122) used to get a product from the company to the customer. For example, whether it is sold through retailers or sold straight to a customer.

4) Depending on the situation, some of the Ps might be more important than others.
5) For example, if customers really want the product, or it's in a really convenient place, they may be prepared to pay a higher price.
6) Alternatively, customers may be prepared to go to a less convenient place, or buy a product that isn't exactly what they want, if the price is lower.
7) A business can use information about the different elements of the marketing mix to help it make decisions. Changing elements of the marketing mix is a way for a business to carry out its decisions.
8) By having the right combination of the four different elements, a business can have an advantage over its competitors (called a competitive advantage), by attracting and selling to more customers.

There's more on the factors that affect the marketing mix on the next page.

Businesses need to consider all the P's in the marketing mix...

A good marketing mix makes customers want to spend money on your product. The marketing mix won't be the same for all products, but companies should still think about all the elements when they choose their mix.

The Marketing Mix

There are lots of things that a business needs to think about when choosing a marketing mix. For example, things such as what is likely to appeal to customers and how the different elements will influence one another.

Lots of Factors Can Affect a Business's Marketing Mix

1) Changes in technology may affect different parts of the marketing mix. For example, improvements in e-commerce (selling products through the internet — see p.123) means that more companies are selling their products online rather than in stores. Changes in digital communication (see page 37) have also affected how companies promote their products online.

2) Customers' needs and wants usually change over time — a business should adapt its marketing mix to meet these changing needs. E.g. companies may have to lower their prices for products that use older technology as these products no longer meet the needs of customers.

You need to be able to say how well a business has adapted to changing needs over time, and also suggest what changes it should make to its marketing mix.

3) How competitive the market is and what a business's competitors are doing will also affect how a firm balances the elements of its marketing mix. For example, if competitors are offering the same products at lower prices, a business may need to lower its own prices to stay competitive. If a competitor starts selling a brand new product, a business may need to develop its own version of the same product in order to offer a similar range of products to its customers. In a really competitive market, customers may have lots of products to choose from, so businesses may choose to spend more money on promotion to make their products seem more appealing than their competitors'.

The Different Parts of the Marketing Mix Affect Each Other

1) A business may have to make a compromise between the different elements of the marketing mix. E.g. the quality of the product will affect how much it costs to make, and therefore the price it will be sold for.
2) The channel of distribution that a product is sold through will also affect its pricing and promotion. Products sold online are likely to be cheaper than those sold in stores since the business may have lower fixed costs (e.g. rent). High-street retailers are likely to use displays in their store fronts to attract customers, whereas businesses that sell products online may use more online advertising.
3) The quality and price of the product will also affect how it is promoted — if a product is of low quality but it is quite cheap, then price may be emphasised in promotional material. However, if the product is of higher quality or is more expensive, then the promotional material may emphasise its quality.

The marketing mix may involve compromises...

Getting the right marketing mix should increase a company's sales and help it get ahead of the competition. But customers' needs change — businesses need to adapt their marketing mix to respond to these changes.

Markets

Before making decisions, a company needs to identify what their market is and the features of that market, such as how large it is and the type of people in it, e.g. their age or gender.

Different **Markets** Have Different **Structures**

Market research can help to identify the size of a market and the market shares of different businesses within that market.

1) You might remember from p.47 that a market can be a meeting place, trade in a particular type of product (e.g. the oil market), or a group of people.
2) Businesses often want to know about the structure of a market.
3) For example, it can be useful to know the market size and a business's market share.

- The market size is the number of individuals (including companies) within the market which are potential buyers or sellers of products. It can also mean the total value of products in the market.

- The market share of a business is the proportion of total sales within the market that is controlled by the business.

Markets are **Segmented** into **Different Groups** of People

1) As well as knowing market size and shares it can be useful to know how a market is segmented.
2) Segmentation is when people within a market are divided into different groups.
3) Knowing the different market segments can allow businesses to identify their target market — this is the specific group of people that a product is aimed at (see below).
4) They can then create a marketing strategy aimed at their target market (a targeted marketing strategy) to make sure that their marketing is as effective as possible.
5) A market can be segmented by its demographics. These are identifiable characteristics that people within one population might have. For example:

- Age — for example the teenage market, or "grey power" (the over-55s).
- Income — how much different people earn will affect what they are willing to buy.
- Gender — for example, chocolate manufacturers target some items at women (e.g. Flake) and some at men (e.g. Yorkie®).

6) But demographics isn't the only way to segment a market. Other ways include:

- Location — try selling stottie cakes outside the North East, or jellied eels outside London.
- Lifestyle — whether or not people enjoy certain activities, e.g. walking, cycling or reading.

Sport England segmented the market by gender when they launched their This Girl Can marketing campaign. The campaign was designed to encourage women of all ages and abilities to play more sport.

Segmenting the market helps a business find its target market...

Next time you're in a newsagent's, pick out a couple of magazines. Then describe how each of the magazines you've picked out has segmented the market to target a particular group of people.

Market Data

Knowing what the market they're selling to is like can be very useful if a business wants to stay competitive.

Businesses Map the Market to Find Information

1) Mapping the market helps a business understand its location within it, and the market's key features.
2) A business can use a market map to find out the following bits of information:

- Competitors selling similar products — and how customers perceive them.
- Any gaps in the market — see p.6.

3) Market maps are often in the form of a diagram (see the one on the right).
4) Market maps show two variables — here they're price and quality, but they could be almost anything.
5) The map allows a business to see how customers perceive key features of its competitors' products — e.g. their pricing and quality strategies.
6) They can also easily see if there is any part of the map with no products — i.e. a potential gap in the market.
7) Once they have spotted a potential gap in the market, the business will need to carry out research to confirm whether or not there is demand for the type of product which they have identified.
8) If they identify that there is demand for this type of product, then there is a gap in the market. So the business can focus on creating products with the features needed to fill the gap. This will help the business to be different from the competition and so increase its sales.

Market Map for Instant Coffee

A gap in the market can also be called a market opportunity.

Market Data can Inform Business Decisions

Managers might look at data about the market they're working in to inform and support the decisions that they make for a business. For example:

- Knowing the market share of different businesses, the costs of supplies and prices of competitor products may help a business to see if it should, e.g. lower its prices, or reduce the cost of its supplies.
- Segmentation helps a business to decide on the best marketing approach for its target market.
- Market mapping can show if a new product will be in competition with existing products on the market.
- Businesses may also investigate how demand for a product is changing over time. E.g. they might investigate the effect of a promotion by seeing whether it has led to an increase in demand for a product.
- A business might want to study the effect of changes it makes to its products, such as changing the packaging or adding extra features. The business will also want to keep up-to-date with any new products its competitors are selling, so that it can respond to these changes and doesn't lose customers to the competition.

Market maps tell businesses how customers perceive them...

Mapping the market may seem strange, but it's a great way for businesses to get to grips with the competition.

Market Research

Now it's time to have a look at the benefits to firms of carrying out market research into their customers.

Market Research is Used to **Understand Customers**

1) All businesses need their customers to buy their products, otherwise they won't survive.
2) Market research is really important because it helps a business to understand its customers and competitors.
3) One purpose of market research is to identify who the business's customers are. They can use market segmentation to help them do this (see p.97).
4) Market research can then be used to give businesses an understanding of their customers — e.g. what their needs are and how to satisfy them. Market research can also give an indication of how customer preferences are changing over time.
5) Customers' needs may include things like: the type of product, the quality of a product, the price, the convenience of where it is sold and how much choice they have of a range of products (e.g. different colours).
6) By understanding customers' needs, businesses will be better able to make products that meet these needs.

Market research data is a type of marketing data.

Market Research Helps Businesses to:

Make informed decisions

Market research provides data that can be used to support and inform decisions, such as choosing the correct marketing mix. E.g. it can help them make sure they have a marketing strategy that is targeted at the right market. They need to consider things such as:

- what products to sell
- where to sell them and how to promote them
- what price to sell them for

Increase sales

The demand for a product or service is how much of it people will be willing to buy at a given price. Knowing the demand for a product can help businesses to increase sales by adjusting their pricing (see p.111). This should help ensure the business survives.

Stay competitive

1) Gathering information on the products and prices of competitors can help to show how they are different. This can help a business to improve its strategies to be more competitive.
2) For example, it might help a business to spot when a group of customers have a need that isn't being met (a gap in the market — see p.6). A business will want to develop a way to meet the customers' needs before its competitors do.
3) This might mean developing a new product. Or it might mean selling an existing product in a new place or at a new price, or promoting it in a new way to convince customers they need it.

Reduce risks

1) If a business sells a product that customers don't want or tries to sell products at a price that's too high or in the wrong location, it could end up losing a lot of money.
2) Using market research to make informed decisions will help the business to avoid this and therefore help to reduce the risk of making costly mistakes.
3) This should help to ensure the business's survival.

Businesses need to identify and satisfy the needs of their customers...

By now you should understand what market research is, and why it's important for businesses to do. Coming up, it's time to find out how businesses might choose to carry out market research...

Market Research

Businesses can use different types of market research to understand the needs and wants of their customers. One type is primary market research — there are many different methods of primary market research.

Primary Research is Collecting Information Yourself

1) Primary research involves getting information from customers or potential customers.
2) This could involve asking customers questions, or watching how people behave.
3) Primary research is useful for finding out new information, and getting customers' views.
4) But a business can't ask every potential customer for their views — usually just a sample of people.
5) Large samples are the most accurate but also the most expensive. Small businesses may have to compromise here and use small sample groups to keep their costs down.
6) Businesses can also save on costs by carrying out research over the telephone or internet rather than in person — this is especially useful for small businesses.
7) Primary research provides data that's up-to-date, relevant and specific to the needs of your business. The research can also be specific to the target market.
8) But on the downside, it's expensive, and can be time-consuming.
9) Different types of primary research have different advantages and disadvantages. For example:

Questionnaires

These are documents with questions that are given to people. They're cheap and can be used to sample a large geographic area, but it's likely that many people won't respond.

Surveys

Surveys are used to collect information from people, e.g. over the phone or using questionnaires. Phone surveys have a much higher rate of response than questionnaires but they can be more expensive.

Interviews

Interviews involve asking people questions face-to-face. They have a good rate of response but can be expensive.

Focus groups

Focus groups are where a small group of people discuss their attitudes towards a product. They're faster than surveying several people individually, but may mean that quieter individuals do not get their opinion heard.

Observation

Observation involves observing what people do or say, instead of asking them. Observations are really cheap and give accurate information, but also don't allow customers to give opinions — so the business will know what customers are doing, but not necessarily the reasons why.

Trialling

Trialling is where a business launches a product to a small selection of people to begin with (e.g. in one particular location) and records how it sells. They can then make changes to improve sales before launching it to a larger market. Trialling lets a business test in a real market how their product is received, and reduces the risk of costly mistakes once it is launched on a larger scale. However, it means that competitors will be able to get an idea of what the business is doing.

Some forms of primary research are cheaper than others...

It can take a long time to collect data using primary research. But it allows a business to ask exactly the questions they want to the right type of people. So the results they get should be pretty useful.

Market Research

There's a little more here on methods of market research that businesses can use to collect data on their customers. It's important that businesses collect the right kind of data and also have data that's reliable.

Secondary Research is Looking at Other People's Work

1) Secondary research gives businesses access to a wide range of data — not just the views of their sample groups. It's useful for looking at the whole market, and analysing past trends to predict the future.
2) It involves looking at things like market research reports (such as from Mintel), government publications (such as the Family Expenditure Survey, Social Trends or census data), and articles in newspapers and magazines and on the internet.
3) Businesses can also look at their own internal data, for example past sales reports.
4) Secondary research is often used by small businesses as it's cheaper than primary research, and the data is easily found and instantly available.
5) Disadvantages of secondary research are that it's not always relevant to your needs, it's not specifically about your products, and it's often out of date.

A census is an official survey of a country's population — including how many people there are and information about them.

Social Media Can be Used for Market Research

1) Social media includes websites such as Facebook® and Twitter. These sorts of sites allow people to create profiles of themselves on the internet. That includes putting the things that they enjoy.
2) Businesses can sometimes collect this information and use it for their market research. For example, they can see what sorts of things are popular or are increasing in popularity.

Data Can be **Quantitative** or **Qualitative**

1) Suppose you want to do some market research about chocolate pizza. You can find out two kinds of information.

- Quantitative information is anything you can measure or reduce to a number. Asking "How many chocolate pizzas will you buy each week?" will give a quantitative answer.
- Qualitative information is all about people's feelings and opinions. Asking "What do you think of chocolate pizzas?" will give a qualitative answer. Qualitative data is tricky to analyse because it's hard to compare two people's opinions. However, allowing customers to voice their opinions is likely to give a greater depth of information.

2) Good market research will use both types of information.
3) All market research data needs to be reliable — this means that its results can be repeated by another researcher. Reliable market research represents the people that the business is interested in accurately. The more reliable the data is, the more useful it is for a business.

Businesses should only use data that's reliable...

Being able to interpret data is just as important as knowing why and how it's collected. Make sure you understand the types of data businesses might look at, and how they'd use this data to make decisions.

Using Market Research

Now it's time for an example of some market research data and how you could interpret it.

You Need to be Able to Interpret Market Research

In an exam, you could get asked to look at the results of some market research and come up with ideas for how a business could improve its marketing mix (see p.95) based on the research. E.g.

BUSINESS EXAMPLE

1) 'Crazy Juice Ltd' wanted customers' views of their damson juice. They sent a questionnaire to 2000 of their existing customers.
2) The collected data is shown below.

Q1a: How many times have you purchased damson juice?	
Never	1290
Once	580
Twice	80
Three times	40
Four or more times	10

Q1b: If you answered 'once', are you planning to buy it again?	
Yes	60
No	520

3) An analysis of this data could look something like this:

'The results show that more than a quarter of the sample group have made a trial purchase of damson juice. This shows that the company's advertising for the product is successfully attracting customers. However, very few of these customers go on to make repeat purchases. This suggests that there is a problem with the product itself. Crazy Juice Ltd need to consider changing the product, or dropping it altogether.'

4) These pie charts show the results of Crazy Juice Ltd's research into why people buy their products, carried out in 1992 and 2016.

Reasons for buying Crazy Juice — 1992

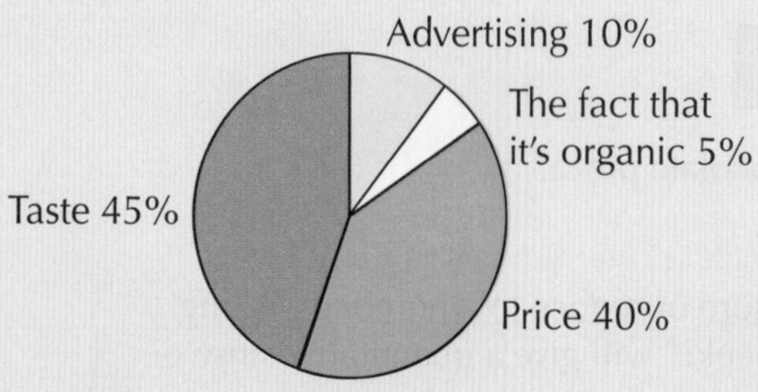

Reasons for buying Crazy Juice — 2016

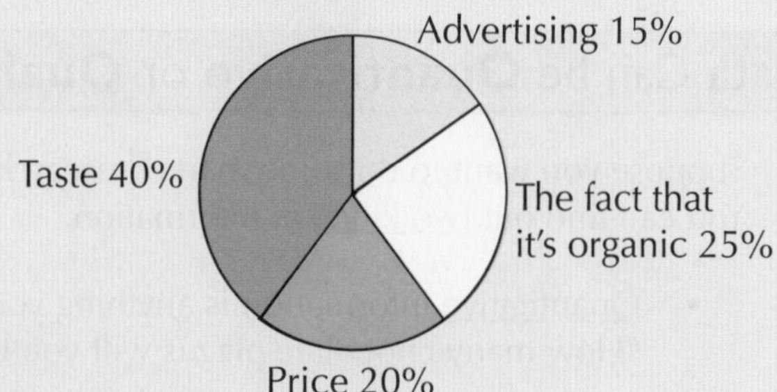

5) An analysis of the charts would include points like...
   - Taste was the most important factor in both years.
   - More people bought Crazy Juice because it's organic in 2016 than in 1992.
   - Price decreased in importance from 1992 to 2016.
6) Because of this research, Crazy Juice might change their promotional material to emphasise the taste and environmental friendliness of the drink.
7) The quality of the product needs to stay the same, but price has become less important to customers, so it might be possible to increase the price of the drink, without decreasing sales by too much.

Market research data can be used as evidence to support decisions...

You might get a question that gives you market research data to help you recommend a decision or explain an effect. You should mention the data in your answer, and use it to support your reasoning.

Worked Exam Questions

Have a look at the following worked exam questions. They'll give you an idea of the types of question you may see in the exams, and there are lots of hints here on how to go about answering them.

1 Look at **Item A** below.

> **Item A — WorkOut Ltd.:**
> Ananda owns a sportswear company, WorkOut Ltd. Ananda's clothes are targeted at individuals who are 25-35 years old, and who exercise regularly. He spends a large amount of money researching customer preferences in sportswear and ensuring that customers who own his products enjoy them and find them attractive. His products are relatively expensive. His brand is not very well known except amongst fitness experts. He sells his products directly to the owners of gyms, who are then responsible for selling the products to the customers in their gyms.

a) Outline **one** aspect of the marketing mix that has been prioritised by Ananda.

[2]

Sample answer:

Ananda prioritises place since WorkOut Ltd. sells its products in places that are convenient to his customers.

You could have also said here that Ananda prioritises product by making sure his customers like the products.

b) Outline **one** way in which Ananda has segmented the market.

[2]

Sample answer:

Ananda has segmented the market by age, as he is targeting people who are aged between 25 and 35 years old.

You could also say lifestyle here, as he's targeting people who regularly exercise.

c) Outline **one** reason why it's important for WorkOut Ltd. to correctly identify its target market.

[2]

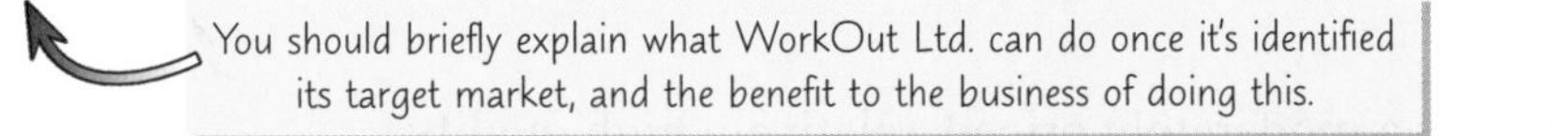

You should briefly explain what WorkOut Ltd. can do once it's identified its target market, and the benefit to the business of doing this.

Sample answer:

Identifying its target market means that WorkOut Ltd. can create a targeted marketing strategy, which will mean that it doesn't waste money by creating ineffective promotional material.

There are lots of advantages to identifying a target market, such as making the business more likely to succeed, and reducing risks.

Exam Questions

1 Explain **one** advantage to a small business of using secondary market research rather than primary market research.

....

....

....

[Total 3 marks]

2 Look at **Item A** and **Figure 1** below.

Item A — MetroMusic:
MetroMusic is an established small business which sells CD players and other sound equipment. Playing vinyl records has become more fashionable in recent years, so the business has decided to start selling record players which can be used to play old vinyl records. It decides to sell a brand called The Groove. **Figure 1** on the right shows the market map for some brands of vinyl record players in the market based on price and quality. MetroMusic has used market segmentation to identify its target market.

Figure 1

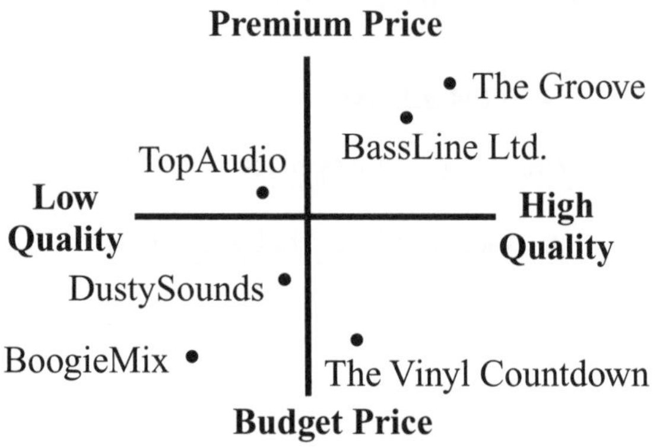

Premium Price
The Groove
BassLine Ltd.
TopAudio
Low Quality
High Quality
DustySounds
BoogieMix
The Vinyl Countdown
Budget Price

a) Define the term 'market segmentation'.

....

....

[1]

b) Identify which of the other products on the market The Groove would be in competition with.

....

[1]

c) Outline **one** reason why a moderately priced, relatively high quality record player may sell well.

....

....

[2]

[Total 4 marks]

Product Life Cycles

It's back to the four Ps of the marketing mix (see p.95) and it's time to look at the product again. Even firms that come up with great products will find that they don't sell well forever — all products have a life cycle.

Demand for a Product Changes Over Time

All products go through the same life cycle — but the sales life of some products is longer than others'. For example, the sales life of most cars is about ten years, but the sales life of many computer games is only a few months. Whatever the product, its marketing mix will need to change during its life cycle.

1 Research and Development (R&D)

R&D is the first stage of a product's life cycle. It's used to develop an idea into a marketable product.

- Scientific research is often vital for product development. A lot of scientific research is done in universities. It's often "pure" science — without any kind of commercial aim.
- Large businesses often then have teams of "applied" scientists, who try to use recent scientific discoveries to develop new or improved products to sell.
- One aim during product development is to find the most cost-effective materials and methods to use.

R&D can lead to innovation, where people invent new products, or come up with new ways of doing things.

2 Introduction

The product is launched and put on sale for the first time. This is usually backed up with lots of advertising and sales promotions. Place is also an important P here — there's no point launching a product in places where nobody will be interested in buying it.

3 Growth

During this phase, demand increases, until the product becomes established.

4 Maturity

Demand reaches its peak during this stage. Promotion becomes less important — businesses will continue to advertise the product, but less than at its launch. As the product's popularity grows, businesses will try to make the product more widely available. Towards the end of this phase, the market becomes saturated and there's no more room to expand.

5 Decline

Eventually demand starts to fall as rival products take over.

Firms will change elements of the marketing mix over a product's life cycle...

Understanding how demand changes during the product life cycle can help a business to choose the correct marketing mix. This should help to increase sales, reduce unnecessary costs and reduce risks for the business.

Product Life Cycles

The sales and profit a product makes for a business will change over the course of its life cycle.

You Can Use Graphs to Show a Product's **Life Cycle**

1) At different points in a product's life cycle, a business will have different costs associated with the product.
2) The demand for a product will also change over its life cycle. This means the amount of revenue it brings in will change.
3) So the stage of its life that a product is in will affect the revenue and profit of a business. You can see how this happens on the following graphs:

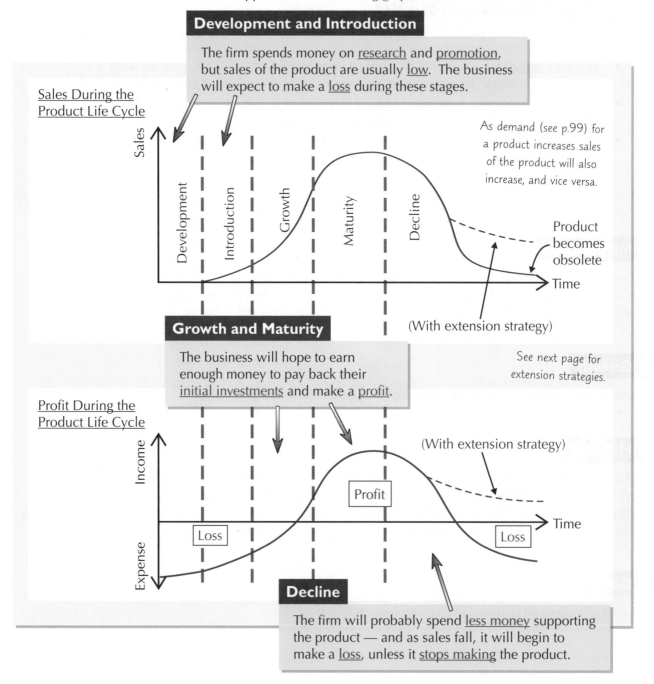

Development and Introduction

The firm spends money on research and promotion, but sales of the product are usually low. The business will expect to make a loss during these stages.

As demand (see p.99) for a product increases sales of the product will also increase, and vice versa.

Growth and Maturity

The business will hope to earn enough money to pay back their initial investments and make a profit.

See next page for extension strategies.

Decline

The firm will probably spend less money supporting the product — and as sales fall, it will begin to make a loss, unless it stops making the product.

Products won't make a profit to begin with...

Make sure you understand how the product life cycle can affect a firm's sales and profit. Try sketching out both graphs yourself, and labelling each one with the stages of the product life cycle.

Extension Strategies

Over time the sales of products may eventually decline, as you saw on the previous page. But there are lots of things that businesses can do to keep their products selling. These are called extension strategies.

Firms May Try to **Extend the Life** of Products in **Decline**

1) Although the sales of all products will eventually decline, firms can take action to extend their life.
2) They might decide to use an extension strategy during the decline phase of the life cycle.
3) If the extension strategy works, the product will make profit for longer.
4) However, it means spending more money on the product — this takes away cash from other parts of the business.
5) Firms have to strike a balance between investing money in supporting old products and in designing new ones.

There are **Several Types** of Extension Strategy

There are lots of ways that firms can extend the life of their products, for example:

- Adding more or different features — adding new features may increase demand for the product by making it more useful or more appealing to customers.
- Using new packaging — creating a new packaging design for the product may make it more eye-catching, so that customers are more likely to see it and choose it over competitors' products. A new image for the product may also attract a new target market...
- Targeting new markets — businesses can find new markets for their products, for example a different age group or country. They can then target their promotional material at the new markets to extend the life of the product.
- Changing advertisements — by running a new advertising campaign, businesses may be able to make more people aware of the product, or promote it in a way that makes it more appealing to the original market or to a new market.
- Lowering price — businesses can reduce the price of the product, or use special offers or competitions.

1) Several of these extension strategies are related to each other. For example, changing the packaging of the product may help to target a new market. Businesses may use a combination of several strategies.
2) However, certain strategies may be more beneficial to a business or a certain situation than others.
3) You need to be able to evaluate how useful different strategies will be for a business, or suggest strategies that a business could use.

BUSINESS EXAMPLE

- Bubbletime is a company that sells shower gels and shampoos.
- One of its shower gels for babies entered the decline phase of its life cycle.
- Therefore the company decided to rebrand the product as a shower gel for people with sensitive skin.
- It designed new packaging and also changed TV adverts and posters for the shower gel, so that they were targeted towards all ages with sensitive skin.
- This meant that the company was able to extend the life of the product.

Extension strategies should increase the sales of a product...

If an extension strategy is successful, demand for a product should increase, and a business's sales should increase more quickly than if it had spent the same money developing a new product instead. Firms will hope that the increase in sales covers the costs of the extension strategy, so their profits shouldn't be affected overall.

Product Portfolios

A firm's product portfolio is basically a list of all the products that it sells. Companies need to make marketing decisions not just for single products, but for their whole product portfolio.

A **Product Portfolio** is a **Range** of Products

1) A product portfolio is the range of different products that a business sells.
2) Businesses aim to have a balanced product portfolio. What this means is that they ideally want to be selling a variety of different products, all at different stages of the product life cycle.
3) This means that if one product fails, they should still be able to depend on the others.

Boston Matrix — Market Share and Market Growth

The Boston Matrix (or Boston Box) is a way for a firm to analyse its product portfolio. The market share of each product is considered, as well as how fast the market the product is in is growing. Then each product is assigned a slightly silly name.

Each circle in the matrix represents one product. The size of each circle represents the revenue (see p.24) of the product.

Question marks

All new products are "question marks" (sometimes called "problem children" or "wildcats"). They have a small market share but high market growth. They aren't profitable yet and need heavy marketing to give them a chance of success.

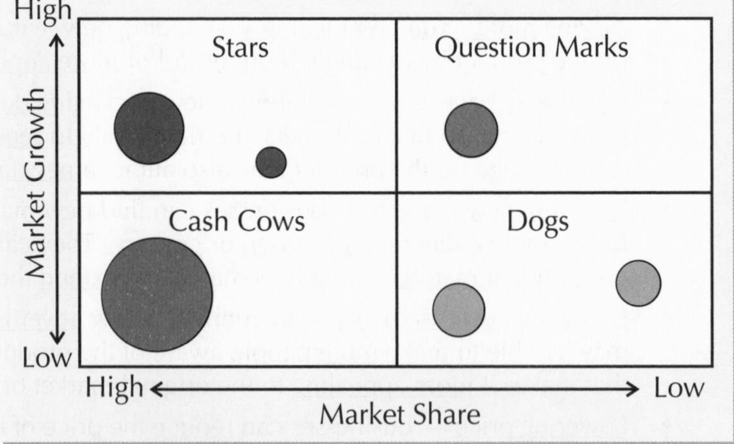

Stars

"Stars" have high market share and high market growth — they're future cash cows (see below).

Cash cows

"Cash cows" bring in plenty of money. They have high market share but low market growth — they're in their maturity phase. Costs are low, since they've already been promoted and are produced in high volumes.

Dogs

"Dogs" have low market share and low market growth — they're pretty much a lost cause. The business will either get what profit it can before discontinuing them, or sell them off.

The Boston Matrix Helps to **Analyse** a **Product Portfolio**

1) The Boston Matrix helps a business see whether it has a balanced product portfolio.
2) A balanced product portfolio means that a business can use money from its cash cows to invest in its question marks so they can become stars.
3) The Boston Matrix has its limitations though. For example, a dog may still have strong cash flow and be profitable despite falling sales and a low market share.

A company should have a range of different product types...

The names should help you here — you can keep 'milking' cash cows for more money, stars are doing well, dogs are the pets that don't pay their own way and question marks are... well, question marks...

Product Development

It's not wise to put all your eggs in one basket — that's why businesses try to make sure they're selling a few different products at any time. In other words, they make sure they have a broad product portfolio.

Businesses Need a **Variety** of **Products**

1) Most large businesses will have products at different stages of the product life-cycle, giving them a balanced portfolio.
2) They'll have some products that have reached the peak of their sales — bringing in lots of money with little investment. These are responsible for most of the business's income.
3) However, at some point these products will start to decline and will have to be replaced. So the firm needs to have products in the development and introduction stages that will later grow to maturity and take their place. These products still need lots of investment.

Firms May **Broaden** Their **Product Portfolios**

1) Businesses may broaden (expand) their portfolios in order to increase sales, target a different segment of the market or compete with other companies.
2) A business may use the Boston Matrix (see previous page) to see if they need to broaden their portfolios (e.g. if they have too many "dogs" and not enough "stars" or "cash cows").
3) Businesses can broaden their portfolios by...

- adding products to an existing range by developing new products based on their current ones. For example, a company that sells fruit smoothies made from local produce could launch some new flavours of smoothies.
- increasing their range of products by developing products that are different from their current ones. For example, they could launch some smoothie ice-lollies made from locally-produced fruit.

4) Designing and producing more products is known as diversification. It reduces the risk that a decline in sales of one product will harm the business, meaning that there's less threat to the firm's profits.

Be **Market-Driven** — Not Product-Driven

1) Market-driven firms will use market research to find out what the target market wants, then make it. This usually means the product is useful — like an MP3 player with a built-in radio.
2) Product-driven firms will design or invent a new product and then try to sell it. This often means they make something nobody really wants — like an MP3 player with a built-in toaster.
3) With very few exceptions, market-driven firms do best.

Businesses need to develop products that customers want to buy...

Having loads of products is no good if they're not selling well, so businesses have to be careful when they're investing in new products. There's a bit more on how they can make sure they get things right on the next page.

More on Product Development

Businesses need to have balanced product portfolios, but developing products isn't completely risk free...

Differentiation Can Attract Customers

Differentiation is about making your products or services distinctive in the market — e.g. by changing elements of the marketing mix. These differences should make customers want to buy your product instead of competing products.

A company may not be able to differentiate itself for long — competitors may copy the idea which removes their competitive advantage.

1) Without differentiation, customers will think your product is identical to others.
2) One way to differentiate a product is to give it a unique selling point (USP) — see p.6. This could be a special feature or a service provided by the company, such as fast delivery.
3) You can promote your product in a way that makes it seem different, even if it's not.
4) You can also change the price of the product. Cheaper usually means more appealing to a mass market, but it also means less profit per unit sold. Having a really expensive product can actually make it appear much more luxurious than competitors' products and more appealing to a niche (small and specialised) market.
5) A business can also develop a good brand image (the impression customers have about a business or product — see p.118). If customers recognise and like a business's brand, they're more likely to buy their products.
6) Product design is hugely important for product differentiation. The DESIGN MIX has three main elements:

Function

The design must be fit for its purpose. A car without an engine would be a non-starter. Unique features can also help — a razor with seven blades shaves better than a razor with one.

Cost

A good design will lead to low manufacturing costs. This means higher profits.

Aesthetics (appearance)

A good product should look attractive and distinctive. Packaging can also help a product to stand out (and protect it till it reaches the customer).

Developing New Products Has Benefits and Risks

Product development makes firms rely less on one product's sales. There are also other benefits as well as risks:

Benefits

- New products will increase overall sales for the business and may extend the life cycle of existing products (see p.107).
- They may appeal to a new market segment and so open up business opportunities.
- Businesses can initially charge higher prices for new products before their competitors bring similar products to the market.
- It can be good for a firm's reputation — if they've been the first to launch exciting new products in the past, people will naturally be interested in their future products.

Risks

- It can be a very costly and time-consuming process — businesses risk running out of money if they invest too much into research and development and don't get the products to market quickly enough.
- Businesses can end up wasting resources by developing something customers don't want.
- Businesses might not be able to produce the new product on a large scale at a low enough cost.
- Businesses risk ruining their reputation if the new product is of poor quality.

Product design is about more than looking good...

Think about the latest thing that you bought and work out how the business that made it have used differentiation to make it appealing. E.g. is it great value for money, or does it have a unique feature?

Price

Time for another of those P's now and it's the one that customers usually think is most important — price. First up it's time to think about how the demand for a product and the size of a company can affect pricing decisions.

Businesses Need to Think About **Demand** When Setting **Prices**

1) Most businesses aim to make a profit — this means that the money they get from selling their products has to be more than the business's costs.

2) The easiest way to do this is to make the price of each product higher than the total cost of making it.

The total cost of making a product includes the cost of getting it to market too — e.g. marketing and distribution costs.

3) However, firms need to think about how the price of a product will affect demand (the quantity of a product that customers are able and willing to buy). As prices rise, demand for a product tends to fall. So firms need to make sure that the price of a product isn't so high that they won't sell many.

4) Sometimes, a firm may need to set the price of a product lower than the total cost of making it so that there is still a decent level of demand for the product (see page 113). In this case the firm may have to rely on making lots of profit on other products in its portfolio so that it doesn't go bust.

The **Size** of a Firm may Affect its **Prices**

As a firm grows, it may be able to change how it prices its products. For example:

- A business's pricing decisions are likely to change as it grows. E.g. once it has developed loyal customers and a good reputation, it might be able to increase prices without demand falling too much.
- On the other hand, as a business grows it can benefit from economies of scale (see page 28). This means that the average cost of making each product falls, so the business can afford to lower prices.

Without demand, products won't sell...

A business needs to be careful when choosing how to price its products. Price them too high, and people might not be interested. Too low, and the business might not make enough to cover its costs. It's all a careful balance.

Price

There are lots of things that a firm should think about when setting prices — both inside and outside the business. Many factors relate to different costs for the business, but there are other types of factor which also matter.

Internal and External Factors Influence Pricing Decisions

There are many factors to consider when deciding on the price of a product. Some of these factors are internal (controlled by the business) and some are external (not controlled by the business).

Internal Factors Come From Inside the Business

- Technology — The technology used by the business in every step of its process of making and marketing the product will affect pricing. For example, if expensive machinery is needed to make the product, then this may increase the price that it needs to be sold at in order to make a profit. However, in the long-term, machinery may help to reduce costs since, e.g. processes may be more efficient or fewer employees may be needed (see p.60).
- Method of production (see p.58-59) — Flow production may require expensive machinery but it will also be more likely to benefit from economies of scale (see p.28) compared to job production so products may be cheaper.
- Product life cycle — Where a product is in its life cycle will affect its price. For example, when the product is in the introduction and growth phases a firm may charge a very low or very high price to encourage people to buy it (see p.113-114). When it's in the maturity phase, a firm may need to bring its price in line with competitors' prices (see below). When it's in the decline phase, the firm may need to reduce the price in order to increase demand for the product again.

External Factors Come From Outside the Business

- Competition — If the product is sold in a competitive market, the firm needs to look at what competitors are charging for similar products. If a firm puts its prices too high, customers will just choose a competitor's product. If it puts its prices too low, customers will query whether the quality is as good as its competitors'.
- Market segments — The nature of the market segment that a product is being targeted at will affect its price. For example, if the product is aimed at a segment with a high income, its price will be higher than a similar product aimed at a segment with a lower income.
- Cost of raw materials — This will affect the cost of each unit (individual product). High quality raw materials will lead to high unit costs and so high prices will be needed to cover these costs.

There are lots of things to think about when making pricing decisions...

There are things that a business can do to reduce the costs of internal factors which affect price. For example, using more efficient processes, or trying to take advantage of economies of scale. But there are some things that a business can't do anything about. For example, if a competitor starts selling a similar product at a much lower price, the business will have to adjust its pricing as well, or it could find itself losing out on sales.

Pricing Strategies

Once a firm knows how much a product costs, it can start thinking about its pricing strategy. This will depend on things such as what the competition is like and the impression the firm wants to give customers about its product.

Here are **Six Pricing Strategies** a Business Could Use

1) Price Penetration

1) This is where a firm charges a very low price when a product is new to get lots of people to try it.

2) It's a good way to establish a market share for a product in a competitive market.

3) The product will make very little profit at first but once it has become established the firm increases the price. Loyal customers should continue to buy the product despite the price increase.

2) Loss Leader Pricing

1) This is when the price of a product is set below cost. The firm doesn't make a profit on it, but the idea is that customers will buy other products as well (which it does make a profit on).

2) E.g. games consoles are often priced below cost but firms make profit on games that go with them.

3) Promotional Pricing

1) This is when products are put on offer for a limited period of time. For example, their price could be reduced, or they could be sold as part of a buy-one-get-one-free offer.

Promotional pricing can also be used as a type of sales promotion — see p.121.

2) This should help to increase demand in the short term, so is good for businesses that are aiming to increase their market share or sales revenue, but don't mind if the amount of profit they make per product is less.

3) However, if customers start expecting the product to be on offer, they may stop buying it when it's full price.

Pricing Strategies

4) Price Skimming

1) This is where firms charge a high price to begin with — they can usually do this when they know there will be a high demand for the product (e.g. goods that use new technology and have a desirable USP, such as smart TVs).
2) It often works for established firms as they'll have loyal customers who will be willing to pay.
3) The high price helps the firm to increase revenue and to cover any research and development costs.
4) Having a high price also helps to make the product more desirable to people with high incomes or to a more niche market (e.g. professionals), which can help to improve the firm's image and status.
5) Once the product's established, the firm lowers the price to help it become a mass-market product.

5) Competitive Pricing

1) This is where the firm has to charge similar prices to other firms.
2) It happens most when there is lots of choice and not much product differentiation — e.g. petrol.
3) The firm may make very little profit and have to find ways other than price to attract customers.

6) Cost-Plus Pricing

Firms may use this method if they're not in price competition with other producers. The firm works out the total cost of making the product, and then adds on a certain amount depending on how much profit they want to make while still having reasonable demand. There are two main ways it can be done:

Using a Mark-Up

Work out how much the product costs and then add a percentage mark-up. So if the product costs £2 to make, and you want a 25% mark-up, you'd sell it for £2 + 25% = £2.50.

Using a Profit Margin

Work out how much the product costs and increase it to get the profit margin you want. So if the product costs £2 to make, and you want a 20% profit margin, this means that £2 is 80% of your required selling price.
So 80% = 200p, 1% = 200 ÷ 80 = 2.5p, 100% = 2.5p × 100 = 250p.
So you'd sell it for £2.50.

Note: mark-up is expressed as a % of cost. Profit margin is expressed as a % of the selling price.

Sometimes a company will choose to charge a high price...

Next time you're in a supermarket, have a search to find two products with a promotional pricing strategy and two products with a competitive pricing strategy. Then write down all the reasons why you think those pricing strategies may be suitable for those particular products.

Worked Exam Question

For some exam questions, you'll need to think about how a business is affected by lots of different factors. Read through the example below for some help with how you might structure these types of answers.

1 Look at **Item A** below.

Item A — Nestlé®:
Nestlé® KitKat® chocolate bars were among the most popular chocolate bars in the UK for many years. However, since the late 1990s their popularity has fallen due to other competitor brands taking over the market.

To extend the life of the *KitKat* brand, *Nestlé* launched a new variation on the product called a *KitKat* Chunky. They also made the chocolate bars available in different flavours, including orange and mint.

However, in 2014 sales of *KitKat* decreased compared to the previous year, and other chocolate brands increased their market share. *Nestlé* spent £10m on marketing *KitKat* in 2015, including launching a partnership with the video website YouTube. It created new packaging with a link to online videos that the consumer could watch while enjoying their *KitKat*.

Evaluate whether using extension strategies for *KitKat* is likely to have been beneficial for *Nestlé*. You should use the information provided, as well as your knowledge of business.

[12]

There's lots to think about for these types of questions. You should discuss the extension strategies that Nestlé® have used, and analyse whether or not they have been successful. You should also finish your answer with a conclusion about whether Nestlé® will have benefited overall from their extension strategies.

Sample answer:

An extension strategy is a method used by a company to extend the life of a product that has declining sales.

Start with a brief introduction to show the examiners you know what extension strategies are.

A company can extend the life of a product by adding more features. A company can also extend the life of a product by targeting a different market. Nestlé® originally extended the life of its KitKat® range by developing new products in the range, such as the KitKat® Chunky and new flavours of KitKat®. These new products may have appealed to a different target market interested in different forms of chocolate bar, so would have increased demand for KitKat®.

State the extension strategies that Nestlé® have used to show you can apply your knowledge of extension strategies to the context.

Explain how the extension strategies that Nestlé® used would have worked.

Worked Exam Question

Although Nestlé® would have increased their costs by developing the new products, they will have benefited from the increased sales revenue, and from maintaining KitKat® as one of the most popular brands in the UK. However, the extension strategy was not enough to ensure KitKat®'s continued success, as in 2014 KitKat® sales and market share decreased.

Use information from the item to back up your answer.

Nestlé® could have used the money spent on the extension strategy to develop and launch a completely new product. However, it would have taken a long time to establish a new product to have a market share similar to KitKat®'s. The increase in revenue from KitKat® before 2014 is likely to have been greater than the revenue that would have been generated from a completely new product in the same time.

By talking about other things Nestlé® could have done, you can draw comparisons to show whether or not the extension strategies were beneficial. This will show the examiner that you're really thinking about business decisions and their possible consequences.

A company can extend the life of a product by updating packaging. In 2015, Nestlé® changed the packaging of KitKat®. This is likely to have made KitKat®s more eye-catching to consumers. They also added a feature to the packaging that included a link to an online video. This may have meant customers were more interested in buying the chocolate in order to watch the videos, therefore increasing demand for the product.

Updating the packaging and launching a partnership with YouTube were both extension strategies that may have increased demand for KitKat®. The extension strategies were expensive, costing £10m. This would have increased Nestlé®'s costs. However, the campaign should have increased the revenue of KitKat® by increasing demand, which should have covered these costs. Choosing to extend the life of one of its current products may have been less costly for Nestlé® than spending money developing and promoting a new product.

You should talk about the benefits of these extension strategies, and also the costs.

As KitKat® is a popular chocolate bar, it is likely to be an important source of revenue for Nestlé®. Despite the costs associated with the extension strategies, the increase in revenue they cause should be enough to cover these costs. So using extension strategies should ultimately have increased profits and so benefited Nestlé®.

Make sure you finish your answer with a conclusion about whether or not the extension strategies would have benefited Nestlé® overall — make sure you've looked thoroughly at all the information given.

Exam Questions

1 Awoocar are a car company. They currently only make one model of car. It is a small car with a one-litre engine, and is available in four colours.

a) Awoocar are thinking of expanding their product portfolio. Explain why it is important for Awoocar to study the target market of their cars before creating new products.

....

....

....

[3]

b) One of the directors of Awoocar wants to develop a new car to compete in the luxury car market. Explain why this approach might be risky for Awoocar.

....

....

....

[3]

[Total 6 marks]

2 Look at **Item A** below.

Item A — Pottery Wheel:
Jerome runs Pottery Wheel, a small pottery company. He employs a small team of potters and sellers, rents a studio and a warehouse and owns several pieces of pottery-making equipment.

He regularly orders clay and glazes for his team. The prices his suppliers offer for clay orders are shown in **Figure 1**. He generally orders 100 kg of clay at a time.

Figure 1

Size of order	100 kg	250 kg	500 kg
Price (£)	50	110	200
Average price per kg (£)	0.5	0.44	0.4

Explain why Jerome may be able to lower the prices of the pottery collections as the business starts producing more units.

....

....

....

....

[Total 4 marks]

Methods of Promotion

Businesses use promotion to tell customers what the company and their products are all about. Promotion should persuade customers that they want to buy the products, which should help to increase sales.

Promotion is **Really Important** for a Business

Firms spend lots of time and money on promotion. There are many reasons why they do it:

1) To inform customers about the product — customers need to know that the product exists, what it is or does and what its USP is. Even if it's been on the market for some time, customers may still need reminding about a product.
2) To persuade customers to buy the product — firms have to make customers really want the product and to choose it over competitors' products. Firms use many different tactics to do this, such as tempting descriptions, displaying positive results of customer surveys, and special offers.
3) To create or change the image of a product — for example, the use of humour and bold colours creates a fun and vibrant image, whereas darker colours and classical music might create a more sophisticated, luxurious image. The image that a firm wants a product to have will largely depend on who it's aimed at.
4) To create or increase sales — this one is usually the ultimate reason for promotion — more sales can lead to more profit and a greater market share.

Good Branding is Important

1) A firm's brand image is the impression that customers have of the firm or products sold by the firm — e.g. the firm may have a reputation for high quality, luxury products. There may also be a recognisable logo that customers associate with the company or products.
2) Products with a strong brand image are easily recognised and liked by customers. A strong brand image is usually built up over a number of years. It's important that a firm's products, prices, methods of promotion, and the places they sell in all build the right brand image.
3) A firm may create different brand images for different products to target different market segments.

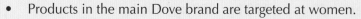

BUSINESS EXAMPLE

- Dove is a company that produces toiletries such as skin care and hair care products.
- Products in the main Dove brand are targeted at women.
- It has a separate brand for its products that are aimed at men — Dove Men+Care.
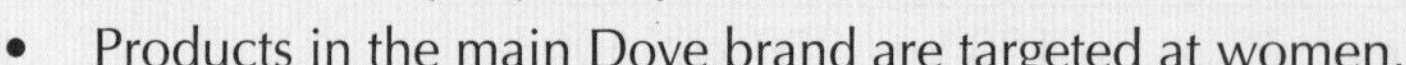
- It also has Baby Dove — a brand aimed at parents looking for products for babies.

4) Developing a brand image and promoting products is expensive for a business, but both should increase the revenue of a firm — through first time purchases and repeat purchases. The business will have planned for this increase in revenue to cover the costs of promotion and branding.

Businesses need to build the right brand image for their customers...

Promotion's crucial, especially in a very competitive market. It's the way that businesses are able to persuade possible customers that they're better than the competition. There are more methods of promotion coming up...

Methods of Promotion

Adverts might just be the first thing you think about when someone mentions promotion. They're a great way for a business to get its message out, and as you're about to see, they can be found all over the place.

Firms **Promote** Their Products by **Advertising**

One way that businesses can establish a good brand image is through effective advertising. Advertising is any message that a firm pays for which promotes the firm or its products. Methods of advertising include:

1) Newspapers — local ones can reach a market segment in a specific geographical area and national ones can reach a wide audience. They're printed often so they're a good way to promote temporary offers. However, the print quality is usually poor and the number of people reading newspapers is declining.
2) Magazines are often aimed at a particular market segment, e.g. people in the same age group or people with similar hobbies. Businesses can use adverts in these magazines to target these specific market segments. Magazine adverts can be pricier than newspaper adverts, but they're better quality and people tend to hang on to magazines for longer.
3) Posters and billboards can be placed near a target audience, stay in place for a long time and be seen daily by lots of people. But people might not look at them for long, so messages need to be short.
4) Leaflets, flyers and business cards are cheap to produce and distribute. They can be targeted at certain areas (which is useful for targeting a market segment in a particular location) and people can keep them until they need the information. But many people see them as 'junk' and throw them away quickly.
5) Television adverts can be seen by a wide audience and include sounds and moving images. They can deliver long messages and help to emphasise the firm's image. On the downside, they're very expensive.
6) Internet adverts can be seen at any time by a large, targeted audience, can include sounds and moving images, and customers can visit the firm's website immediately after viewing the advert. However, there are so many adverts online, people may stop looking at them properly or choose to block them.
7) Radio adverts can be heard by a wide audience, and include sound. Adverts on local radio stations are good for companies that want to target a market segment in a particular location. Some national radio stations play particular types of music, e.g. classical music. So businesses who want to appeal to people they think will listen to these certain types of music can choose to advertise via these stations.

Businesses Can **Sponsor** Organisations and Events

Firms sometimes give money to organisations and events — e.g. schools, TV production firms and exhibitions. In return, their name is displayed by the organisation or at the event. This is called sponsorship. E.g.:

- SPORT — A large firm might stamp its brand name all over an international competition. A smaller firm might only be able to afford to sponsor the local Sunday League team, but the aim is the same.
- TELEVISION — Some soap operas and weather reports are sponsored by well-known brands.

Sponsorship can create a high profile for your business or brand name, it's also a good way to target a market segment that is characterised by lifestyle (e.g. hobbies). But if the thing you're sponsoring starts to get bad publicity, your company's image might suffer too.

Businesses have to pay to advertise or sponsor...

Businesses need to think about who they want to promote themselves to when they choose how to advertise. It's likely to be a waste of money displaying adverts somewhere where your target market is unlikely to see them.

More Methods of Promotion

Sometimes, a firm will rely on other people spreading the word for them. For example, they could get articles written about them in newspapers or magazines, or have information about them shared on social media.

Public Relations (PR) Gets a Firm Noticed in the Media

1) PR involves communicating with the media, e.g. doing a TV interview or issuing a press release.
2) It can be a cheap and easy way to get a firm noticed by a wide audience.
3) But once the firm has spoken to the media, it has little control over what the public get to see or hear. E.g. the full TV interview might not be shown or journalists may use the press release to criticise the firm's activities.

A press release is a piece of writing about a firm's activities (e.g. the launch of a new product), which is sent to the media in the hope that they will run a story on it.

Firms Can Also Use New Technology for Promotion

The internet is becoming more important as a method of promotion. Here are some ways in which it can be used:

Social Media

- Social media is a quick, easy and cheap way for firms to promote their products.
- Firms can use their social media pages to do things like advertise products, offer sales promotions, share news stories about their products and build up excitement for new products being launched.
- They are also able to make separate accounts for different parts of the business, and so may be able to target specific market segments.
- They can add information whenever they like, so they can respond quickly to internal or external changes.
- Customers can go quickly from the social media page to the firm's website where they can buy products.
- However, any mistakes or negative customer comments can be seen quickly by lots of people, so time and money needs to be spent carefully monitoring the site.
- Firms can also use social media to try and launch viral adverts. Viral advertising is when adverts are shared on social media and are viewed many (perhaps millions) of times in a short time period. This is good for targeting segments of a market that use social media frequently (e.g. younger age groups).

Targeted Advertising

- An individual's internet search history can be used to create targeted advertising.
- Web pages have spaces for adverts, but the adverts found in these spaces will depend on what an individual has searched for in the past. So the adverts will be more likely to be something that the individual is interested in, and therefore will be more effective.
- Technology can also track an individual's location for use in targeted advertising. Although some individuals dislike this, and may be put off the brand.

E-newsletters

Individuals may also decide to be a part of a business's mailing list. This means that they will get e-newsletters from the business about promotions and offers.

A lot of promotion now takes place online...

Technology has opened up new ways for firms to promote themselves. Being able to use the internet as a method of promotion is a really quick way for a firm to get its message out to a large number of people. It's so important that many firms even employ people just to manage their social media accounts.

More Methods of Promotion

Even more methods of promotion coming up on this page. As you might have realised, there are lots of things a business can do to promote itself. The trick is to choose the best method for the business and product in question.

Sales Promotion is a Short-Term Method Used to Boost Sales

1) You need to know these seven sales promotion methods that firms use:

- competitions
- free samples (product trials)
- special offers, e.g. 2 for 1 offers or price reductions
- coupons, e.g. 20p off a product
- point of sale displays, e.g. a branded display case at the front of a shop
- free gifts, e.g. a cuddly toy that comes with the product
- loss leaders, e.g. reducing the price of one product so it's below cost (see p.113)

2) An advantage of sales promotion is that it should encourage new customers to try a product. This will boost sales in the short term but could also increase sales in the long term if customers like the product and continue to buy it once the promotion has ended.
3) A disadvantage of sales promotion is that customers get used to seeing products on promotion and may be reluctant to buy them at other times. Also, using regular sales promotions might not be suitable for certain market segments. E.g. it might make a product in a luxury market seem like less of a luxury item, so it won't be useful for targeting a higher income segment that are looking for luxury.

Firms Must Choose the Best Promotional Mix

Firms use a combination of different promotional methods (advertising, sponsorship, PR, etc.) to promote a product — this is called the promotional mix. You need to be able to analyse the different factors that might influence a firm's promotional mix. Here are some things you should think about:

1) Finance available: E.g. large firms can usually afford to spend more than smaller ones.

2) Nature of the product or service: E.g. some products need lots of description to say what they are.

3) What competitors are doing: E.g. a firm might want to use social media if all of its competitors are.

4) Nature of the market: E.g. if a market is growing rapidly, a firm may be willing to spend more on promotion as they are predicting a large increase in sales, which will cover the costs.

5) Target market: promotions might need to be in a place where they'll be seen by the right people, and need to be presented in a way that they'll appeal to the right people.

The right promotional mix should appeal to the right market...

If you're asked to choose a method of promotion for a certain business, have a think about all the information you've been given before you recommend anything. A small business selling to a local area isn't likely to have the money needed for a TV advert, and doesn't need to advertise to that many people. And it may not be best for a firm selling luxury products to have lots of sales promotions.

Place

Place (the final P) is all about channels of distribution — how products get from manufacturers to consumers.

Firms Need to Choose the Most Suitable Channel of Distribution

1) Firms need to make sure that their products are available to consumers at the right place. To do this, they need to choose the most appropriate channel of distribution. This depends on things like where the consumer is likely to shop, how many consumers they want their products to reach, how quickly they want the product to get to the consumer, and how much customer service the consumer will need.
2) Here are three common channels of distribution:

1 Selling to wholesalers

Wholesalers buy products in bulk and store them in a warehouse. Manufacturers sell products to a wholesaler, then consumers or retailers buy the products from the wholesaler. This channel is good for manufacturers that make lots of a particular product and don't need to communicate much with the consumer — e.g. a baked beans manufacturer. Selling to a wholesaler means the manufacturer gets bulk orders and doesn't have to store lots of stock. The wholesaler will already have customers, so products can reach lots of potential consumers quickly. And if retailers buy from the wholesaler, it means the product will end up being sold in even more places, so reach even more customers. The problem with this channel is that consumers may get lower levels of customer service compared to the other channels.

Wholesalers and retailers need to make a profit, which can push up prices for consumers.

2 Selling directly to retailers

Retailers sell products to consumers. Selling directly to retailers means that the manufacturer can provide the retailer with product knowledge so the retailer can provide better customer service. So the customers have higher satisfaction with the products. The retailer can help to promote products (e.g. with point of sale displays), which may help to increase sales. Also, using retailers means that products are sold in more places, so more potential customers are exposed to them (especially if the retailer already sells similar products). However, it can be hard for new firms to persuade many retailers to stock their products.

3 Selling directly to customers

1) Firms that sell directly to customers will have lower fixed costs than retailers, since they won't have to pay to have stores open. This may mean that they can charge less for products. But it can be time-consuming for firms to sell products to individual customers, especially if each customer only buys small quantities. They also have to arrange delivery of the goods, which can be difficult and expensive if the customers are in lots of different places. This channel is good for firms who don't have loads of customers or firms selling one-off items, e.g. custom-made wedding dresses.
2) One way firms can sell directly to customers is using telesales. This is when companies sell products to consumers via the phone.
3) E-tailers sell products via the internet — i.e. they use e-commerce (see p.123). They can sell to a global market so they have more potential customers than if they used stores.

Place is about getting products from the company to the consumer...

Each channel of distribution has its own pros and cons — the one that's best depends on the business.

E-Commerce

If you've ever bought anything on the internet, then you've used e-commerce. It's really important for businesses.

E-Commerce and M-Commerce Involve Selling Products via the Internet

E-commerce allows goods and services to be bought on the internet — and it's growing fast.

1) Firms put details of their products on their website. Customers may be directed straight to the product they want if they follow a link placed elsewhere, e.g. in an advert. Alternatively they can use the website to browse through the product range or use a search box to find the products they want.
2) Products are ordered online and are usually paid for using a credit or debit card or with PayPal.
3) The products are then delivered to the customer.

PayPal is an online payments system.

- M-commerce (mobile commerce) allows goods and services to be bought using a wireless mobile device, such as a smartphone or tablet.
- It's pretty much the same as e-commerce (customers can find and buy products on the internet), but the fact that they can do this in a wider range of locations and situations is making m-commerce more and more popular.

Customers often prefer to use a firm's app on a mobile device rather than their website.

Businesses Can Reach International Markets More Easily

The internet means that people in more places can buy a business's products.

1) The internet can be accessed all over the world. As part of its marketing strategy, a business may want to target markets in foreign countries with online promotions.
2) Even small companies can do this, since it's much cheaper than buying advertising space in foreign newspapers, magazines, etc.
3) For all businesses, selling to international markets may lead to higher profits.

E-Commerce and M-Commerce are Becoming More Important

1) The internet is always growing — more and more businesses are creating websites.
2) The number of consumers on the internet is also increasing — more people have access to the internet (either at home or on a mobile device) and improvements in technology mean the service is becoming more reliable.
3) As a result, an increasing number of people are turning to the internet to buy products.
4) Businesses need to keep up with this changing trend — they need to make sure they can meet the changing expectations of customers and adapt to changing competition within the market.

Higher Customer Expectations

1) Customers expect to be able to buy products from a firm online. If they can't, it's often easy to find an online competitor selling what they want.
2) They also want things like low prices, free delivery and returns, and a website that's easy to use. If they can't get these, it's often easy for them to shop elsewhere.

More Competition

1) Customers can buy products from firms around the world, so there are a lot more firms to compete with.
2) It's easy for customers to go from one firm's website to another, so it's easy for them to compare products and prices. Therefore firms need to work harder to persuade customers to buy from them.

Businesses need to keep up with e-commerce...

When it comes to marketing, e-commerce has given firms access to places that would previously have been out of their reach. If a business wants to stay competitive in modern markets, e-commerce is the way forward.

More on E-Commerce

There are loads of good reasons to use e-commerce and m-commerce, but selling online isn't always easy.

E-Commerce and M-Commerce Have Many **Advantages**

E-commerce has some big advantages over traditional methods of doing business — mostly to do with increasing sales, reducing costs and prices, and becoming more competitive.

1) A big advantage of e-commerce is that businesses can access wider markets — e.g. markets in other parts of the world. This means businesses have more potential customers, so sales may increase.
2) The growth of m-commerce also means that a business's sales may increase further, as it's becoming easier for customers to buy products online.
3) E-commerce saves money on paper. Things like sales brochures and product information no longer need to be printed and posted by the firm — they can be viewed online, on apps, or downloaded by the customer.
4) Some firms that traditionally employed staff to sell products over the telephone have been able to cut costs by making these people redundant and allowing customers to buy online instead.

BUSINESS EXAMPLE

- In 2004, British Airways closed two of its call centres in the UK.
- In the two years before the decision was made, British Airways had seen a 34% decrease in calls to its call centres, as people were booking more flights online.
- British Airways predicted that closing the call centres would save them more than £10 million within five years.

5) Businesses that sell successfully online may be able to close (or not have to open) high street shops. This saves the business money on things such as property and staff costs.
6) If firms rely more on online sales than sales from customers visiting their shop, they may be able to locate in more remote areas where wages tend to be lower.
7) All these savings mean that firms which only sell goods or services online can offer lower prices than high street shops — this is one of the main reasons that sales from many internet shopping sites are increasing.

There are Some **Drawbacks** of E-Commerce and M-Commerce

There are plenty of benefits to a firm of selling over the internet, but it's not completely straightforward. Setting up the facilities needed for e-commerce can be expensive and time-consuming.

1) Special equipment may need to be bought and installed, especially for large businesses with many customers. (A sole trader may be able to launch a website from their home computer with no problems.)
2) Firms may need to employ specialist website or app designers, who'll have to be paid. Other staff might need to be trained in using the equipment and in providing good customer service.
3) Some consumers are reluctant to buy online — they might not have internet access, or they might prefer to visit a shop where they can see what they're getting. As a result, firms might have to spend more on marketing to try to persuade more people to use their online services.

E-commerce can be expensive to set up but can reduce costs over time...

When a company decides to sell products over the internet, there are lots of things to think about. For example, how the website will work and how to get products to the customers. If these systems aren't thought about properly, things are likely to go wrong, and the company could end up with lots of unhappy customers.

Worked Exam Questions

Before you read through the answers below, have a go at the questions yourself. Then see how your answers compare to the sample answers, and try to work out if there's anything you should have done differently.

1 Look at **Item A** below.

Item A — Cushion Company:
Lisa is setting up a small business selling handmade cushions and other small furniture accessories. She designs and makes each product herself — on average, she can produce three items per day. Lisa is planning to sell her products directly to her consumers using e-commerce.

a) Define the term 'e-commerce'. *[1]*

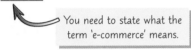

You need to state what the term 'e-commerce' means.

Sample answer:

E-commerce is when products are sold over the internet.

b) Outline **one** disadvantage for Lisa of selling products directly to her customers. *[2]*

There are two marks available here — one mark for giving a disadvantage of selling directly to customers and one mark for explaining this disadvantage.

Sample answer:

It may be time-consuming, because she will have to arrange all the sales with individual customers.

You could also have said it may be expensive as she will have to arrange the delivery of goods to different customers.

c) Outline why selling to a wholesaler might not be suitable for Lisa's business. *[2]*

Sample answer:

Wholesalers order products in bulk and Lisa doesn't make products in large enough quantities to sell to a wholesaler.

You know from the item that Lisa's business is small, and she makes products slowly. So you should link your explanation back to this information.

Exam Questions

1 Look at **Item A** below.

Item A — Mamo Ltd.:
Mamo Ltd. is an established company which makes food and drink products. One year it launches a new brand of energy drink for sports. It decides to celebrate the launch of its new product by sponsoring a marathon running event in a major UK city.

Outline **one** reason why Mamo Ltd. may have chosen to sponsor the marathon instead of another kind of event.

....

....

....

[Total 2 marks]

2 Look at **Item B** below.

Item B — British Bikes Ltd.:
British Bikes Ltd. is a UK company which makes and sells bicycles and bicycle accessories. It has recently developed a new website and a mobile phone app that allows customers to buy products from the company. Its competitors also have similar apps available.

a) Outline how British Bikes have used m-commerce.

....

....

[2]

b) Outline **one** possible effect of using m-commerce on the sales of British Bikes Ltd.

....

....

[2]

c) Outline **one** reason why it's important that British Bikes Ltd. keeps developing its website and app.

....

....

[2]

[Total 6 marks]

Revision Summary for Section 5

Right, you've reached the end of Marketing — time to see how much of it you can remember.

- Try these questions and tick off each one when you get it right.
- When you've done all the questions for a topic and are completely happy with it, tick off the topic.

The Marketing Mix and Market Research (p.95-102) ☐

1) What are the four elements of the marketing mix? ☐
2) Why is a firm's marketing mix for a product likely to change over time? ☐
3) Give four different ways of segmenting a market. ☐
4) Give two pieces of information which a business might find out from a market map. ☐
5) Give two customer needs that a business might want to identify. ☐
6) Give three benefits to a business of identifying and satisfying customer needs. ☐
7) Give four methods of primary market research. ☐
8) Give two methods of secondary market research. ☐
9) What is the difference between quantitative and qualitative market research? ☐

Products (p.105-110) ☐

10) What is the first stage in a product life cycle? ☐
11) Sketch a graph to show how sales of a product are likely to change throughout its life cycle. ☐
12) Give five different types of extension strategy. ☐
13) What is a firm's 'product portfolio'? ☐
14) Give two ways in which a firm might broaden its product portfolio. ☐
15) State three benefits and three risks to a firm of developing a new product. ☐

Price (p.111-114) ☐

16) Explain how a firm's costs will influence the price it charges for a product. ☐
17) Give three internal factors that will influence a firm's pricing decisions. ☐
18) Describe the main features of each of the following pricing strategies:
    a) price penetration, b) price skimming, c) competitive pricing, d) cost-plus pricing. ☐

Promotion (p.118-121) ☐

19) Explain two reasons why firms choose to promote their products. ☐
20) Explain why it's important that a firm develops a strong brand image for a product. ☐
21) Explain how leaflets and flyers may be used to target a particular market segment. ☐
22) How can firms use sponsorship for promotion? ☐
23) Give one advantage and one disadvantage of a firm using PR as a method of promotion. ☐
24) List six sales promotion methods a firm might use to boost sales. ☐

Place and E-commerce (p.122-124) ☐

25) What is a 'channel of distribution'? ☐
26) What is 'm-commerce'? ☐
27) Give three ways in which the use of e-commerce might reduce a firm's costs. ☐

Sources of Finance

There are lots of different sources of money for firms. The different sources can be classed in a number of different ways, such as whether they come from inside or outside the business and how long they last.

Firms **Need Finance** for Five Reasons

1) New firms need start-up capital (the money or assets needed to set up a business).
2) New firms often have poor initial cash flow — this means that they find it hard to cover their costs (see p.24), so they need additional finance to cover this.
3) Sometimes customers delay payment, so finance is needed to cover this shortfall in (lack of) liquidity.
4) If a business is struggling, it may need additional finance to meet its day-to-day running costs.
5) Firms may need finance in order to expand, e.g. to buy larger premises or to recruit new staff, or for things such as new marketing campaigns.

Liquidity is how easily the business can access cash — see page 145.

Finance can be Classed as **Internal** or **External**

1) Internal finance comes from inside the business. It can be a quick and easy way to get money. It saves borrowing and having to pay back interest. However, some businesses may not have enough and have to find external sources instead.
2) External finance comes from outside the business. It usually needs to be paid back (e.g. loans) — sometimes with high interest.

Internal Sources include...

- Personal or business savings
- Retained profits
- Selling fixed assets

These different sources of finance are covered in more detail below and on the next page.

External Sources include...

- Bank loans, overdrafts and mortgages
- Loans from family and friends
- New partners
- Share capital, venture capital and stock market flotation
- Trade credit
- Government grants
- Hire purchases
- Crowd funding

Sources of Finance Can be...

Sources of finance can be classed by how long they last — short-term, medium-term or long-term (see next page).

1) **Short-Term** Sources of Finance

Short-term sources will lend money for a limited period of time. Examples of short-term sources include:

- TRADE CREDIT — businesses may give firms one or two months to pay for certain purchases. This is useful for a small firm as they have time to earn the money needed to pay the debt. However, if the firm makes the payment too late, they could end up with a large fee.
- OVERDRAFTS — these let the firm take more money out of its bank account than it has paid into it. Overdrafts can allow businesses to make payments on time even if they don't have enough cash. However, they usually have a higher interest rate than other loans (see next page) and the bank can cancel the overdraft at any time. If it isn't paid off, then the bank can take some of the business's assets.

2) **Medium-Term** Sources of Finance

Selling FIXED ASSETS is an example of a medium-term source of finance. This is when firms raise cash by selling fixed assets (assets that a business keeps long-term, e.g. machinery/buildings) that are no longer in use. There's a limit to how many assets you can sell, though — sell too many and you can't go on trading.

Sources of Finance

3) Long-Term Sources of Finance

Long-term sources are paid back over a long period of time (more than a year). Some don't need to be paid back.

GOVERNMENT GRANTS are often given to qualifying new or small firms. Unlike loans, they don't have to be repaid. However, there are fewer options than for loans, strict criteria may have to be met to qualify for them, and the money may have to be spent in a specific way.

LOANS
- Bank loans are quick and easy to take out. Like with overdrafts, they are repaid with interest, and if they aren't repaid, the bank can repossess the firm's assets. However, the interest rate for loans is usually lower than for overdrafts.
- It may be easier to get loans from friends and family than from a bank. The money lent will go into the firm immediately, however the lender may want a share in the profits of the firm.
- Mortgages are loans used to finance buying property. The property is used as collateral — this means that the property can be taken by the bank if the individual can't pay off the mortgage. Interest payments are relatively low compared to other sources of finance. A sole trader might use their house as collateral to borrow money — but they risk losing it if their business fails.

HIRE PURCHASES — these are when a firm purchases something by first paying a deposit, then paying the rest in instalments over a period of time, while they have use of the product. This allows firms to purchase useful things for their business that they otherwise couldn't afford, such as expensive machinery. It also means that they have use of the product over a longer period of time.

PERSONAL SAVINGS and FORMING PARTNERSHIPS — A business owner may put some of their own capital into the business to get it started or if it is having cash flow problems (see page 138). They may also go into partnership with someone (see p.9). This will mean that the new partner can also contribute their own capital towards the business. However, it's risky for business owners to use their own capital as they could end up losing their money if the business fails.

SHARE CAPITAL — If a business becomes a limited company (see p.10) it can be financed using share capital — money raised by selling shares in the business. Individuals who buy shares will have part ownership in the business. Finance from share capital doesn't need to be repaid (unlike a loan). However, selling shares means that the original owner(s) will lose some control over how the business is run and new shareholders will also expect to be paid dividends.

RETAINED PROFIT — these are profits that the owners have decided to plough back into the business after they've paid themselves a dividend (see p.20).

VENTURE CAPITAL — This is money raised through selling shares to individuals or businesses who specialise in giving finance to new or expanding small firms. Venture capitalists will usually buy shares in businesses that are risky but have the potential to grow quickly. They will take a stake in the business, and may expect returns more quickly than other shareholders would.

STOCK MARKET FLOTATION — When a private limited company decides to sell its shares on the stock market, it becomes a public limited company (see p.11). Trading shares on the stock market means that shares in the company can be bought and sold by anyone. This can bring a lot of extra finance into the business, especially if the shares are in high demand, as this will increase their value.

CROWD FUNDING — This is when a large number of people contribute money towards starting up a business or funding a business idea. It's often used for creative or innovative businesses and usually takes place online. Normally each person only contributes a small amount of money. Sometimes, the people that contribute money may get a reward in return.

Sources of Finance

It's not just the length of time that a source of finance lasts for which matters to a business.
This page has a summary of some of the different factors that determine the best source of finance for a firm.

Four Factors Affect the Choice of Finance

1 Size and type of company

Not all companies have access to all types of finance:

- Established firms are more likely to use retained profits (see previous page) than smaller firms. But larger companies (e.g. PLCs — see page 11) are under pressure from shareholders to give large dividends, reducing the profit they can retain.
- A limited company (see page 10) can issue more shares (called new share issues). Private limited companies can only sell shares if all the shareholders agree to sell them. Whereas in public limited companies shares are sold on the stock market by anyone, to anyone (see previous page). Small businesses are unable to issue new shares and may also find it hard to get loans or overdrafts.
- Established firms may find it easier to get loans than new firms because they can prove to the bank that they've been profitable over a longer period of time. This means banks will see them as less risky. Banks need security for a loan, usually in the form of assets such as property. If things go wrong, these assets can be sold to pay back the loan. Large firms can normally take out larger loans than small firms, as they usually have more valuable assets. Some types of business may not have fixed assets available to use as security for a loan (or to sell).

2 Amount of money needed

A company wouldn't issue more shares to buy a toaster. Small amounts of money usually come from internal sources. For larger amounts of money (e.g. for new property or machinery), the firm is more likely to need an external source of finance.

3 Length of time the finance is needed for

It'd be daft to take out a mortgage because a customer is a week late paying an invoice. Using savings or an arranged overdraft from a bank are common ways to see a business through a short-term lack of finance.

4 Cost of the finance

Some sources, e.g. bank loans and overdrafts, are more expensive than others as the money has to be paid back with interest.

Firms need to make sensible financial choices to avoid difficulties...

Make sure you know the details of the different sources of finance on the previous three pages and that you can identify the right source of finance to meet the needs of a business. That includes understanding the factors that affect which source of finance a firm should choose.

Break-Even Analysis

Break-even analysis allows firms to find out the minimum amount they need to sell to get by.

Breaking Even Means **Covering Your Costs**

1) The break-even level of output or break-even point in units is the level of sales (or output) a firm needs in order to just cover its costs. In other words, the point at which total costs = total revenue

The break-even level of output can also be called the break-even quantity.

2) It can be measured by the number of units a firm needs to sell to break-even:

$$\text{break-even point in units} = \frac{\text{fixed cost}}{\text{sales price} - \text{variable cost}}$$

This is the variable cost per unit.

3) Or it can be measured by the revenue the firm needs to make to cover its costs:

break-even point for revenue (or costs) = break-even point in units × sales price

4) If a firm sells more than the break-even point, it'll make a profit — if it sells less, it'll make a loss.

5) New businesses should always do a break-even analysis to find the break-even level of output.

- Pin-Chit Ltd. make padlocks. They have fixed costs of £2000, and the variable cost per unit is £2. The selling price is £4.
- Their break-even output = 2000 ÷ (4 – 2) = 2000 ÷ 2 = 1000 units
- So the firm will break even if it makes and sells 1000 units.
- The break-even point for revenue = 1000 × 4 = £4000
- This means that the firm should have a revenue of £4000 in order to break even.

6) A low break-even output is good for a business as it won't have to sell as much to make a profit.

If you can't make a profit, breaking even is the next best thing...

Don't be put off learning this page by the different terms used for the amount of units that a business has to sell to break even, i.e. the break-even level of output, the break-even point in units or the break-even quantity — they all mean the same thing. Also, remember that you can work out the amount of money that the business has to earn to break even (the break even point for revenue).

Break-Even Analysis

Now that you know what break-even analysis is, it's time to see how you could use a break-even diagram.

Break-even Diagrams Show the Effect of Output Changing

1) A break-even diagram has number of sales or output on the x-axis, and costs and revenues on the y-axis.

2) If the output is lower than the break-even output, the firm will make a loss.

3) If the output is higher than the break-even output, the firm will make a profit.

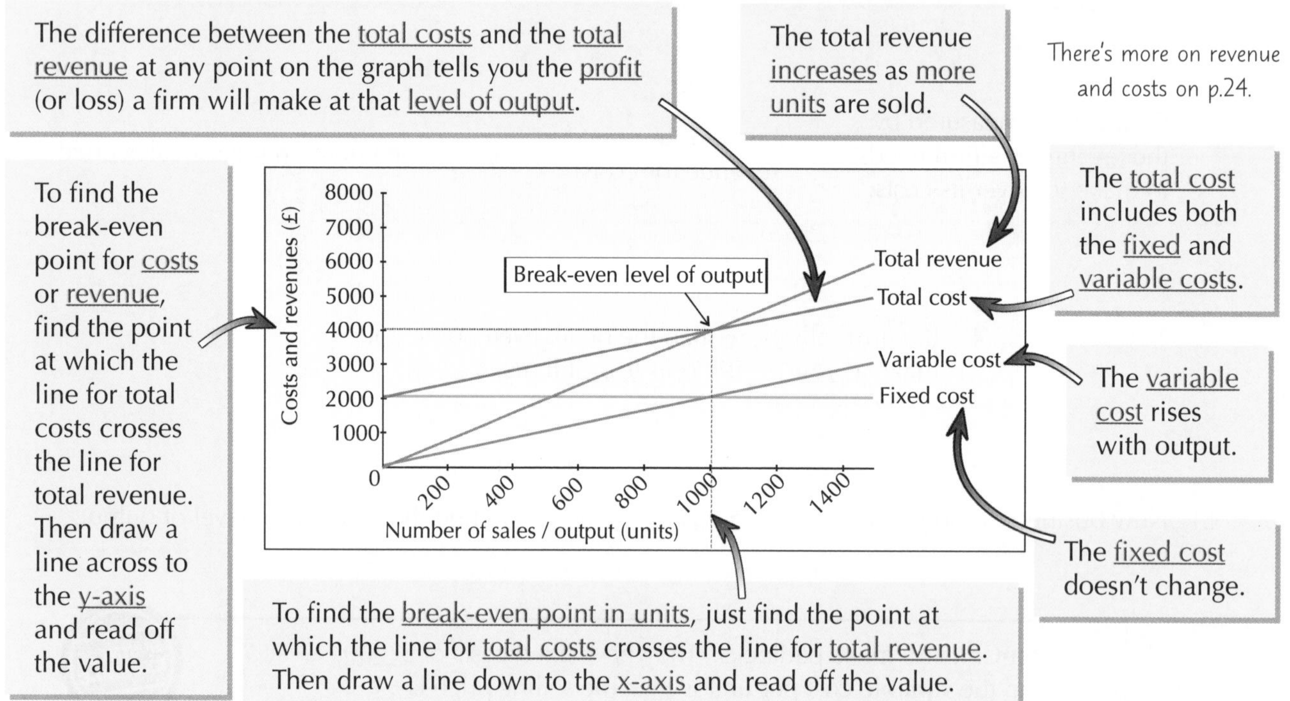

The difference between the total costs and the total revenue at any point on the graph tells you the profit (or loss) a firm will make at that level of output.
The total revenue increases as more units are sold.
There's more on revenue and costs on p.24.
To find the break-even point for costs or revenue, find the point at which the line for total costs crosses the line for total revenue. Then draw a line across to the y-axis and read off the value.
Costs and revenues (£)
8000
7000
6000
5000
4000
3000
2000
1000
0
Break-even level of output
Total revenue
Total cost
Variable cost
Fixed cost
200
400
600
800
1000
1200
1400
Number of sales / output (units)
The total cost includes both the fixed and variable costs.
The variable cost rises with output.
The fixed cost doesn't change.
To find the break-even point in units, just find the point at which the line for total costs crosses the line for total revenue. Then draw a line down to the x-axis and read off the value.

BUSINESS EXAMPLE

The break-even diagram above is for Pin-Chit Ltd. You can see that:

1) Fixed costs are £2000. Variable costs increase £2 for every unit sold. So, total costs start at £2000 and increase £2 for every unit sold.
2) Total revenue rises £4 for each unit sold (since the price of each padlock is £4).
3) The break-even level of output is 1000 units or £4000.
4) Total costs (and variable costs) are rising at a slower rate than revenue. So, as output increases, profit per unit also increases.

Break-even diagrams — an easy way to put a lot of information in one place...

The diagram above may seem confusing, but if you take the time to go through each of the labels, it should become clearer. The most important thing to notice is the point where the line for total cost and the line for total revenue cross each other. You can use it to find the break even point in units or for revenue (or cost).

More Break-Even Analysis

Even more on break-even analysis here — this time, how to find the margin of safety for a given level of output. This is an easy way of seeing how much a business's output can fall before it starts making a loss.

Break-Even Analysis Can be Used to Find the Margin of Safety

1) The margin of safety for a firm is the gap between the current level of output and the break-even output.
2) You can find the margin of safety using the following equation:

margin of safety = actual sales (or budgeted sales) – break-even sales

3) The firm will use budgeted sales if it is trying to forecast its future margin of safety. The budgeted sales will be the sales that it expects to make.

Firms forecast how much they are likely to sell in a given period of time. These predictions are often based on previous sales and their best guess.

You Can Also Use a Break-Even Diagram to Find the Margin of Safety

1) You saw on the previous page how a firm can create a break-even diagram to help them calculate their break-even point in units or the break-even point for revenue or costs.
2) Using the same example, here's how you could use one to find a firm's margin of safety.

1) Pin-Chit Ltd. need to sell 1000 units in order to break even (see previous page).
2) In one financial year, the company sold 1800 units.
3) The margin of safety for the company was therefore 1800 – 1000 = 800 units.
4) This means that the firm's output would have to fall by 800 units the next year before it would start to make a loss.
5) You can also show Pin-Chit Ltd.'s margin of safety using a break-even diagram:

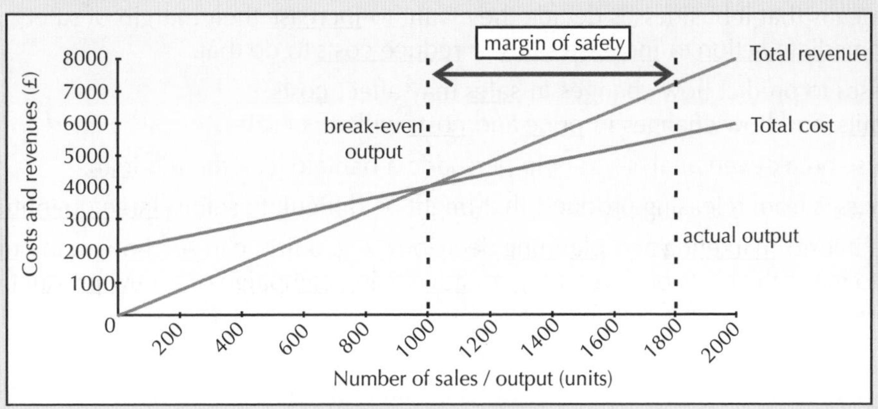

The bigger the margin of safety, the less likely that a firm will make a loss...

A big margin of safety means that a firm can afford to sell fewer units before it starts to make a loss, this means that a sudden dip in revenue is less likely to cause big problems. So it can be useful for firms to know what their margin of safety is, in case they need to make some changes to reduce the risks they face.

More Break-Even Analysis

Businesses can use break-even analysis to see the effects of changes that they may make to their business, e.g. increasing their prices, but there are advantages and disadvantages to break-even analysis.

Revenue and Costs May **Change**

1) A firm's revenue, costs and profit or loss are all important for how it makes decisions.
2) High revenue or profits may lead to a business being more likely to take risks than if it has a low revenue or profit or makes a loss.
3) Break-even diagrams can be useful for seeing how changes in revenue and costs may affect break-even output.
4) For example, the rate at which revenue changes may decrease if the firm decides to lower its prices. The rate at which costs change may also increase or decrease, e.g. if the cost of supplies changes.

The two break-even diagrams below show the effect of Pin-Chit Ltd. lowering its prices from £4 per unit in 2015 to £3.50 per unit in 2016 on the break-even output.

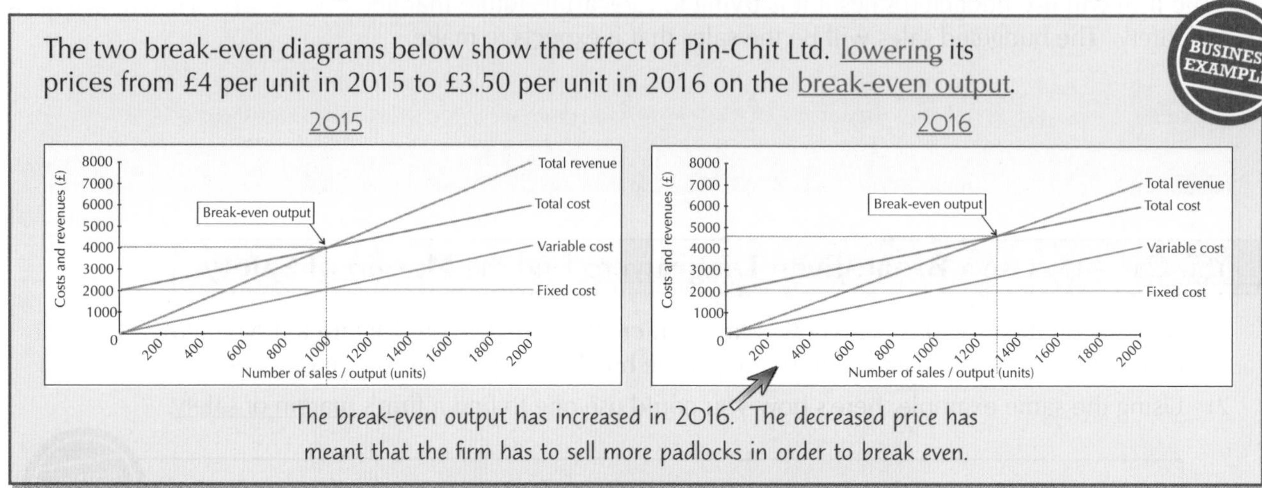

The break-even output has increased in 2016. The decreased price has meant that the firm has to sell more padlocks in order to break even.

Break-Even Analysis has **Advantages** and **Disadvantages**

Advantages

1) It's easy to work out.
2) It's quick. This means that if businesses decide they want to increase their margin of safety, they can take immediate action to increase sales or reduce costs to do that.
3) It allows businesses to predict how changes in sales may affect costs, revenue and profits, and how changes in price and costs will affect sales.
4) Businesses can use break-even analysis to help persuade a bank to give them a loan.
5) It can stop businesses from releasing products that might be difficult to sell in large quantities.
6) It can be used to inform marketing and planning decisions, e.g. a firm can see how many units would have to be sold to make the costs of developing an advertising campaign or a new product worthwhile.

Disadvantages

1) It assumes that the firm can sell any quantity of the product at the current price.
2) Break-even analysis assumes that all of the products are sold, without any waste.
3) If the data is wrong, then the results of the analysis will be wrong.
4) It can be complicated if it involves more than one product.
5) It only shows how much a business needs to sell, and not how much it actually will sell.

REVISION TASK

Break-even analysis is pretty good, but it isn't perfect...

Try covering the page and writing down all the advantages and disadvantages of break-even analysis that you can remember. Then check your work and read through the ones you've missed.

Cash

Cash flow — a handy thing for a business to know, and also GCSE Business students as it happens...

Cash is Not the Same Thing as Profit

1) Cash is the money a company can spend immediately. A business needs cash in order to pay off short term debts (e.g. bank loans), its employees, its suppliers and overheads (these are ongoing expenses, e.g. rent or lighting).

2) Cash is important to a business as it provides it with liquidity. This means that it can be much more quickly traded than other assets. This gives the firm the ability to buy things from other companies more quickly. Many other assets would have to be converted into cash before they could be used to trade with other companies.

3) A lack of cash could lead to the firm failing, because it may be unable to pay its debts (this is called insolvency), unless it sells off its assets.

4) Profit is the amount of money a company earns after costs have been taken into account. So a business can make a profit if it earns more than it spends but still run out of cash if it uses its cash to invest in other assets for the business.

5) Cash flow is the flow of all money into and out of the business.
When a firm sells its products, money flows in (cash inflow).
When it buys materials or pays wages, money flows out (cash outflow).

Net cash flow = cash inflows – cash outflows for a given period of time

6) If a company has positive cash flow then there is more cash inflow than cash outflow for a particular time period. Positive cash flow means that a company has no problem in making payments. However, it may also mean that the company is losing opportunities to invest in ways that might improve it (e.g. in new equipment).

7) Positive cash flow is still not the same thing as profit, though — a company may make a profit if overall it earns more than it spends, but still have poor cash flow (e.g. if cash inflow does not occur in time to make cash outflow requirements — see page 136).

Positive cash flow and a good profit — that's when you know it's going well...

So a business can have a lot of cash but not have made much profit and vice versa. This can be a bit confusing, so make sure you really understand the difference between cash, profit and cash flow before you move on.

Cash Flow Forecasts

Cash flow in a business can change quite a lot from one month to the next, so it's important that a business keeps track of its cash flow and can identify any periods during which it might have problems.

Cash Flow **Forecasts** Help Firms to **Anticipate Problems**

1) A cash flow forecast is a good way of predicting when a firm might face a liquidity problem (lack of cash). It lists all the inflows and outflows of cash that appear in the budget (a forecast of all of the firm's likely expenses and revenue).
2) The firm will see when an overdraft or other short-term finance might be needed.
3) The forecast can also be used to help the business to make plans, e.g. decide when to order from suppliers throughout the year. It can also provide targets to the business, such as a minimum amount of cash for it to try to have throughout the year so that there is always enough cash in the business to prevent cash flow problems from arising.
4) The forecast needs to be watched carefully — to monitor what the impact of unexpected cash flows might be.

Businesses forecast how much they are likely to sell in a given period of time to estimate what their revenue will be — these predictions are often based on sales from previous months or years, and the firm's best guess.

BUSINESS EXAMPLE

Here's an example of a cash flow forecast for a firm publishing football magazines.

Cash Flow Forecast — Footy Fanzines Ltd.

	April	May	June	July	August	Sept
Total receipts (cash inflow)	15 000	12 000	5000	5000	16 000	16 000
Total spending (cash outflow)	12 000	12 000	10 000	10 000	12 000	12 000
Net cash flow (inflow – outflow)	3000	0	(5000)	(5000)	4000	4000
Opening balance (bank balance at start of month)	1000	4000	4000	(1000)	(6000)	(2000)
Closing balance (bank balance at end of month)	4000	4000	(1000)	(6000)	(2000)	2000

Numbers in brackets are negative.

closing balance = opening balance + net cash flow

1) In June and July, when the football season's over, the net cash flow is negative because more money flows out than in.
2) The firm can see it will need a source of extra finance to get it through from June to September.
3) It's useful to know this in advance because it means the firm can plan — it won't suddenly have to panic in June when it starts to run out of money.

Keeping an eye on those brackets should help to spot any problems...

Cash flow is quite easy once you've understood how the figures are worked out. Make sure you can understand the figures in the table above, and also that you know why cash flow is super important.

Cash Flow — Credit

A firm's cash flow will change if they give their customers longer to pay for products — this is called credit.

Credit Terms Can Affect Cash Flow

Credit terms tell you how long after agreeing to buy a product the customer has to pay.
This can affect the timings of their cash flows.

BUSINESS EXAMPLE

1) Stuffin's Turkeys Ltd. sell most of their products in December.
2) This table assumes customers pay when they purchase the product.

	October	November	December	January	February	March
Total receipts (cash inflow)	800	1500	12 000	300	500	300
Total payments (cash outflow)	3000	4000	2000	300	200	150
Net cash flow	(2200)	(2500)	10 000	0	300	150
Opening balance (bank balance at start of month)	3000	800	(1700)	8300	8300	8600
Closing balance (bank balance at end of month)	800	(1700)	8300	8300	8600	8750

3) The table below assumes customers are given two months credit to pay.
4) It's a bit more complicated as the total receipts come in two months after the sale is made.

	October	November	December	January	February	March
Total sales this month (for payment in 2 months)	800	1500	12 000	300	500	300
Total receipts (cash inflow)	200	200	800	1500	12 000	300
Total payments (cash outflow)	3000	4000	2000	300	200	150
Net cash flow	(2800)	(3800)	(1200)	1200	11 800	150
Opening balance (bank balance at start of month)	3000	200	(3600)	(4800)	(3600)	8200
Closing balance (bank balance at end of month)	200	(3600)	(4800)	(3600)	8200	8350

Payment made in 2 months

In February, the total receipts are for the turkeys bought in December. So net cash flow is 12 000 – 200 = 11 800

5) The main differences are:
- when customers pay immediately there is only one month where short-term finance is needed.
- when they pay on 2 months credit the business will need to arrange short-term finance for 3 months.

Credit means that businesses have to carefully plan things in advance...

Make sure you remember that credit terms with customers affect cash inflow for a business.

Cash Flow — Problems

Unfortunately, lots of firms go out of business sooner or later. And poor cash flow is the most common cause of bankruptcy in firms that are more profitable. So solving cash flow problems is really important for firms.

Poor Cash Flow Means You've Got **Big Problems**

1) Poor cash flow means there is not enough cash in a business to meet its day-to-day expenses — there's a lack of working capital.
2) Staff may not get paid on time — this will cause resentment and poor motivation.
3) Some suppliers offer discounts for prompt payment of invoices — the business may not be able to take advantage of these.
4) Creditors (people or firms that are owed money) may not get paid on time — they may insist on stricter credit terms in future.
5) Some creditors may not wait for payment — they might take legal action to recover the debt. If the business does not have the money it may go into receivership (a 'receiver' is appointed to reclaim money owed to the creditors by selling off the struggling firm's assets) or be forced to cease trading.

There are **Three Main Reasons** for Poor Cash Flow

1) POOR SALES — There's a lack of demand from consumers for the firm's products, so the firm has less money coming in and it cannot pay its creditors.
2) OVERTRADING — The firm takes on too many orders — as a result it buys in too many raw materials and hires too many staff. Something goes wrong with the orders and the firm doesn't get the money from its customers quickly enough to pay its debts.
3) POOR BUSINESS DECISIONS — For example, the firm decides to bring out new products or expand into new markets but they do not bring in as much money as forecast. Bad business decisions are usually caused by not doing enough planning or market research.

There are Ways to **Improve Cash Flow**

1) By rescheduling payments:
   - A business could "reschedule their receipts of income". For example, they could give their customers less generous credit terms or insist they pay immediately.
   - They could try to reschedule the payments they make to their suppliers. This could include negotiating better credit terms — ideally, the credit period given to customers should be less than the credit period obtained from suppliers.
2) By reducing cash outflow. Most firms carry a stock of unsold products — they could simply sell these instead of making more.
   - By destocking, the cash inflows will be the same — but cash outflows will be reduced as less will be spent on raw materials.
   - However, eventually they'll run out of stock. At this point, they'll have to start paying out money to make more products.
3) By firms arranging to have an overdraft with their bank (see p.128).
4) By finding new sources of finance (such as a new business partner) in order to make payments.
5) By increasing cash inflow, e.g. by increasing the selling price.

Smart businesses make good business plans first to avoid these issues...

Making good cash flow forecasts is key to preventing some of the problems on this page. By seeing the problems ahead of time a business is able to organise cash flow to prevent cash flow problems in the first place.

Worked Exam Questions

Next up, a page on exam questions, but with answers written in for you. It's a good idea to have a read through them as the questions are similar to what you might get in your exams.

1 Look at **Item A** below.

> **Item A — IceChips**
> Jess runs a business, IceChips, which makes and distributes frozen chips to restaurants and hotels in her local area. She buys potatoes from Johnson's, a local farm. The business spends £50 000 each year on fixed costs. In 2015, the total variable costs came to £0.85 per kg of chips and each packet of chips was sold for £1.80 per kg. Using these figures and her actual sales in 2015 Jess worked out her break-even level of output and her margin of safety.

a) Calculate Jess's break-even level of output for 2015.
Give your answer to the nearest whole number.
Show your working.

[2]

The question says to give your answer to the nearest whole number so make sure you follow these instructions when writing your answer.

Sample Answer:

Break-even level of output = fixed cost ÷ (sales price – variable cost)

= 50 000 ÷ (1.80 – 0.85)

= 50 000 ÷ 0.95

= 52 631.578 = 52 632

Break-even level of output = 52 632 units

b) State **one** benefit to a firm of knowing its margin of safety for a financial year.

[1]

This is just a "state" question, so you just need to write down a benefit — you don't need to explain it.

Sample Answer:

The firm will know how much its output can fall by before it starts to make a loss.

c) A year later, Jess calculates that her break-even level of output will be 48 000 kg of chips. She keeps the price of the chips the same as the previous year. Calculate the revenue that Jess's business will have to make in order to break even.
Show your working.

[2]

Sample Answer:

Break-even point for revenue = break-even output × sales price

= 48 000 × 1.80 = 86 400

Remember to double check your calculations after you've done them, to avoid mistakes.

Revenue = £ 86 400

Exam Questions

1 Which of the following describes a short term source of finance? Put a cross (X) in **one** correct box.

- **A** overdraft ☐
- **B** retained profit ☐
- **C** share capital ☐
- **D** bank loan ☐

[Total 1 mark]

2 Look at **Item A** below.

> **Item A — Shoesies Ltd.:**
> Shoesies Ltd. is an online company specialising in shoes for children.
> It gives customers 30 days' credit on all purchases and also operates a generous returns policy of a full refund on all items returned within 60 days.
>
> Shoesies Ltd. observed that it had falling sales over its final quarter of 2014 and that the number of returns of items had increased.
>
> At the beginning of its financial year in 2015, Shoesies Ltd. had three outstanding loan repayments and a lack of cash in the business. It was also unable to meet its supplier's 10 day credit agreement for purchases of fabrics.

a) Explain **two** reasons why Shoesies Ltd. is facing cash flow problems.

1. ....

....

....

2. ....

....

....

[4]

b) Shoesies Ltd. is considering two possible ways of solving its cash flow problems:

- Rescheduling their payments.
- Obtaining another source of finance.

Recommend which is the better option for Shoesies Ltd. to take. Give reasons for your advice.
Write your answer on a separate piece of paper.

[9]

[Total 13 marks]

Investments

When business make investments, they have to be careful that they don't go spending too much money...

Businesses Have to Make **Investments**

1) An investment is money which is put into a business to make improvements in order to make the business more profitable.
2) Here are a few examples of investments that businesses may make:
   - New machinery — buying new machinery may make processes more efficient, or may enable a business to make new products.
   - New buildings — new, larger premises will enable a business to expand by increasing the number of employees it can have, the amount of machinery it can keep or the amount of stock it can store.
   - New vehicles — businesses that rely on vehicles, e.g. delivery services, can expand by buying more vehicles, or by getting larger vehicles that can transport more products.
3) But spending money can be risky as the investment may not bring in more money to the business, and may even result in a loss of money.
4) So businesses often want to make sure that their investments are worthwhile.
5) To do this, they calculate the return on an investment...

You Can Find the **Average Rate of Return** on an **Investment**

An investment's lifespan is the length of time over which it earns money for the firm.

1) The return on an investment is how much a business makes or loses as a proportion of the original investment that it puts in.
2) The average rate of return is a calculation of the average return on an investment each year over its lifespan.
3) To calculate it you first have to work out the average annual profit — you can do that using this formula:

$$\text{average annual profit} = \frac{\text{total profit}}{\text{number of years}} \times 100$$

4) Then you can put your value for average annual profit into this formula, to find the ARR.

$$\text{ARR (\%)} = \frac{\text{Average annual profit}}{\text{cost of investment}} \times 100$$

BUSINESS EXAMPLE

The table below shows the investment that a business made in a project that lasted 5 years. It also shows the profit the business made each year as a result of the investment. Calculate the average rate of return (ARR) for the investment.

	Profit				
Investment	Yr 1	Yr 2	Yr 3	Yr 4	Yr 5
(£10m)	£4m	£5m	£6m	£7m	£5m

1) First calculate the total profit of the project — this is the sum of the profit made by the project each year minus the cost of the initial investment: 4 + 5 + 6 + 7 + 5 – 10 = £17m
2) Then divide the total profit of the project by its lifespan in years to find the average annual profit: 17m ÷ 5 = £3.4m
3) Next, you use the formula above to find the ARR:

$$\text{ARR (\%)} = \frac{\text{average annual profit}}{\text{initial investment}} \times 100 = \frac{3.4}{10} \times 100 = 34\%$$

5) The bigger the ARR for an investment, the more successful the investment for the business. But a good ARR will depend on the firm involved, as well as the amount of money invested — an ARR of 6% would be a significant return for a £1m investment, but probably not for a £100 one.

There's no set percentage for a good ARR, it just depends on the firm...

The ARR is one of the trickier calculations in this book, so make sure you're ok with it before going on.

Income Statements

An income statement is a type of financial statement showing how income has changed over time. It's split into three clear sections to make it easier to see the different costs of a business and what is left over at the end.

There are **Three Parts** to an **Income Statement**...

Here is an example of an income statement for Yummo Chocolates Ltd.

- The yellow box shows the trading account,
- the blue box is the profit and loss account,
- and the pink box is the appropriation account.

These figures just mean that the numbers below them are in thousands of pounds.

Numbers in brackets are negative.

Income Statement
Yummo Chocolates Ltd.
Year ending 31st March 2016

	£000	£000
Revenue..............................		180
Cost of sales:		
Opening stock.........	3	
Purchases...............	15	
	18	
Minus closing stock.........	(5)	
Cost of sales = ...		(13)
Gross profit =......................		167
Minus expenses		
Wages and salaries....	93	
Rent and rates...........	10	
Office expenses.........	28	
Advertising...............	5	
Depreciation............	8	
Other expenses.........	3	
Expenses = ...		(147)
Operating profit = ...		20
Interest payable		(2)
Profit before tax (Net profit)...		18
Taxation		(3)
Dividends		(9)
Retained profit		6

1) The **Trading Account**

1) This records the firm's gross profit or loss.

2) Revenue (or turnover) is the value of all products sold in a given period of time (see p.24).

3) Cost of sales records how much it cost to make the products sold during the year — the direct costs.

4) To find the cost of sales, first add up the value of the opening stock (the stock present at the start of the year) and the stock purchases made throughout the year. Then take away the value of the closing stock (the stock left over at the end of the year).

5) Gross profit is the difference between the revenue from selling the chocolate and the direct costs of making it. This means:

gross profit = revenue – direct costs

Income statements show how income has been spent and how much is left...

Income statements can be a bit tricky to get the hang of. You need to add up the numbers as you go down each column to get the number on the next row. The numbers in brackets are negative, so you take them away.

Income Statements

On this page you'll cover the remaining two bits of the income statement. Then you'll need to think about how businesses might use different parts of the income statement to analyse their performance.

2) The **Profit and Loss** Account

Minus expenses	
Wages and salaries....	93
Rent and rates...........	10
Office expenses.........	28
Advertising................	5
Depreciation.............	8
Other expenses.........	3
Expenses = ...	(147)
Operating profit = ...	20
Interest payable	(2)
Profit before tax (Net profit)...	18

1) This records all the indirect costs of running the business.
2) It doesn't cover the cost of buying machinery, but it does cover depreciation — this is the amount of value which an asset has lost over a period of time due to wear and tear. Calculating depreciation allows businesses to set aside money for replacing assets.

There are two methods of calculating depreciation:

1) Straight line method. This is the easy way. If a machine costs £5000 and will wear out after about 5 years, the depreciation is simply £1000 each year.
2) Reducing balance method. This depreciates the machinery by a percentage of its value each year — a £5000 machine might depreciate by 25% each year.
   - Depreciation in year 1 = 25% of £5000 = £1250. The value is now £5000 – £1250 = £3750.
   - Depreciation in year 2 = 25% of £3750 = £938. The value is now £3750 – £938 = £2812.

3) The money left after paying all the indirect costs is called the operating profit.
4) Finally, any interest paid or received is included. What is left is true profit — net profit.

3) The **Appropriation** Account

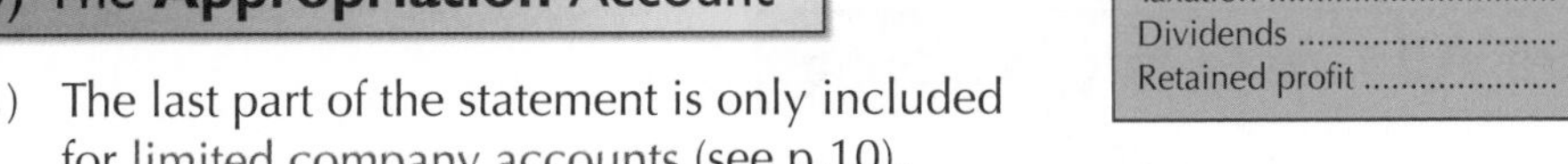

Taxation	(3)
Dividends	(9)
Retained profit	6

1) The last part of the statement is only included for limited company accounts (see p.10).
2) It records where the profit has gone — to the government as tax, to shareholders as dividends, or kept in the business as retained profit.

Values on the **Income Statement** Show Business **Performance**

1) Gross profit — If gross profit is low, managers need to look at ways of reducing the cost of making the product, or increasing the revenue, to make gross profit higher.
2) Operating profit — If this is significantly lower than gross profit, it could show that the company's operating expenses are a weak area, e.g. it may invest a lot of money in people or buildings. Management could take steps to reduce these expenses. Banks and investors will look at this figure to assess the risk of lending to or investing in the business. If the operating profit is too low then they may be too worried about losing their money to make an investment.
3) Retained profit tells you if the company is profitable or not — shareholders and potential investors will look at this figure to assess investments. It also shows how much internal finance the company has available to invest, and so what potential it has to get bigger.

The different types of profit depend on what costs are considered...

Make sure you know what the different terms on income statements mean before moving on. There's more on net profit and gross profit on the next page so get familiar with them now to avoid confusion.

Profit Margins

You covered a little bit on gross and net profit on page 25. Now, just to throw some more numbers at you, here's a page on profitability ratios. These show what happens to each pound spent by a customer.

Gross Profit Margin Ignores Indirect Costs

Gross profit margin is the fraction of every pound spent by customers that doesn't go directly towards making a product:

Gross profit margin = gross profit ÷ sales (revenue) × 100

Here's how to calculate the gross profit margin using this equation:

BUSINESS EXAMPLE

1) Yummo Chocolates makes and sells chocolates. In 2016, its gross profit was £167 000 and its revenue was £180 000.
2) This means the gross profit margin was:
   167 000 ÷ 180 000 = 0.92777...
   0.92777... × 100 = 92.78% (2 d.p.)
3) Or, if you prefer, you can think of it like this...

For every £1 spent by customers...

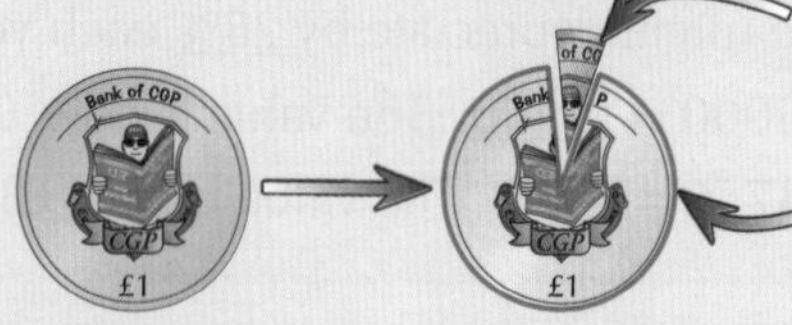

...7.22p was used to make the product...

...leaving 92.78p — but this still has to pay for expenses like salaries, interest, and so on.

What counts as a good gross profit margin depends on the type of business, but the higher the percentage the better. The margin can be improved by increasing prices or reducing the direct cost of sales. Some businesses (e.g. a supermarket chain) can have a low gross profit margin because they sell in high volumes and they need to keep their prices competitive to survive.

Net Profit Margin Takes All Costs into Account

Net profit margin is the fraction of every pound spent by customers that the company gets to keep (after all its costs have been paid):

Net profit margin = net profit ÷ sales (revenue) × 100

1) In 2016, Yummo Chocolates had operating expenses of £147 000 and the interest it paid on loans totalled £2000. Its gross profit was £167 000, which meant that it had a net profit of £18 000 (£167 000 – £147 000 – £2000).
2) The revenue in 2016 was £180 000, so the net profit margin was:
   18 000 ÷ 180 000 = 0.1
   0.1 × 100 = 10%

For every £1 spent by customers...

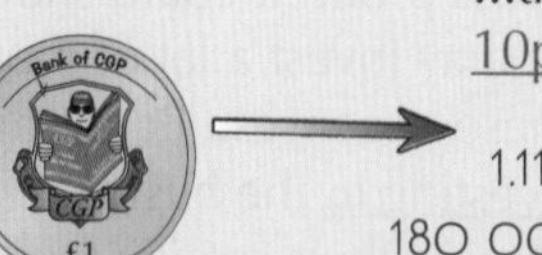

...the company gets 10p as net profit.

1.11p (= 2000 ÷ 180 000) paid off interest

7.22p was spent making the product (see above)

81.67p (= 147 000 ÷ 180 000) paid off other expenses (e.g. salaries)

Just like for gross profit margins, what counts as a good net profit margin depends on the business, but the higher it is, the better. Net profit margin is often larger for new companies which are still small and don't have many indirect costs. As businesses grow, these costs go up and net profit margin decreases.

Knowing what fraction of income goes into costs can be pretty useful...

The gross profit margin and net profit margin vary a lot between different types of firms, so there's no set rule for what makes a good profit margin. If you're asked to calculate them in the exam remember that gross profit margin should be larger than net profit margin, otherwise your calculation is wrong.

Statements of Financial Position

The statement of financial position (or balance sheet) records where the business got its money from, and what it has done with it. It is calculated at a particular date — usually the last day of the financial year. This page deals with the first part of the statement — that's everything in the blue box in the example below.

Fixed Assets will Last for More Than One Year

1) The business has used some money to buy fixed assets — premises, machinery, vehicles.
2) This figure is what they're worth on the date of the statement of financial position — they'll have depreciated since they were bought, but that's all taken care of in the income statement (see p.143).

Statement of Financial Position
Yummo Chocolates Ltd., 31st March 2016

	£000	£000
Fixed Assets		
Premises		80
Machinery		40
Vehicles		30
		150
Current Assets		
Stock	5	
Debtors	12	
Cash	3	
	20	
Current Liabilities		
Creditors	(14)	
Unpaid Corporation Tax	(1)	
	(15)	
Net Current Assets (Working Capital)		5
Net Assets		155
Financed by		
Shareholders' Funds		
Share Capital		80
Retained Profit and Reserves		50
Long-term Liabilities		
Bank Loan		20
Mortgage		5
Capital Employed		155

Current Assets – Current Liabilities

Fixed Assets + Net Current Assets

This purple bit is the Capital Employed section — see the next page.

Current Assets Last a Few Months

These are listed in increasing order of liquidity:

Brackets around a number means it's negative.

1) Stock is the least liquid. It includes raw materials and finished products that the firm has spent its money on but which have not yet been sold.
2) Debtors refers to the value of products sold — usually on credit — that have not yet been paid for by customers. What's happening here is that the firm is lending its money to customers so they can buy its products.
3) Cash is the most liquid. This is money the firm hasn't spent on anything yet — it's just sitting in the bank.

The liquidity of an asset tells you how quickly it can be bought or sold.

Current Liabilities are Bills the Firm Has to Pay Soon

1) These are any payments the firm will have to make within one year of the date on the balance sheet. Creditors is the opposite of debtors — it is money the firm owes to its suppliers. Also included is any unpaid corporation tax — payable to the government out of the previous year's profits — as well as any unpaid dividends to shareholders (there aren't any for Yummo this year, so this figure's not shown).
2) This is money which doesn't really belong to the firm, since it's going to have to pay it to someone else pretty soon. So you take this away from the current assets figure...

Current Assets – Current Liabilities = Net Current Assets

1) The net current assets figure is what you get when you subtract those current liabilities from the current assets — this is the money available for the day-to-day operating of the business. It's also called working capital.
2) Add the net current assets to the fixed assets and you get the net assets, or net worth, of the business. This is the amount the firm would make if it sold all its assets (in theory) — it's what the firm is worth.

Both these calculations are labelled on the statement of financial position above.

This statement shows everything the firm has and what it owes...

You're going to finish this off on the next page — but try to make sure you've understood everything so far. Why not give yourself a quick test on what the difference is between assets and liabilities.

Statements of Financial Position

Now for the second part of the statement of financial position — where all the money came from to create the net worth of the business. Originally it came from shareholders buying the shares, and money loaned to it by other people — over the years retained profit will be added to this, and possibly more loans.

Shareholders' Funds Came from the **Firm's Owners**

Shareholders' funds include share capital and retained profit and reserves on the statement:

Share Capital

- This is the money put into the business when shares were originally issued. This might have been years and years ago for long-established companies.
- This is not the same as what the shares are currently worth. Most shares traded on the stock exchange are second-hand — the person selling them gets the cash, not the firm.
- Firms can raise new capital by issuing new shares (see p.129). The usual way is to have a rights issue. This is where existing shareholders are offered new shares at a reduced price.

This is the Capital Employed section from Yummo Chocolates' statement of financial position (see previous page).

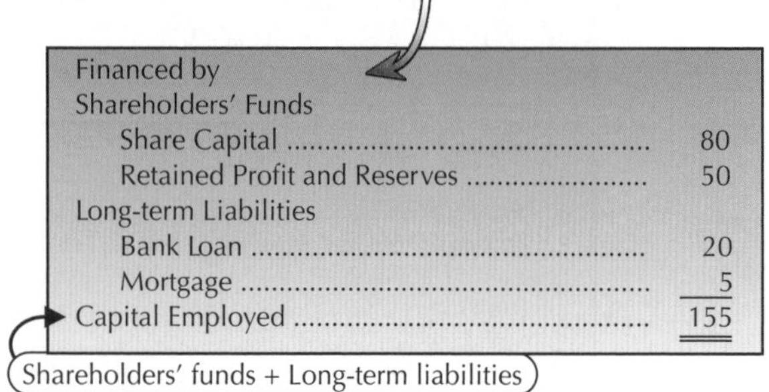

Financed by	
Shareholders' Funds	
Share Capital	80
Retained Profit and Reserves	50
Long-term Liabilities	
Bank Loan	20
Mortgage	5
Capital Employed	155

Retained profit and reserves

- This shows all the profit that the firm has made over the years that it has decided to keep instead of paying in dividends.
- Firms retain profit to finance future investment or to protect the firm against future problems.
- This comes under "shareholders' funds" because profits are really the shareholders' money — they've just decided to leave it in the firm rather than taking it out as dividends.

See pages 128-130 for more on sources of finance.

Long-term Liabilities — Money **Owed to Others**

1) Firms don't just get money from their shareholders — they borrow it from other people as well. Included here are any debts that will take more than one year to repay, e.g. bank loans.
2) Debts payable in less than a year come under current liabilities instead — see the previous page. It's all money the company owes, but it's conventional to split it up like that.

Capital Employed is the **Total** Put into the Business

1) Capital employed is what you get when you add shareholders' funds to long-term liabilities. This is equal to net assets (see previous page) because it shows where the money to fund them came from.
2) If you're confused, think about it this way — all the money the business has got (from shareholders and borrowing from other people) is accounted for by capital employed. And everything it's done with the money it got (bought premises, kept it as cash, etc.) is listed under net assets. They have to be the same — because money doesn't just vanish.

The capital employed value should be the same as net assets...

When you're revising statements of financial position, remember that the sources of finance that a business uses depends on several factors — e.g. the size or type of business (see p.130 for more). So the values in the second part of the statement will also depend on those factors.

Statements of Financial Position

Now that you've seen what's shown on a statement of financial position, here's a little bit on how they are used.

Statements of Financial Position Show a **Snapshot in Time...**

1) The statement of financial position can be used to assess a business's performance at a point in time.

2) It shows the sources of capital for the business (see pages 128-129). Long-term loans and mortgages are better sources than overdrafts, since they are less expensive.

3) It can also be used to work out the working capital and liquidity of the business, which can be useful in making business decisions. E.g. if the business has a large amount of working capital, they could invest this money in new equipment or use it to pay off some loans.

See p.145 for how to find the working capital and liquidity of a business from its statement of financial position.

...and Can be Used to Show **Trends Over Time**

1) Statements of financial position can also be compared across several consecutive years.
2) Here are some examples of pieces of information that can be compared and what they can tell you:

Fixed assets

A quick increase in this indicates that the company has invested, e.g. in property or machinery. As a result, this means that the company's profit may increase in the future.

For a reminder of these terms, flick back to pages 145-146.

Retained profits or reserves

Increases in this suggest an increase in profits.

Liabilities

The amount and type of liabilities can indicate how well-managed a business is. A company with a high value of loan capital and a relatively low value of share capital or reserves would be in trouble if interest rates went up. If long-term liabilities have increased, the business might reduce its borrowing in the future.

3) This comparison can be used to make business decisions. For example, if a business shows slow growth by not having more assets year on year, the company may decide to reduce dividends and retain more of their profit to invest in the business. There's more on this on the next page.

Statements of financial position are useful for comparisons over time...

There are many ways that businesses can use their statements of financial position — only a few are shown here. They can also be used alongside income statements and other financial data (see next page) to give firms a much better insight into how they are performing and how they need to improve.

Financial Data and Business Performance

Businesses collect a lot of information as they go along, about their own and their competitors' finances. This is important for businesses as it helps them to keep track of how well they're doing, and how they might improve.

Financial Data Can Help a Business to **Plan** and **Make Decisions**

1) The finance function of a firm is the part of the firm that deals with its finances (e.g. the finance department).
2) One of its main roles is to provide the business with financial data and to analyse this information.
3) Analysing financial data shows a firm how well it is doing, and helps it to plan and make good decisions.
4) For example, financial data can help to inform a business about the impact of a decision, and so help to support or justify it, or prevent the business from making a mistake.
5) When a firm is doing well financially, it is more likely to plan to make investments and to take riskier decisions than when its finances are not doing so well.
6) As well as the financial statements on pages 142-143 and 145-147, the following types of financial data may be used by businesses to plan and make decisions:

- Cash flow forecasts (p.136-138) can show whether or not a business decision (e.g. investing cash in new equipment) would lead to cash flow problems.
- Calculations of profit and loss (p.25) and profitability ratios (p.144) can help a business to see if it should reduce costs or try to increase revenue.
- Predicting the average rate of return (p.141) of an investment can help a business to determine if an investment would be worthwhile.

Several **Stakeholders** Will be Interested in a Business's **Financial Data**

1) Stakeholders (see p.20) can use the financial analysis of the income statement or the statement of financial position to check how healthy the business is. E.g. growing net assets may indicate that the business is healthy, whereas low net assets may indicate that the business is borrowing too much.
2) Here are some examples of possible stakeholders and other ways they might use a financial analysis:

- Existing shareholders — these are entitled to a share of the profits (the share dividend). They may use the income statement to assess the performance of the directors of the business, to see if they have made sensible decisions (e.g. reducing expenses when revenue falls).

- Potential shareholders or lenders — these may look at how much profit the business makes. If the business makes enough profit, they may consider investing in it or lending it money.

- Employees — these will be interested in whether the company makes a profit or a loss. A profitable business will be able to afford to give employees a pay rise, but a loss-making business might make some workers redundant.

- The government — the government receives corporation tax from the business. It uses the income statement to calculate how much tax the business needs to pay.

- Suppliers — these are likely to be interested in the liquidity of a business — the more liquid it is, the better it will be at paying bills, so they will be more likely to sell it goods.

Financial Data and Business Performance

You've read lots of information in this section on how useful financial information is for a business and all the different ways that it can be used. For this last page, it's time to think about some of its limitations.

There are Some **Limitations** to **Financial Data**

1) As you saw on the previous page, there are lots of different types of financial data that can be used to understand how well a business is performing, and make decisions about the running of the business.

2) In order to use some types of financial data, it's important that there is another source of appropriate data to allow a comparison. For example, a firm could compare how their financial data has changed over time, or they could compare it against a competitor who produces similar products.

BUSINESS EXAMPLE

1) TheRulerCo. is a company that makes and sells stationery.
2) It uses the bar chart on the right to compare its financial performance with two of its competitors.
3) The bar chart shows that TheRulerCo. has a lower gross profit margin than two of its competitors. So either its cost of sales is higher, or it is charging relatively less for its products.
4) This will mean that TheRulerCo. will be able to make decisions about certain parts of the business, e.g. reducing the cost of raw materials, to help improve its profit margins.

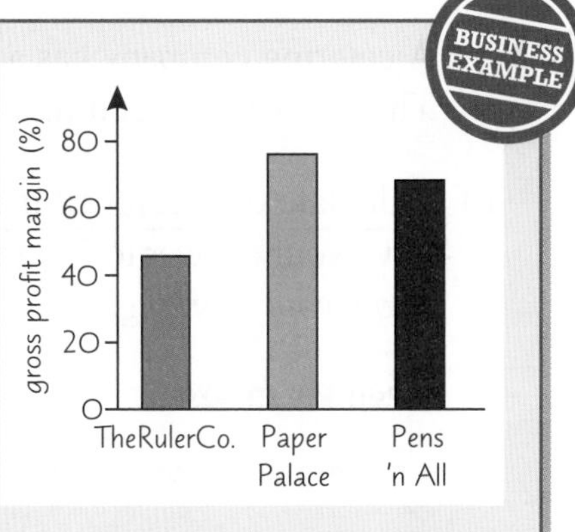

3) However, using financial data to understand business performance isn't perfect. In some cases it may not be possible to directly compare two different sources of data. For example, one firm in the comparison may be much larger or operate in a different country.

4) Even if the same firm's financial performance for different years is compared, it can still be hard to tell exactly what may have caused any changes. That's because there are often lots of different variables which may affect a company's financial performance — such as how well the economy is doing.

5) Another limitation to using financial data to assess business performance is that it only includes quantitative data and not qualitative data (see p.101). Qualitative data can include things like customers' opinions, which can be useful for determining what changes a business should make.

By comparing themselves with other firms, firms can plan improvements...

Using financial data isn't foolproof as you can see, but without it businesses wouldn't be able to get much of an idea of their performance. Businesses can use their financial data alongside other forms of data such as market research, to get a more well-rounded idea of how their business is performing compared to their competitors.

Worked Exam Questions

It can be very useful when you're learning material to think about how you might answer questions on it. For each of these worked exam questions, try thinking of the answer to each one before reading the sample answer.

1 Explain why investors may be interested in how the operating profit of a business compares with its gross profit.

The question is asking about investors, so make sure that your answer applies to investors and not another type of stakeholder.

[3]

Sample Answer:

If the operating profit is significantly lower than the gross profit, then this suggests that the company spends too much on indirect costs and therefore may be risky for investors to invest in.

2 A catering company has a sales revenue of £700 000 and a gross profit of £490 000. The cost of its operating expenses (other than cost of sales) and interest are £436 000.

a) Calculate the net profit margin for the company.
Give your answer to 3 significant figures.
Show your working.

[3]

Sample Answer:

net profit = gross profit – (other operating expenses and interest)

= 490 000 – 436 000 = 54 000

net profit margin = (net profit ÷ sales revenue) × 100

= (54 000 ÷ 700 000) × 100 = 7.7142...%

Make sure you keep the different steps involved in a calculation separate and clear — you may get marks for your working if your answer is wrong.

net profit margin = 7.71%

b) A year later, the company calculates its gross profit margin to be 25% and its net profit margin to be 4%. Explain why the company may have decided to find cheaper insurance, based on this information.

The question is telling you to use the information it has given you, so make sure the answer you give is based on the gross and net profit margins for the company and not just your own knowledge.

[2]

Sample Answer:

The business has a relatively low net profit margin compared to its gross profit margin. Reducing the amount the business spends on its indirect costs, such as insurance, would help to increase its net profit margin.

For this question, you need to remember that the lower a firm's indirect costs are, the higher its net profit margin will be.

Exam Questions

1 Look at **Item A** and **Figure 1** below.

> **Item A — Speedy Wheels:**
> Speedy Wheels is a courier company that delivers items in parts of the United Kingdom. Speedy Wheels is considering investing £20 000 in new delivery vans. It predicts that these vans will last for approximately five years before they will need to be replaced.
>
> The managers of Speedy Wheels forecast the increase in profit as a result of the new vans in the five years following this investment. Their results are shown in **Figure 1**.

Figure 1

	Year 1	Year 2	Year 3	Year 4	Year 5
additional profit (£000)	17	13	15	15	12

a) Identify **two** other investments that could help Speedy Wheels to expand their business.

1. ....

2. ....

[2]

b) Use the information above to calculate the average rate of return of the delivery vans.

average rate of return = ...

[4]

c) Explain how the predicted average rate of return may affect Speedy Wheels' decision to expand the business.

....

....

....

....

[3]

[Total 9 marks]

Revision Summary for Section 6

Some parts of this section are a bit tricky, so take your time with these questions and flick back if you need to.

- Try these questions and tick off each one when you get it right.
- When you've done all the questions for a topic and are completely happy with it, tick off the topic.

Sources of Finance (p.128-130) ☐

1) Give one advantage of using internal sources of finance over external sources of finance. ☐
2) Give one disadvantage of using fixed assets to raise finance. ☐
3) Give one difference between a government grant and a loan. ☐
4) Describe what is meant by a hire purchase. ☐
5) Give one factor that may affect the source of finance used by a company. ☐

Break-Even Analysis, Cash Flow and Investments (p.131-141) ☐

6) Write the equation for finding the break-even point for revenue for a company. ☐
7) Explain how to find the break-even point in units for a firm from a break-even diagram. ☐
8) What is the margin of safety on a break-even chart? ☐
9) Give one disadvantage of using break-even analysis. ☐
10) What is meant by net cash flow? ☐
11) How do you calculate the closing balance for a period on a cash flow forecast? ☐
12) Describe how credit can affect cash flow for a business. ☐
13) Give one reason why poor cash flow can make running a business difficult. ☐
14) Describe one reason why a business may have poor cash flow. ☐
15) Give one reason why a business might invest money in new premises. ☐
16) Write the equation for finding the average rate of return for an investment. ☐

Income Statements and Profit Margins (p.142-144) ☐

17) How is gross profit calculated on an income statement? ☐
18) Give two pieces of information that are within the profit and loss account of an income statement. ☐
19) Give two pieces of information on an income statement that can be used to analyse a business's performance. ☐
20) a) What does the net profit margin represent?
    b) How is the net profit margin calculated? ☐

Statements of Financial Position, and Financial Data and Business Performance (p.145-149) ☐

21) What are meant by fixed assets? ☐
22) Is cash more or less liquid than stock? ☐
23) Describe what is meant by share capital. ☐
24) What would a rapid increase in the value of fixed assets on a statement of financial position indicate to potential investors? ☐
25) Give one stakeholder that would be interested in the performance of a business and explain why they would be interested. ☐
26) Give one reason why it may be difficult to directly compare financial data from two competitors. ☐

Practice Exams

Once you've been through all the questions in this book, you should feel pretty confident about the exams. As final preparation, here's a set of **practice exams** for you to try. Your real exams may be structured slightly differently, but these papers will still give you a taste of what they might be like.
The time allowed for each paper is 1 hour 45 minutes.

GCSE Business

Paper 1

In addition to this paper you should have:
- A calculator.

Centre name					
Centre number					
Candidate number					

Time allowed:
- 1 hour 45 minutes

Surname
Other names
Candidate signature

Instructions to candidates
- Use black ink or ball-point pen.
- Write your name and other details in the spaces provided above.
- Answer **all** questions in the spaces provided.
- Do all rough work on the paper.
- Cross out any work you do not want to be marked.

Information for candidates
- The marks available are given in brackets at the end of each question.
- There are 90 marks available for this paper.
- You are allowed to use a calculator.

Advice to candidates
- In calculations show clearly how you worked out your answers.

For examiner's use			
Q	Attempt Nº		
	1	2	3
1			
2			
3			
Total			

Section A
Answer all questions.

**For multiple choice questions, put a cross (☒) in the box alongside your answer.
If you wish to change your answer, put a line through your original answer.
For example: ☒. Then mark your new answer with a cross in the box.**

1 a) Which of the following describes the term 'job production'?
Put a cross (☒) in **one** correct box.

- ☐ **A** When a firm manufactures unique products one at a time.
- ☐ **B** When a firm produces items in a way that keeps stock levels to a minimum.
- ☐ **C** When a firm produces items in a way so that they have buffer stocks of items at every stage in the process.
- ☐ **D** When a firm manufactures identical products on an assembly line.

[1]

b) Which of the following is a form of post-sales service?
Put a cross (☒) in **one** correct box.

- ☐ **A** Training customers in how to use the product.
- ☐ **B** Getting the contact details of potential customers.
- ☐ **C** Providing customers with information about the product they're interested in.
- ☐ **D** Calling customers to find out if they're interested in a product.

[1]

c) Which of the following is a benefit of having an organisational structure with very few layers?
Put a cross (☒) in **one** correct box.

- ☐ **A** There are likely to be lots of managers to organise tasks.
- ☐ **B** Each manager will only be in charge of a small number of employees.
- ☐ **C** Communication between the top and bottom of the organisational structure will be fast.
- ☐ **D** There is no need for any managers.

[1]

d) Which **two** of the following actions might a business take to improve its ethics? Put a cross (X) in **two** correct boxes.

☐ **A** Making sure factory workers work at least 10 hours per day.

☐ **B** Criticising competitor products in advertising material.

☐ **C** Setting up codes of conduct for factories.

☐ **D** Buying the cheapest raw materials possible from farmers in developing countries.

☐ **E** Paying staff in low-income countries above the minimum wage.

[2]

e) Which of the following businesses is most likely to prioritise the location of the market when choosing where to locate? Put a cross (X) in **one** correct box.

☐ **A** A company that sells stationery over the internet.

☐ **B** A hairdresser.

☐ **C** A courier service that delivers items nationally.

☐ **D** A company that arranges package holidays over the phone.

[1]

f) Explain **one** reason why an entrepreneur might find setting up a business rewarding.

....

....

....

[3]

Question 1 continues on the next page

g) Explain **two** disadvantages of a sole trader business structure.

1. ....

....

2. ....

....
[4]

h) Explain **one** way in which high unemployment may cause problems for a business.

....

....

....
[3]

i) Explain **two** benefits to a business of managing its supply chain effectively.

1. ....

....

2. ....

....
[4]

j) Look at **Figure 1** below.

Figure 1

Costs and Revenue for a Business in 2015 and 2016

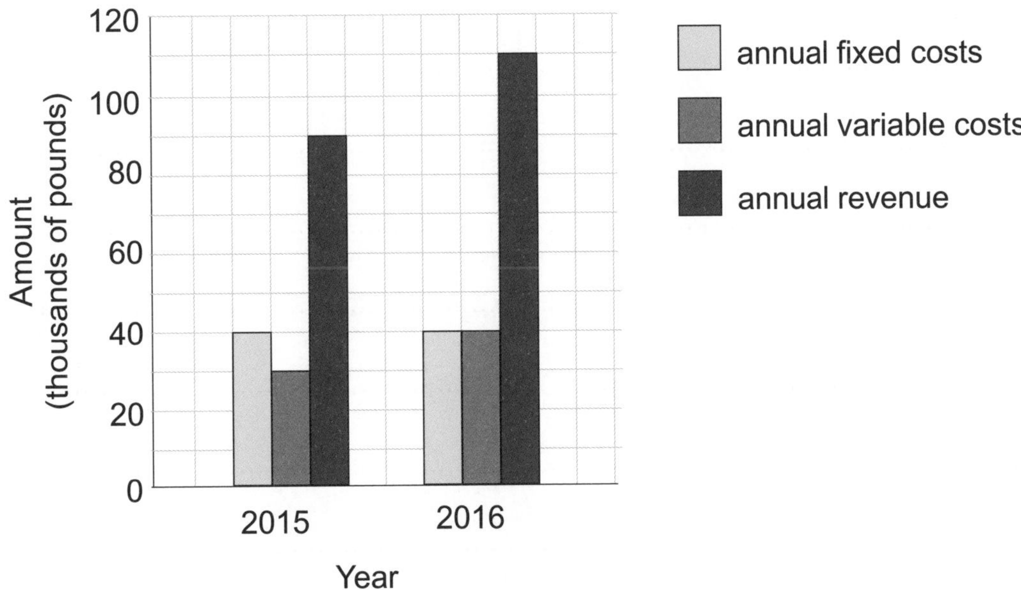

Calculate the percentage increase in profit between 2015 and 2016.
Show your working.

Percentage increase = ...%
[4]

Question 1 continues on the next page

k) Discuss the likely benefit to a business of training staff.

....

....

....

....

....

....

....

....

....

....

....

....

....

....

[6]

[Total 30 marks]

Section B
Answer all questions.

2 Look at **Item A** below.

> **Item A — Amazon®:**
> Amazon® is a successful online retailer that has seen huge growth since it was founded in the 1990s. Much of its success is due to the effects of globalisation, although company bosses regularly invest in new products, processes and technology to ensure the firm continues to grow.
>
> In 2012, *Amazon* bought a robotics company called Kiva Systems® for $775 million. *Kiva Systems* specialised in making robots for use in locating and delivering products in warehouses. The robots receive orders from the computer database system. They are then programmed to locate the shelf with the correct products and to lift the shelf and bring it to the worker who can locate the products. *Amazon* employs members of staff to manage the robotics system.
>
> In addition to the use of robots, *Amazon* also has an advanced computer system which tracks each product as it is packaged and labelled with an address for each customer.
>
> Largely due to heavy investments, in the final quarter of 2012 *Amazon's* net profit had fallen 45% from the 2011 figure of $177 million.

a) Define the term 'globalisation'.

....

....

[1]

b) Outline **one** advantage to *Amazon* of selling products online.

....

....

[2]

Question 2 continues on the next page

c) Calculate *Amazon's* net profit in the final quarter of 2012.
Show your working.

Net profit = $......................... million
[2]

d) Analyse the possible impact on *Amazon* of investing in new technology.

....

....

....

....

....

....

....

....

....

....

....

....

....

....
[6]

Look at **Item B** below.

Item B — Amazon®:
Amazon employs over 600 000 people worldwide. It has many 'fulfilment centres' in the UK. These huge warehouses employ thousands of people in a range of departments, such as procurement and logistics, IT, quality assurance and warehouse operations.

Amazon offers its employees competitive wages, discount codes to use on their website and an opportunity to own shares in *Amazon*. *Amazon* also allows many of its employees to work flexible hours.

e) State **two** ways in which a company must act lawfully towards its employees.

1. ....

....

2. ....

....

[2]

f) In 2017, Sam starts working in one of *Amazon's* UK fulfilment centres and earns £9.50 per hour. He works his contracted hours in four ten-hour shifts each week. He is entitled to four weeks of paid holiday each year. Calculate how much Sam earns each year before tax.
Show your working.

Amount earned each year before tax = £ ....

[2]

Question 2 continues on the next page

Turn over ▷

g) Explain why *Amazon* offers its employees the benefits mentioned in **Item B**.

....

....

....

....

....

....

....

....

....

[4]

Look at **Item C** below.

Item C — Amazon®:
In 2008, *Amazon* started a programme called Frustration-Free Packaging, to promote sustainable packaging. For a product to be certified as having Frustration-Free Packaging its packaging has to meet certain criteria, such as it must protect the product, be fitted to the size of the product and not require any extra *Amazon* packaging. Other criteria are that it's recyclable and easy to open.

Since 2008, the Frustration-Free Packaging programme has saved over 244 000 tons of packaging material. However, only some products across *Amazon's* range have been certified as having Frustration-Free Packaging. Therefore, in 2018 *Amazon* decided to take this further and required all products of a certain type (e.g. toys, consumer electronics, cleaning materials), which are also a large size or weight, to be in Frustration-Free Packaging by 1st August 2019. This is because larger products tend to have more packaging waste than smaller products.

In 2018, *Amazon* set up helpful tools to help sellers change their packaging to meet the Frustration-Free Packaging criteria, such as a website and support system. The website gives information on how sellers can develop Frustration-Free Packaging. The support system links the sellers to other companies that can help them design and test the packaging. *Amazon* also decided to give sellers credit on items that were certified early, to help with costs involved.

h) Recommend whether or not *Amazon* should go further and require all of its products to be in Frustration-Free Packaging. Give reasons for your answer.

....

....

....

....

....

....

....

....

....

....

....

....

....

....

....

....

....

....

....

....

....

[9]

[Total 28 marks]

Turn over for the next question

Section C
Answer all questions.

3 Look at **Item C** below.

> **Item C — Raymer's Ltd.:**
> Raymer's Ltd. are a baked-bean manufacturer located on the outskirts of a town in the UK. The company was started 15 years ago by Ms Anneka Raymer. Ms Raymer and her family currently own all of the shares in the company.
>
> Raymer's Ltd. use flow production to make their product and employ over 90 staff. The firm's sales have grown each year and the directors have set new objectives for the business which focus on diversification and expansion. They are also considering making Raymer's a public limited company.

a) Outline why flow production is an appropriate production method for Raymer's Ltd.

....

....

....

[2]

The directors of Raymer's Ltd. have produced a break-even chart for the business, as shown in **Figure 2**.

Figure 2

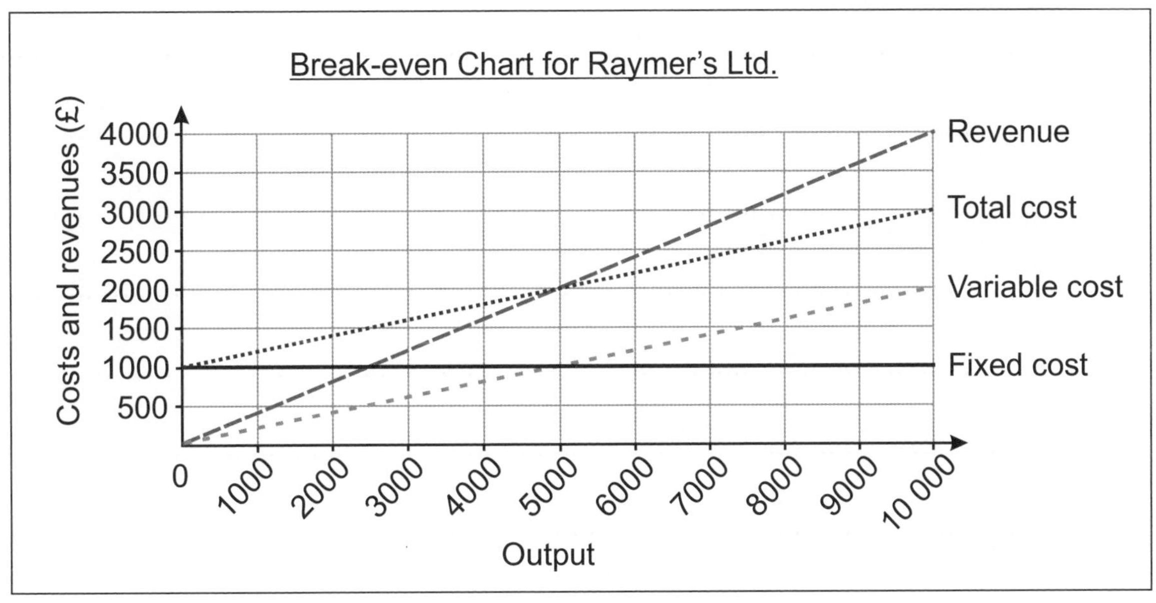

b) Identify the fixed costs for Raymer's Ltd.

....
[1]

c) Raymer's Ltd. currently has an average output of 9000 units.
Use **Figure 2** to calculate Raymer's Ltd.'s current margin of safety.
Show your working.

Margin of safety = ...
[2]

Question 3 continues on the next page

Turn over ▷

d) Analyse the impact on Raymer's Ltd. of becoming a public limited company.

....

....

....

....

....

....

....

....

....

....

....

....

....

....
[6]

Look at **Item D** below.

Item D — Raymer's Ltd.:
Another local food manufacturing company has recently gone out of business. Raymer's Ltd. are hoping they can buy this firm's old factory building so they can expand their business.

If the expansion goes ahead, Raymer's Ltd. estimate that they will need to increase their workforce by 15%. Many of the new staff will be factory workers — the firm are planning to train these staff informally whilst they are on-the-job. Raymer's Ltd. will need some new factory supervisors if the growth goes ahead.

e) Raymer's Ltd. have two options for recruiting their new supervisors:

Option 1: Recruit internally and train existing factory workers to be supervisors.
Option 2: Recruit externally.

Recommend which **one** of these options Raymer's Ltd. should choose.
Give reasons for your answer.

[9]

Question 3 continues on the next page

Look at **Item E** below.

Item E — Raymer's Ltd.:
Raymer's Ltd. bought the old factory building and went ahead with the expansion. After the expansion, they steadily increased the output of their products by 30%. The sales team found several new customers including a supermarket chain, for which Raymer's Ltd. agreed to add the supermarket's own labels to the tins. Due to the growth of the firm, Raymer's Ltd. recruited two customer service assistants to deal directly with customer queries.

However, following the expansion, the percentage of products that were returned by customers increased. Common complaints included loose labels, dented tins, and tins that contained a lower weight of produce than was stated on the label.

f) Analyse the impact of the expansion on the reputation of the business.
In your answer you should consider:

- customer service
- consumer law

You must evaluate which area would have had the biggest impact on the business.
Use evidence to support your answer.

....

....

....

....

....

....

....

....

....

....

....

....

....

....

[12]

[Total 32 marks]

END OF QUESTIONS

GCSE Business

Paper 2

In addition to this paper you should have:
- A calculator.

Centre name					
Centre number					
Candidate number					

Time allowed:
- 1 hour 45 minutes

Surname	
Other names	
Candidate signature	

Instructions to candidates
- Use black ink or ball-point pen.
- Write your name and other details in the spaces provided above.
- Answer **all** questions in the spaces provided.
- Do all rough work on the paper.
- Cross out any work you do not want to be marked.

Information for candidates
- The marks available are given in brackets at the end of each question.
- There are 90 marks available for this paper.
- You are allowed to use a calculator.

Advice to candidates
- In calculations show clearly how you worked out your answers.

For examiner's use			
Q	Attempt N°		
	1	2	3
1			
2			
3			
Total			

Section A
Answer all questions.

For multiple choice questions, put a cross (X) in the box alongside your answer.
If you wish to change your answer, put a line through your original answer.
For example: ☒. Then mark your new answer with a cross in the box.

1 a) Which of the following is an example of primary market research?
Put a cross (X) in **one** correct box.

- ☐ **A** reading an article in a magazine
- ☐ **B** a focus group
- ☐ **C** researching the market on the internet
- ☐ **D** reading government publications

[1]

b) Which of the following is an example of advertising?
Put a cross (X) in **one** correct box.

- ☐ **A** a strong brand image
- ☐ **B** special offers for products
- ☐ **C** selling products online
- ☐ **D** posters

[1]

c) Which of the following is the correct description of a merger?
Put a cross (X) in **one** correct box.

- ☐ **A** When one firm expands by buying more than half the shares in another firm.
- ☐ **B** When a firm expands by opening a new outlet.
- ☐ **C** When a firm grows by expanding its own activities.
- ☐ **D** When two firms join together to form a new firm.

[1]

Question 1 continues on the next page

d) Which of the following statements about globalisation are true?
Put a cross (X) in **two** correct boxes.

☐ **A** Globalisation means that businesses face more competition.

☐ **B** Globalisation makes it harder for people to communicate around the world.

☐ **C** Globalisation means it's free for companies to import goods into other countries.

☐ **D** Globalisation means that businesses can only sell products to peòple in countries where they have shops.

☐ **E** Globalisation means that it's easier for businesses to locate parts of their business abroad.

[2]

e) Which of the following describes what is meant by retained profits?
Put a cross (X) in **one** correct box.

☐ **A** Profits that are paid to the shareholders of the business.

☐ **B** Money from personal savings.

☐ **C** Profits that are invested back into the business.

☐ **D** The amount of profit that is paid as tax.

[1]

f) State **two** examples of different forms of digital communication.

1. ....

2. ....

[2]

g) Explain the impact of increasing prices on the gross profit margin of a firm if costs stay the same.

....

....

....

....

[3]

h) Explain **two** ways in which a business might be damaged if its products don't meet legal requirements.

1. ....

....

2. ....

....
[4]

i) Look at **Figure 1** below.

Figure 1

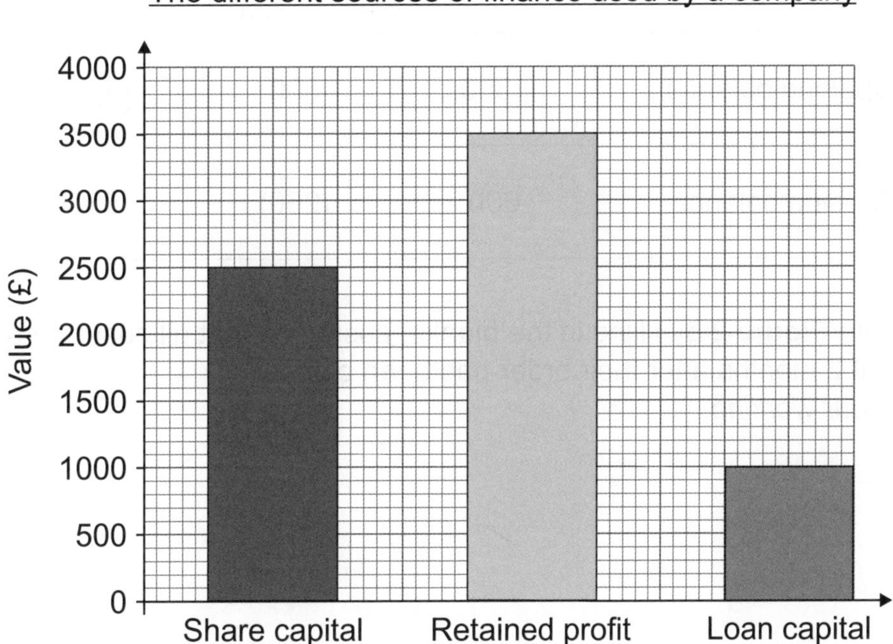

Calculate the percentage of the total amount of finance that is share capital.
Give your answer to 3 significant figures.
Show your working.

share capital = ...%
[2]

Question 1 continues on the next page

Turn over ▷

j) **Figure 2** shows an incomplete cash flow statement for a company that gives its customers 2 months credit to pay.

Figure 2

Cash Flow Statement				
£	April	May	June	July
Total orders this month (for payment in 2 months)	1000	1300	1400	1500
Cash inflow	300	350	ii)	1300
Cash outflow	1000	1200	1300	1350
Net cash flow	(700)	i)	(300)	(50)
Opening balance	1300	600	(250)	(550)
Closing balance	600	(250)	(550)	(600)

Complete **Figure 2** by filling in the blanks, assuming that all customers make their payment 2 months after their order has been placed.
Show your working.

[2]

k) Explain **one** benefit to a business of carrying out market research.

....

....

....

....
[3]

l) Calculate the gross profit margin for a company that has a sales revenue of £3m and a gross profit of £690 000.
Show your working.

gross profit margin = ... %
[2]

m) Discuss the purpose to a business of writing a business plan.

....

....

....

....

....

....

....

....

....

....
[6]

[Total 30 marks]

Turn over for the next question

Section B
Answer all questions.

2 Look at **Item A** below.

Item A — Heyshore Sports Ltd.:
Heyshore Sports Ltd. are a company that own a sports centre in the town of Heyshore. In the last five years, their revenue has increased by 36% and profits have increased by 20%. As a result of this success, they have increased staff wages by 5% and cut the membership fees they charge their customers by 3%. They have also invested in refurbishing their changing rooms.

In 2017, Heyshore Sports Ltd. carried out a survey of some of their customers by giving them a questionnaire to fill in. They had carried out the same survey five years previously. The results for one of the questions on the questionnaire are shown below.

Q1 What is the most important aspect of a sports centre for you?

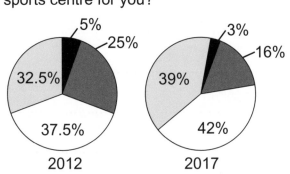

Before the survey, Heyshore Sports Ltd. had flyers for the sports centre that showed a picture of the outside of the centre and displayed the price of monthly membership. Afterwards, they changed the flyers to show an image of the gym room, and a list of activity classes that they provide.

a) Identify which aspect of a sports centre saw the biggest change in perceived importance between 2012 and 2017.

....

[1]

b) Outline **one** way in which Heyshore Sports Ltd. may have satisfied the objectives of their customers.

....

....

[2]

c) State **two** advantages of using questionnaires over other forms of primary research.

1. ....

2. ....
[2]

d) Analyse the effect that changing the flyers is likely to have on Heyshore Sports Ltd.'s sales.

....

....

....

....

....

....

....

....

....
[6]

Question 2 continues on the next page

Turn over ▷

e) Heyshore Sports Ltd. are considering two options for improving the business:

Option 1: Buying up-to-date exercise machines.
Option 2: Extending the opening hours from 08:30-20:00 to 07:00-22:00.

Recommend which **one** of these two options Heyshore Sports Ltd should choose. Give reasons for your answer.

....

....

....

....

....

....

....

....

....

....

....

....

....

....

....

....

....

....

....

....

....

[9]

The changing room refurbishment cost Heyshore Sports Ltd. £250 000.
Figure 3 shows how Heyshore Sports Ltd. forecast their profits will increase as a result of refurbishing the changing rooms, over the lifespan of the refurbishment.

Figure 3

	Year 1	Year 2	Year 3	Year 4	Year 5	Year 6	Year 7
additional profit (£000)	74	87	82	68	48	30	22

f) Calculate the average rate of return for the changing room refurbishment.
Show your working.

average rate of return = ... %
[4]

Question 2 continues on the next page

Look at **Item B** below.

Item B — Heyshore Sports Ltd.:
Heyshore Sports Ltd. would like to expand their business by building more outdoor facilities. They are considering using an area of meadowland directly behind the sports centre. The land is currently a popular picnic spot for families, although a local environmental group tries to dissuade people from using the land as it's home to lots of wild plant and animal species. Another option is to use land 500 metres down the road from the sports centre. The land is currently occupied by a derelict factory, which would need knocking down and removing before any building could begin. This site is twice the size of the meadowland and the building work is expected to be more expensive.

g) Heyshore Sports Ltd. want to avoid too much conflict from stakeholders when they decide on a site for their expansion. They need to choose between:

Option 1: The area of meadowland behind the sports centre.
Option 2: The disused factory site 500 metres down the road from the sports centre.

Recommend which **one** of these two options Heyshore Sports Ltd. should choose. Give reasons for your answer.

....

....

....

....

....

....

....

....

....

....

....

....

....

....

....

....

....

....

....

....

....

[9]

[Total 33 marks]

Turn over for the next question

Section C
Answer <u>all</u> questions.

3 Look at **Item C** below.

> **Item C — L'Oréal:**
> L'Oréal are a multinational cosmetics company. One of their growing markets is in India, where they grew on average 21.7% each year between 2009 and 2016.
>
> In 2004, L'Oréal set up a factory in Pune, India to manufacture products for sale in India. 90% of the products sold in India are made in this factory. Many of the raw materials used to make products in the factory come from India.
>
> Since 2005, L'Oréal have been aiming to increase the sustainability of their business operations, for example by installing solar cells to heat water and recycling waste water at the factory. In 2015, the Pune factory was certified as reaching internationally recognised standards for efficient energy use.

a) State **two** aims that L'Oréal might have in India.

1. ....

2. ....

[2]

b) Define the term 'sustainable'.

....

....

[1]

c) Outline **one** benefit to L'Oréal of making its factory in Pune more sustainable.

....

....

....

[2]

d) Analyse the impact that setting up a factory in India is likely to have had on L'Oréal's costs.

....

....

....

....

....

....

....

....

....

....

[6]

Look at **Item D** below.

Item D — L'Oréal:
Market research has shown that in less affluent areas of India, people are more likely to buy products in small sachets for a single use, which are cheaper than buying larger bottles. As a result, L'Oréal sell their shampoo in a larger range of sizes and prices in India than they do in other countries, including sachets. Although L'Oréal prices its shampoo cheaply, it is slightly more expensive than competitor products.

L'Oréal distribute their products through a number of channels in India. Research has shown that the majority of sales in India are made through small, independent retailers. L'Oréal supplies its products through these stores as well as large chain stores and supermarkets. They are also targeting e-commerce at customers in more rural areas.

Question 3 continues on the next page

e) Explain why L'Oréal may have chosen to invest in the design of their new shampoo sachets.

....

....

....

....

....

....

[4]

f) Evaluate whether L'Oréal is likely to benefit from its marketing strategy in India. You should use information provided as well as your own knowledge of business.

....

....

....

....

....

....

....

....

....

....

....

....

....

....

....

[12]

[Total 27 marks]

END OF QUESTIONS

Note on Answers:

A lot of the time in Business, there isn't really a "right answer". Instead, it's about being able to explain yourself and justify your decisions.

Section 1 — Business in the Real World

Page 15

Exam Questions

1 B ***[1 mark]***

2 How to grade your answer:

Level 0: Nothing worthy of credit. ***[No marks]***

Level 1: There is some attempt to state the qualities that Bushra has shown, but there is little or no explanation to back up these statements. ***[1 to 2 marks]***

Level 2: There is a basic analysis of the qualities that Bushra has shown, but the explanations are lacking in detail, or points have been missed. ***[3 to 4 marks]***

Level 3: There is a thorough analysis of the qualities that Bushra has shown, with detailed explanations of how she has shown them. ***[5 to 6 marks]***

Here are some points your answer may include:

Bushra has quit her job as a journalist to start her own company. This shows that she is willing to take risks.

Bushra has identified a gap in the market for fashionable, vegan-friendly and ethically produced shoes. This shows that she is innovative/creative.

Bushra has chosen a manufacturer who suits her needs. This shows she is able to make business decisions.

Bushra has made sure the manufacturers provide her with quantities of stock that she's able to store in her office. She's also prepared a successful presentation to a nationwide retail firm. This shows that she is organised.

By successfully presenting to a nationwide retail firm, Bushra has also shown that she is confident.

Bushra has worked hard to find the right manufacturer for her shoes, by visiting many trade shows. She also worked hard before the presentation to the nationwide retail store, as she didn't take a day off for two weeks. This shows that she is hardworking and determined.

Page 23

Exam Questions

1 Aims are overall goals that a business wants to achieve ***[1 mark]***. Objectives are more specific targets ***[1 mark]*** which are used to help measure how well a business is achieving its aims ***[1 mark]***.

2 a) E.g. the residents will benefit from the roads Better Energy Plc. are planning to build ***[1 mark]*** as it may improve access to the area ***[1 mark]***. / The residents will benefit if the wind farm creates jobs in the area ***[1 mark]***, as it may mean more people have money to spend in local shops ***[1 mark]***.

b) How to grade your answer:

Level 0: Nothing worthy of credit. ***[No marks]***

Level 1: There is a basic description of a conflict that Better Energy Plc. might have considered, but with little explanation of why the options for where to build their wind farm may have caused this conflict. ***[1 to 2 marks]***

Level 2: There is a detailed description of a conflict that Better Energy Plc. might have considered, with a detailed explanation of why the options for where to build their wind farm might have caused this conflict. ***[3 to 4 marks]***

Here is an answer you could have written:

Better Energy Plc. may have considered the conflict between the opinions of the local residents of Madingborough and their shareholders. This is because the local residents of Madingborough have protested against the wind farm being built near them, because it could spoil the views in the local area. However, the shareholders are likely to support building the wind farm near Madingborough, as it will be cheaper than building it offshore and can be finished faster, so their dividends are likely to increase sooner.

Page 32

Exam Questions

1 B ***[1 mark]***

2 C ***[1 mark]*** and E ***[1 mark]***

3 Hint: for the reason you choose, make sure you explain why it would harm the business.

E.g. locating near businesses of the same type means the business will be in direct competition with its neighbours ***[1 mark]***, so customers may choose to shop at the competitor businesses ***[1 mark]*** causing the business to lose sales ***[1 mark]***.

4 E.g. internal growth is slow ***[1 mark]*** as the business grows by expanding its own activities ***[1 mark]***, so it may take a long time for profits and sales to increase ***[1 mark]***.

Section 2 — Influences on Business

Page 43

Exam Questions

1 Advantage: by having a minimum wage, staff are more likely to be motivated ***[1 mark]*** and therefore may be more productive for a business ***[1 mark]***.

Disadvantage: businesses may have increased costs ***[1 mark]***, which may mean that their profit is reduced ***[1 mark]***.

2 How to grade your answer:

Level 0: Nothing worthy of credit. ***[No marks]***

Level 1: There is some attempt to state the effects of using Fair Trade products on the financial success of Beancraft Ltd., but there is little or no explanation of the causes of these effects. ***[1 to 2 marks]***

Level 2: There is a basic analysis of how using Fair Trade products might affect the financial success of Beancraft Ltd., but the explanations are lacking in detail, or points have been missed. ***[3 to 4 marks]***

Level 3: There is a thorough analysis of how using Fair Trade products might affect the financial success of Beancraft Ltd., with detailed explanations of the causes of these effects. ***[5 to 6 marks]***

Here are some points your answer may include:

Workers on coffee bean plantations that are Fair Trade certified will get a fair wage, which will allow them to afford a better quality of life. However, buying only from Fair Trade certified plantations may mean that Beancraft Ltd. will have to pay more for coffee beans than its competitors.

This could mean that the prices of its coffee products are higher than those of its competitors. This may mean that consumers choose its competitors' coffee instead of Beancraft Ltd.'s, leading to a loss in revenue.

Beancraft Ltd. will also have a smaller selection of plantations to buy from than its competitors, since a smaller number of plantations are Fair Trade certified than those that are not. This may mean that it won't be able to offer varieties of coffee that its competitors offer, which may mean that customers won't choose its products and it will have a loss in revenue.

However, Beancraft Ltd. may be able to include details of its use of Fair Trade sources of coffee beans in its marketing, in order to emphasise the company's ethical principles. Most of its competitors do not use Fair Trade sources of coffee beans, so emphasising the use of Fair Trade sources in Beancraft Ltd.'s marketing could help it to stand out from its competition. This may mean that customers who want to buy ethical products will choose Beancraft Ltd.'s coffee over its competitors'. This will lead to an increase in revenue for Beancraft Ltd.

Page 54

Exam Questions

1 How to grade your answer:

Level 0: Nothing worthy of credit. ***[No marks]***

Level 1: There is an attempt to describe some scenarios where a business might face very little competition, but with only brief discussion of why there is little competition in these situations. ***[1 to 2 marks]***

Level 2: A number of scenarios where a business might face very little competition have been described, with some discussion of why there is little competition in these situations. ***[3 to 4 marks]***

Level 3: There is a detailed description of the scenarios where a business might face very little competition, and a clear discussion of why there is little competition in these situations. ***[5 to 6 marks]***

Here are some points your answer may include:

A business may face little competition if it has just released a brand new product. This is because, until other businesses start selling similar products, anyone who wants the product will have to buy it from this business. Furthermore, businesses may take out a patent for a new product, which will mean that other businesses won't be able to copy their idea for a set period of time, keeping competition low.

A business may face very little competition if they sell very specialist products that not many people want to buy.

There probably won't be much competition as the market won't be big enough for many businesses to survive.

A business may face very little competition if it's in a market where it is hard to start a business, for example because the cost of setting up a new business is too high. This could be due to the cost of equipment or the cost of training employees to have specialist skills. Not many businesses will be set up to sell to these markets, and there'll be low competition.

2 How to grade your answer:

Level 0: Nothing worthy of credit. ***[No marks]***

Level 1: There is a basic description of the advantages and disadvantages of the changing economic climate on Clear Skin but with little explanation of whether Clear Skin would have benefited overall. ***[1 to 3 marks]***

Level 2: There is a basic explanation of the advantages and disadvantages that the changing economic climate would have on Clear Skin. There is some attempt to conclude whether Clear Skin would have benefited overall, but with little or no explanation to justify the conclusion. ***[4 to 6 marks]***

Level 3: There is a good description of the advantages and disadvantages that the changing economic climate would have on Clear Skin. There is a conclusion as to whether Clear Skin would have benefited overall, but the justification is lacking in detail. ***[7 to 9 marks]***

Level 4: There is a detailed and thorough analysis of the advantages and disadvantages that the changing economic climate may have on Clear Skin. A conclusion has been made as to whether Clear Skin would have benefited overall, which has been fully justified using evidence. ***[10 to 12 marks]***

Here are some points your answer may include:

A rise in unemployment means that more people are out of work, and so many people have less money available to spend.

The unemployment rate increased from 5.2% to 7.8% between the start of 2008 and the end of 2009. This means it's likely that consumer spending would have gone down. Clear Skin's products are not necessities, so it is likely that demand for them may have fallen as the unemployment rate rose.

A low interest rate means that it is cheaper to borrow money, and less interest is paid on money saved in the bank.

This can cause people to spend more and save less.

The Bank of England base rate for interest decreased from 5.5% to 0.5% between the start of 2008 and the end of 2009. This means that most other interest rates are also likely to have fallen sharply within this time period. This means that consumer spending may have increased, which could have caused Clear Skin's sales to increase.

The falling interest rates would also have meant that Clear Skin paid less in interest repayments on their loan. This fall in business costs would have meant they had more money available to invest in the business.

The value of the British pound against the rupee fell by 2.9 between the start of 2008 and the end of 2009.

This would have meant that it became more expensive for Clear Skin to import its raw materials. This would have left them with less money to invest in the business.

If the extra costs of raw materials outweighed the reduced costs of the bank loan, Clear Skin could have increased their prices to cover these extra costs. However, this may have led to a decline in sales, which would have made it more difficult for them to grow the business.

You need to finish your answer with a conclusion as to whether or not Clear Skin would have benefited from the changing economic climate — make sure you've looked thoroughly at all the information given.
E.g. 'Although falling interest rates may have reduced some of Clear Skin's costs, the rise in exchange rate may have increased costs. Also, rising unemployment rates are likely to have reduced consumer spending, meaning that demand for Clear Skin's products may have fallen. This fall in consumer spending is likely to have resulted in Clear Skin suffering overall from the changing economic climate.'

Section 3 — Business Operations

Page 65

Exam Questions

1 E.g. batch production is faster than job production ***[1 mark]***, since it involves making batches of identical products at the same time ***[1 mark]***, so the firm will be more productive ***[1 mark]***.

2 How to grade your answer:

Level 0: Nothing worthy of credit. ***[No marks]***

Level 1: There is some attempt to describe how using just-in-time (JIT) will impact The Reading Shelf, but with little explanation of the advantages and disadvantages to the firm. ***[1 to 2 marks]***

Level 2: There is a good description of how using JIT will impact The Reading Shelf, with some explanation of the advantages and disadvantages to the firm. ***[3 to 4 marks]***

Level 3: There is a detailed description of how using JIT will impact The Reading Shelf, and a clear explanation of the advantages and disadvantages to the firm. ***[5 to 6 marks]***

Here are some points your answer may include:

Switching to JIT means The Reading Shelf will no longer order books in bulk, and will only order the stock they need. It is therefore less likely to make orders over 2000 units and so will not benefit from the discount offered by the supplier on these large orders. Therefore, the costs of their supplies could increase.

However, it means The Reading Shelf won't have as much waste from discarding books that are no longer selling. This could mean their costs go down as they are only spending money on books they know they should sell.

Using JIT means The Reading Shelf will have more frequent deliveries. This means their costs will go up, as they'll have to pay a delivery charge each time.
However, The Reading Shelf will no longer need to rent such a large warehouse to store its books, so costs could go down.
Deliveries from the supplier can occasionally be delayed. By changing to just-in-time stock control, The Reading Shelf will not have stock available when deliveries are delayed and will be unable to fulfil orders to bookshops. This may mean that The Reading Shelf will get a bad reputation. This could reduce The Reading Shelf's revenue.

Page 73

Exam Questions

1 Hint: make sure that your answer definitely relates to quality assurance rather than quality control. Quality assurance stops errors from being made in the first place, whereas quality control is about finding faults that have already occurred.
E.g. the firm should waste less materials making faulty products it can't sell ***[1 mark]*** as products will be checked at each stage in the production process ***[1 mark]*** which should prevent errors from being made ***[1 mark]***.

2 E.g. if customers are satisfied with the level of service they receive from a business, they may be more likely to buy products again from the business in the future / recommend it to friends ***[1 mark]***. This will lead to an increase in revenue ***[1 mark]***. If this increase outweighs any spending on improving customer service, then profits will rise ***[1 mark]***.

3 a) E.g. Bee's Travel employs two employees whose sole job is to answer website enquiries ***[1 mark]*** / Bee's Travel aims to answer website enquiries within 24 hours ***[1 mark]***.

b) Hint: you need to give a brief description of how the training in product knowledge will affect customers or staff for one mark and then the impact that this will have on the business for the second mark.
E.g. it will ensure customer queries are answered quickly/ accurately ***[1 mark]*** which will improve customer satisfaction ***[1 mark]***. / Staff may be able to recommend additional products to suit a customer's needs ***[1 mark]***, which will increase Bee's Travel's sales ***[1 mark]***. / It will make customers will feel confident about buying from Bee's Travel ***[1 mark]*** which is likely to increase sales ***[1 mark]***.

Section 4 — Human Resources

Page 82

Exam Questions

1 E.g. effective communication leads to improved staff motivation ***[1 mark]***, as staff will know what is happening in the firm ***[1 mark]*** and therefore will be more confident that they're doing their job properly ***[1 mark]***.

2 a) E.g. Claire Wilkinson is likely to be responsible for the overall strategy of Houghton & Son Ltd.'s sales department in the UK ***[1 mark]***.

b) E.g. there is a short chain of command ***[1 mark]*** / each manager has a wide span of control ***[1 mark]***.

c) E.g. as the company grew it would have needed more employees ***[1 mark]***, and so more managers to organise and control them ***[1 mark]***.

Page 93

Exam Questions

1 a) salaries / commission ***[1 mark]***

b) Money from commission = (19 000 ÷ 100) × 5 = £950
Total amount paid = £1250 + £950 = **£2200**
[2 marks for correct answer, otherwise 1 mark for calculating the money from commission]

c) How to grade your answer:
Level 0: Nothing worthy of credit. ***[No marks]***
Level 1: Some attempt has been made to recommend what Packman's Glazing should do, but with little justification for why this is the better option. ***[1 to 3 marks]***
Level 2: Some of the advantages and disadvantages of the two pay schemes have been described, along with a recommendation of which one Packman's Glazing should use. There is some reasoning to the recommendation, but it is lacking in detail or not fully justified. ***[4 to 6 marks]***
Level 3: There is a detailed explanation of the advantages and disadvantages of the two pay schemes, with a well-reasoned and fully justified recommendation of which one Packman's Glazing should use. ***[7 to 9 marks]***

Here are some points your answer may include:
Paying sales staff commission will make them more motivated to sell, since the more they sell the more they earn. This will lead to higher productivity in the business.
Having motivated staff can also increase staff retention as workers are less likely to want to leave the business. This can reduce recruitment and training costs for the business.
Having motivated staff may also help to attract new employees to the firm, which will make recruiting new staff easier as there are likely to be lots of applicants for vacancies.
However, two of the sales staff have chosen to leave the business, partly because they would prefer to be paid a higher salary but with no commission.
Workers may prefer this pay scheme as it means they get a higher guaranteed income and they don't have the stress of having to sell lots of products in order to increase their income.
But this scheme may mean that productivity falls as the workers are less motivated to perform well. So moving to this pay scheme could mean that Packman's Glazing's profits would fall, as they would be paying their workers more but may experience falling sales.
As the rival firm is new, it may be too early to tell whether their pay scheme is effective at keeping workers motivated enough to stay with the firm long-term and to sell enough products.

You need to finish your answer with a conclusion recommending what you think Packman's Glazing should do — make sure you've looked thoroughly at all the information given. E.g. 'Packman's Glazing should continue with their current pay scheme. Even though this means that they risk losing staff, their workers are likely to be more motivated to perform well, which could lead to more sales and higher profits for the business.'

Section 5 — Marketing

Page 104

Exam Questions

1 Hint: make sure you clearly describe an advantage of secondary market research over primary market research and explain why this will be particularly advantageous to a small business.
E.g. secondary market research is likely to be cheaper than primary market research ***[1 mark]***, since the data is already available ***[1 mark]***, which is an advantage to small businesses because they are unlikely to have as much money as larger businesses ***[1 mark]***.

2 a) Segmentation is when people within a market are divided into different groups ***[1 mark]***.

b) BassLine Ltd. ***[1 mark]***

c) E.g. there is a gap in the market map for a moderately priced, high quality record player ***[1 mark]***, so there may be high customer demand for it ***[1 mark]***.

Page 117

Exam Questions

1 a) By understanding their target market, they can create cars that they know their target market wants ***[1 mark]***. Therefore they will be more likely to sell their cars to their target market ***[1 mark]***, and so are more likely to get a return on their investment / less likely to make a costly mistake ***[1 mark]***.

b) E.g. it is a completely new product ***[1 mark]***, so they risk running out of money ***[1 mark]*** if they spend too much time and money developing the car and don't get it to market quickly enough ***[1 mark]***.

2 How to grade your answer:

Level 0: Nothing worthy of credit. ***[No marks]***

Level 1: There is a basic description of why prices might be lowered, but with little explanation of what may cause the lower prices. ***[1 to 2 marks]***

Level 2: There is a detailed description of why prices might be lowered, with a detailed explanation of what may cause the lower prices. ***[3 to 4 marks]***

Here is an answer you could have written:

E.g. as Pottery Wheel starts to produce more pottery, it will order clay in larger quantities. As the size of the order of clay increases, it becomes cheaper per kg. So Pottery Wheel's costs per unit will go down and it will be able to lower its prices whilst still making a profit.

Page 126

Exam Questions

1 Hint: make sure that you have properly read the information in Item A — it tells you that Mama Ltd's new product is an energy drink for sports.

E.g. by sponsoring the marathon, Mamo Ltd. will be more likely to be promoted to its target market than sponsoring another kind of event ***[1 mark]***, since individuals at the marathon are likely to be interested in sports ***[1 mark]***.

2 a) M-commerce is when goods and services are bought using a wireless device ***[1 mark]***. British Bikes Ltd. have created a mobile phone app which can be used by customers to buy products ***[1 mark]***.

b) British Bikes Ltd. is likely to have increased sales as a result of m-commerce ***[1 mark]***, since people will be able to access their products in many different locations and situations ***[1 mark]***.

c) E.g. British Bikes Ltd. need their technology to stay up-to-date ***[1 mark]***, or customers may choose to buy their products from a more up-to-date competitor ***[1 mark]***.

Section 6 — Finance

Page 140

Exam Questions

1 A ***[1 mark]***

2 a) E.g. the credit period that Shoesies Ltd. gives its customers is longer than the credit period it has to pay its suppliers ***[1 mark]***. This means it has to pay out money for its supplies before money has come in from sales, which is a problem ***[1 mark]***. Recently, sales have been decreasing ***[1 mark]***, which could be a problem as cash inflow may be going down, while it's unlikely that cash outflow will have changed as much ***[1 mark]***.

b) How to grade your answer:

Level 0: Nothing written worthy of credit. ***[No marks]***

Level 1: Some attempt to recommend which option Shoesies Ltd. should take, but with little explanation for why this should be done. ***[1 to 3 marks]***

Level 2: Some of the advantages and disadvantages of the different options have been described, along with a recommendation of what Shoesies Ltd. should do. There is some reasoning to the recommendation, but it is lacking in detail or not fully explained. ***[4 to 6 marks]***

Level 3: There is a thorough description of the advantages and disadvantages of the different options, with a detailed recommendation for what Shoesies Ltd. should do that has been fully explained. ***[7 to 9 marks]***

Here are some points your answer may include:

Rescheduling payments:

Shoesies Ltd. could reschedule their credit agreements so that the credit period for their customers is shorter than the credit period for their suppliers.

They could also reschedule their loan repayments with their bank, so that they take place when there is enough cash in the business. This would mean that their cash inflow would come in before their cash outflow.

However, they may find it hard to reschedule payments with suppliers and they may find that they attract fewer customers with a less generous credit agreement.

Obtaining another source of finance:

They could also look for new investors to increase the amount of cash in the business. This would be a good way of getting a large amount of cash relatively quickly, but would mean that the owners of the company would get less of their profits.

The owners of Shoesies Ltd. could ask for a loan from a friend or family member. This would help with the business's immediate cash flow problems but the loan would eventually need to be repaid. Therefore, the business would not be able to rely on loans in order to completely solve the cash flow problem.

They could arrange an overdraft with their bank for times in which they know they will run out of cash. This would be a good way of ensuring that they can keep up with payments to suppliers, but overdrafts are also expensive and would eventually have to be paid back. As sales are decreasing, Shoesies Ltd. may find it difficult to get the cash needed to pay back a loan or overdraft. Shoesies Ltd. is already unable to make its loan repayments, so obtaining another loan from its bank would probably drive it further into debt.

Make sure you finish your answer with a conclusion recommending what you think Shoesies Ltd. should do — it doesn't matter which you choose as long as you give reasons. E.g. 'Shoesies Ltd. should reschedule their payments. Although this may be difficult, it would be a longer-term solution than obtaining a new source of finance and would also be less expensive.'

Page 151

Exam Questions

1 a) E.g. new buildings ***[1 mark]*** and more employees ***[1 mark]***.

b) total profit of investment = 17 000 + 13 000 + 15 000 + 15 000 + 12 000 – 20 000 = £52 000

average annual profit = 52 000 ÷ 5 = £10 400

average rate of return = (average annual profit ÷ initial investment) × 100

average rate of return = (10 400 ÷ 20 000) × 100 = 52%

[4 marks for correct answer, otherwise 1 mark for correct total profit of investment, 1 mark for correct average annual profit and 1 mark for using the correct equation to calculate the average rate of return]

c) The average rate of return on the investment is quite large ***[1 mark]***. This means Speedy Wheels should quickly see its profits increase as a result of the investment ***[1 mark]***. So Speedy Wheels is likely to go ahead with its decision to invest in the new delivery vans ***[1 mark]***.

Practice Paper 1

Pages 153-169

1 a) A ***[1 mark]***

b) A ***[1 mark]***

c) C ***[1 mark]***

d) C ***[1 mark]***, E ***[1 mark]***

e) B ***[1 mark]***

A hairdresser will want to be somewhere that its customers can easily get to. The other companies sell over the internet or phone, or deliver nationally, so being near their customers will be less important.

f) E.g. the business may make a large profit ***[1 mark]***. This could mean the entrepreneur earns more money than they did before they started the business ***[1 mark]***, which could give them a better quality of life ***[1 mark]***.

g) Hint: there are four marks here — two marks for giving two disadvantages, and two marks for explaining the impact each disadvantage could have.
Any two from: e.g. sole traders may have to work long hours / not get many holidays ***[1 mark]***, so they may regularly feel tired ***[1 mark]***. / Sole traders have unlimited liability ***[1 mark]***, which means if the business goes bust they are legally responsible for paying back all of the business's debts ***[1 mark]***. / Sole traders are also unincorporated ***[1 mark]***, so if anyone sues the business, the sole trader is sued personally ***[1 mark]***. / It can be hard for a sole trader to raise money ***[1 mark]***, so it may be hard to grow the business ***[1 mark]***.

h) E.g. it may mean that people have less money to spend ***[1 mark]***. This could mean that there is less demand for and fewer sales of the products or services offered by the business ***[1 mark]***, which could lead to lower profits ***[1 mark]***.

i) Any two from: e.g. working closely with suppliers ensures key processes are running efficiently/cost effectively ***[1 mark]***, meaning the business may be more profitable ***[1 mark]***. / Managing the supply chain effectively means that the business can make sure it gets its supplies for the best price/value ***[1 mark]***, which will reduce the firm's costs ***[1 mark]***. / Managing the supply chain effectively means the business can make sure its supplies are good quality ***[1 mark]***, which will help it to attract/keep customers ***[1 mark]***. / Effective management of the supply chain means that the business can get products to customers on time ***[1 mark]***, which will help them to keep/build a good reputation ***[1 mark]***.

j) profit = revenue – costs
profit in 2015 = 90 000 – 30 000 – 40 000 = £20 000
profit in 2016 = 110 000 – 40 000 – 40 000 = £30 000
change in profit = 30 000 – 20 000 = £10 000
Percentage increase = (10 000 ÷ 20 000) × 100 = 50%
[4 marks for correct answer, otherwise 1 mark for correctly calculating profit in 2015, 1 mark for correctly calculating profit in 2016 and 1 mark for correctly calculating change in profit]

k) How to grade your answer:
Level 0: Nothing worthy of credit. ***[No marks]***
Level 1: Some attempt to describe some consequences of training staff, but with little discussion of why these consequences benefit the business. ***[1 to 2 marks]***
Level 2: A number of consequences of training staff have been described, with some discussion of why these consequences benefit the business. ***[3 to 4 marks]***
Level 3: There is a detailed description of the consequences of training staff, and a clear discussion of why these consequences benefit the business. ***[5 to 6 marks]***
Here are some points your answer may include:
Training staff makes them better at their jobs, which can mean they work faster.
This can make a business more productive and lower its average unit costs.
Having staff that are better at their jobs is also likely to mean that they can offer a high level of customer service and produce high quality goods. Both of these things may lead to increased sales for the business.
Training can equip staff with new skills. This may be beneficial if the business currently has skill shortages in certain areas, which hinder its success.
Equipping staff with new skills could also help the development of the business if it needs to change the way it operates.
Training can help staff keep up to date with technology.
This can give the business a competitive advantage, and may make it more productive.
Training staff is likely to motivate staff.
This can increase staff retention, which means the business won't have to recruit and train new staff so often, which will decrease its costs.

2 a) Globalisation is the process by which businesses and countries around the world become more connected ***[1 mark]***.

b) E.g. it allows Amazon® to reach a wider market ***[1 mark]***, since people will be able to buy products from the website anywhere in the world ***[1 mark]***.

c) Fall in net profit since 2011 is 45% of \$177 million
= (177 million ÷ 100) × 45 = \$79.65 million
So, net profit = \$177 million – \$79.65 million
= **\$97.35 million**
[2 marks for correct answer, otherwise 1 mark for correctly calculating 45% of \$177 million]

d) How to grade your answer:
Level 0: Nothing worthy of credit. ***[No marks]***
Level 1: Some attempt to describe the impact that investing in new technology may have on *Amazon*, but with little explanation of why it may have this impact. ***[1 to 2 marks]***
Level 2: There is a good description of the impact that investing in new technology will have on *Amazon*, with some explanation of why it may have this impact. ***[3 to 4 marks]***
Level 3: There is a detailed description of the impact that investing in new technology will have on *Amazon*, and a clear explanation of why it may have this impact. ***[5 to 6 marks]***
Here are some points your answer may include:
Investing in a new robotics system has allowed *Amazon* to locate products in its warehouses more quickly.
This is likely to mean that customer orders can be sent out more quickly, which may lead to higher levels of customer satisfaction and an increase in sales.
Having an advanced computer system which tracks customers' products as they are packaged and labelled is likely to reduce the time it takes products to leave the warehouses and reduce the number of mistakes made by human error.
This is likely to make the packing and shipping process more efficient and may mean that customer orders can be sent out more quickly. Again this may lead to higher levels of customer satisfaction and an increase in sales.
However, investing in new technology has been very expensive for *Amazon*. Buying *Kiva Systems* cost \$775 million and on top of this they have to employ staff to manage the robotics systems.
Amazon's investments contributed to a large reduction in their net profit in the final quarter of 2012, which may have meant they couldn't invest as much in growing the business in the following years.

e) Any two from: e.g. it must not discriminate against any staff member. / It must pay staff at least the legal minimum wage. / It must pay all staff doing work of equal value the same amount. / It must make sure it follows health and safety laws. / It must give employees the minimum level of paid holidays. / It must allow employees to have a written contract of employment within two months of starting work.
[2 marks — 1 mark for each correct answer]

f) Weekly wage = £9.50 × 4 × 10 = £380
Amount earned each year before tax = £380 × 52 = **£19 760**
[2 marks for correct answer, otherwise 1 mark for correctly calculating weekly wage]

g) How to grade your answer:
Level 0: Nothing worthy of credit. ***[No marks]***
Level 1: There is a basic explanation of how the benefits would motivate employees, but with little explanation of how this will benefit Amazon. ***[1 to 2 marks]***
Level 2: There is a detailed explanation of how the benefits would motivate employees, with a detailed explanation of how this will benefit Amazon. ***[3 to 4 marks]***

Here is an answer you could have written:
Amazon offers many benefits to employees to motivate them. For example, offering competitive wages will motivate employees because they are likely to feel more satisfied in their job the more they get paid. Offering fringe benefits such as discount codes will also motivate employees, as they will feel happy that working for *Amazon* means they can save money on purchases. Having motivated staff is beneficial for *Amazon* as staff will be more likely to stay with the business, meaning it will spend less time and money on recruitment.

h) How to grade your answer:
Level 0: Nothing worthy of credit. ***[No marks]***
Level 1: Some attempt has been made to recommend whether or not *Amazon* should roll out their Frustration-Free Packaging programme to all products, but with little justification for why this should be done. ***[1 to 3 marks]***
Level 2: Some of the advantages and disadvantages of *Amazon* rolling out their Frustration-Free Packaging programme to all products have been given along with a recommendation of what *Amazon* should do. There is some reasoning to the recommendation, but it is lacking in detail or not fully justified. ***[4 to 6 marks]***
Level 3: There is a detailed explanation of the advantages and disadvantages of *Amazon* rolling out their Frustration-Free Packaging programme to all products, with a well-reasoned and fully justified recommendation of what *Amazon* should do. ***[7 to 9 marks]***

Here are some points your answer may include:
Amazon's Frustration-Free Packaging programme means that the packaging must protect the product, requires no extra packaging by *Amazon* and is recyclable. *Amazon* is a large company, with lots of products on sale, so rolling this programme out to all of its products would mean that it has the potential to save a huge amount of packaging and reduce waste, which is good for the environment.
Reducing the amount of packaging should have other beneficial environmental effects, such as reducing the amount of transport needed for the same number of products. This should benefit *Amazon* and the sellers of the product, by reducing costs.
If these environmental advantages are promoted well, they may encourage more customers to shop with *Amazon* or to keep using *Amazon*, which could increase sales and profit for *Amazon* and also the sellers.
One of the criteria for the Frustration-Free Packaging is for it to be easy to open, which could also increase customer satisfaction, and increase sales and profit for *Amazon* and the sellers.
The sellers of the products to *Amazon* have access to helpful tools, such as a website and support system, which should mean that sellers find it easier to change their packaging to meet the criteria of the programme where they need to.
Also, if *Amazon* adopts a credit system, like it did for the large and heavy goods to be certified by 1st August 2019, this will help sellers with the costs of changing their packaging.
However, some sellers may find changing their packaging too difficult to carry out. Others may find it too expensive to carry out and that the credit given by *Amazon* may not cover all their costs. For these reasons *Amazon* may lose sellers and their products. If they have fewer products to sell it could affect their overall profit.
Also, the items that Amazon required to be certified as having Frustration-Free Packaging were larger items, because they tend to have more packaging waste than smaller items. This means that, for smaller products, there won't be as many beneficial environmental and cost advantages.

You need to finish your answer with a conclusion recommending what you think Amazon should do — make sure you've looked thoroughly at all the information given. E.g. 'Amazon should roll out their new Frustration-Free Packaging programme to all products. It has a lot of environmental benefits, which make the company more sustainable, should attract more customers and lead to more benefits like reduced transport. All these things should lead to increased sales and/or profit for both Amazon and the sellers, and outweigh the potential disadvantages of losing some sellers due to the programme.'

3 a) Hint: you need to describe what flow production is and explain why this is suitable for the products Raymer's Ltd. make.
E.g. in flow production, products are made continuously on a production line ***[1 mark]***. This is appropriate for Raymer's Ltd. as they are a baked-bean manufacturer so the products are likely to be identical / able to be mass produced ***[1 mark]***.

b) £1000 ***[1 mark]***

c) Break-even output = 5000 units ***[1 mark]***
Margin of safety = 9000 – 5000 = 4000 units ***[1 mark]***

d) How to grade your answer:
Level 0: Nothing worthy of credit. ***[No marks]***
Level 1: There is some attempt to describe how becoming a public limited company will impact Raymer's Ltd., but with little explanation of the advantages and disadvantages to the firm. ***[1 to 2 marks]***
Level 2: There is a good description of how becoming a public limited company will impact Raymer's Ltd., with some explanation of the advantages and disadvantages to the firm. ***[3 to 4 marks]***
Level 3: There is a detailed description of how becoming a public limited company will impact Raymer's Ltd., and a clear explanation of the advantages and disadvantages to the firm. ***[5 to 6 marks]***

Here are some points your answer may include:
Converting the company to a PLC means that the company will be able to raise much more capital through selling shares on the stock exchange. This could help to fund the diversification and expansion that the directors are planning. Growth may mean that the company makes more profit.
Converting to a PLC would make it possible for somebody to buy enough shares to take over the company, meaning the Raymer family could end up losing overall control. If the management were to change, the aims and objectives of the business might also change.
Converting to a PLC would mean Raymer's Ltd. had to publish its accounts each year. This could show competitors if the business is struggling, and so could affect their competitive advantage.

e) How to grade your answer:
Level 0: Nothing worthy of credit. ***[No marks]***

Level 1: Some attempt has been made to recommend which option Raymer's Ltd. should choose, but with little justification for why this should be done. ***[1 to 3 marks]***

Level 2: Some of the advantages and disadvantages of internal and external recruitment have been given, along with a recommendation of which option Raymer's Ltd. should choose. There is some reasoning to the recommendation, but it is lacking in detail or not fully justified. ***[4 to 6 marks]***

Level 3: There is a detailed explanation of the advantages and disadvantages of internal and external recruitment, with a well-reasoned and fully justified recommendation of what Raymer's Ltd. should do. ***[7 to 9 marks]***

Here are some points your answer may include:

Internal recruitment

Promoting and training existing staff would boost staff motivation. This is likely to make staff more productive as they will feel valued and so will want the business to do well. Therefore they will do their jobs as best they can to help that to happen. Increased productivity could lead to increased profits for the firm. More motivated staff are also more likely to stay with the firm. This could reduce Raymer's Ltd.'s recruitment and training costs in the future.

Recruiting internally would mean that Raymer's Ltd. save money on advertising the job externally.

It would also mean that the new supervisors already know a lot about the company, so they may need less training than an external recruit.

It would also mean that managers would know the candidate already, so they would have an idea of how suitable they were for the supervisor role. This may save time and money on recruiting an external candidate and then later finding out that they were not right for the job.

Recruiting internally would mean that Raymer's Ltd. have to recruit new factory workers to replace those that had been promoted to supervisor, but they would need to recruit new factory workers anyway as part of the expansion, so this is unlikely to cost too much more.

External recruitment

Another local food manufacturing company has recently gone out of business, so it's likely that there will be unemployed people in the area with supervisor experience that Raymer's Ltd could employ. These people might require less training than some of the existing factory workers.

Recruiting externally would also mean that the new staff may be able to share some of their ideas and experiences from other jobs and introduce more productive ways of working.

It's likely that recruiting externally would give the firm more candidates to choose from, so they would have more chance of finding someone that is well suited to the role.

However, recruiting externally may take more time, as well as money, than recruiting internally. This might be a problem if the firm wants to expand quickly and needs to find staff as quickly as possible.

You need to finish your answer with a conclusion recommending what you think Raymer's Ltd. should do — make sure you've looked thoroughly at all the information given. E.g. 'Raymer's Ltd. should fill the new supervisor positions by promoting existing factory workers. This will make staff feel more motivated, which may make them more productive and more likely to stay with the firm. It will also save money on recruitment and training costs.'

f) How to grade your answer:

Level 0: Nothing worthy of credit. ***[No marks]***

Level 1: The student has stated some likely impacts that the expansion would have had on the reputation of the business, but with little explanation of why these would happen. ***[1 to 3 marks]***

Level 2: The student has given a basic explanation of the likely impacts that the expansion would have had on the reputation of the business. There is some attempt to conclude which area will have the biggest impact on the business's reputation, but with little or no explanation to justify the conclusion. ***[4 to 6 marks]***

Level 3: The student has explained the likely impacts that the expansion would have had on the reputation of the business. There is a conclusion as to which area will have the biggest impact on the business's reputation, but the justification is lacking in detail. ***[7 to 9 marks]***

Level 4: There is a detailed and thorough analysis of the likely impacts that the expansion would have had on the reputation of the business. A conclusion has been made as to which area will have the biggest impact on the business's reputation, which has been fully justified using evidence. ***[10 to 12 marks]***

Here are some points your answer may include:

Customer service

The expansion meant that Raymer's Ltd. were able to take on some new customers. They agreed to use different labels for the supermarket's orders. Satisfying the customer's individual needs like this shows that Raymer's Ltd. were prepared to offer their customers a high level of customer service. This is likely to have improved the reputation of the business.

Raymer's Ltd. employed two customer service assistants. Having specific staff to deal with customer queries is likely to have improved customer service, as the staff are likely to have been trained so they had good product knowledge and knew how to resolve issues efficiently. This is likely to have made customers happy and improved the reputation of the business.

The percentage of products that were returned increased after the expansion. Supplying customers with poor quality products is a sign of poor customer service and is likely to have harmed the reputation of the business.

Consumer law

Consumer law states that a product must match its description and must be of satisfactory quality.

Following the expansion Raymer's Ltd. had a problem with products being returned because they contained a lower weight of produce than was stated on the label. This is breaking consumer law. They also had more products returned because of loose labels and dented tins. These factors mean that the products weren't of satisfactory quality, which again is breaking consumer law. Regularly breaking consumer law would have damaged the reputation of the business.

You need to finish your answer with a conclusion about whether the expansion's impact on customer service or on consumer law will have had the biggest impact on the reputation of the business — make sure you've looked thoroughly at all the information given. E.g. 'Although the expansion led to quality issues and situations where Raymer's Ltd. broke consumer law, the expansion meant that Raymer's Ltd. improved their customer service by employing extra customer service staff to specifically deal with customer queries. Even when customers did experience quality issues, the customer service staff may have ensured that problems were dealt with promptly, which would have had a positive effect on the reputation of the business.'

Practice Paper 2

Pages 170-185

1 a) B ***[1 mark]***

b) D ***[1 mark]***

c) D ***[1 mark]***

d) A ***[1 mark]***, E ***[1 mark]***

e) C ***[1 mark]***

f) Any two from: e.g. social media / websites / email / mobile apps / live chats / video calls ***[2 marks — 1 mark for each correct answer]***

g) Even though the cost of each product stays the same, the amount of money being spent on each product by customers will increase ***[1 mark]***. Therefore a smaller percentage of the money spent by customers will go towards making the product ***[1 mark]***, resulting in a higher gross profit margin ***[1 mark]***.

h) Hint: as well as giving two different ways in which a business may be damaged by breaking consumer law, you also need to make sure you explain both of your suggestions. Each suggestion is worth one mark and each explanation is also worth one mark.
Any two from: e.g. it may have to give a refund, replace or repair the faulty products ***[1 mark]***, which will cost the business money ***[1 mark]***. / It may have to defend itself in court ***[1 mark]***, which would cost money ***[1 mark]***. / The reputation of the business may be damaged ***[1 mark]***, which could lead to a drop in sales ***[1 mark]***.

i) total finance used = 2500 + 3500 + 1000 = £7000
% which is share capital = (2500 ÷ 7000) × 100
= **35.7%** (3 s.f.) ***[2 marks for correct answer, otherwise 1 mark for correctly calculating total finance]***

j) i) May net cash flow = –850 / (850) ***[1 mark]***

The net cash flow is the cash inflow minus the cash outflow, which is 350 – 1200 = –850.

ii) June cash inflow = 1000 ***[1 mark]***

To find this value, look back to the orders coming in in April — this is because these orders will be paid for after the 2 months of credit has passed. You could also find it by adding the net cash flow and cash outflow together, which is –300 + 1300 = 1000

k) Hint: there are lots of things you could say here, such as identifying customer needs, identifying gaps in the market, reducing risk or making informed decisions. You get one mark for stating one thing the business can use market research for, and an extra two marks for explaining how this will benefit the business.
E.g. market research can be used to identify customer needs ***[1 mark]***. By changing their marketing mix to satisfy these customer needs ***[1 mark]***, the business can increase sales ***[1 mark]***.

l) gross profit margin = (gross profit ÷ sales revenue) × 100
= (690 000 ÷ 3 000 000) × 100 = **23%**
[2 marks for correct answer, otherwise 1 mark for using the correct equation]

m) How to grade your answer:
Level 0: Nothing worthy of credit. ***[No marks]***
Level 1: There is some attempt to describe the purpose of having a business plan, but with little discussion of the consequences to a business. ***[1 to 2 marks]***
Level 2: There is a description of a number of different reasons for writing a business plan, with some discussion of the consequences to a business. ***[3 to 4 marks]***
Level 3: There is a detailed description of the different reasons for writing a business plan, and a clear discussion of the consequences to a business. ***[5 to 6 marks]***

Here are some points your answer may include:
Business plans can help an owner to set up a new business.
This is because they can show whether the business is likely to succeed, and the resources that will be needed to start it.
Business plans can help the owner to make business decisions.
This means that the owner can make decisions that are most likely to benefit the business, which will help it to grow, achieve its aims, and succeed.
Business plans can help the owner to set objectives.
This should help the owner to make decisions that will help the business to succeed.
Business plans can help convince a financial backer that a business idea is a sound investment.
This means it may be easier to raise the funds to start the business.
Business plans can show whether a business idea is likely to fail.
This means the owner can choose not to continue with the idea early, before they have wasted too much time or money.
Business plans can show how a business will be organised.
This means the owner can make sure they have the right resources, such as people and money, for the business to run.

2 a) the price ***[1 mark]***

b) E.g. customers will want lower prices ***[1 mark]***, and Heyshore Sports Ltd. have satisfied this objective by lowering their membership fees by 3% ***[1 mark]***.

c) E.g. questionnaires are cheaper than other methods ***[1 mark]***. They can be used to easily sample a large number of people ***[1 mark]***.

d) How to grade your answer:
Level 0: Nothing worthy of credit. ***[No marks]***
Level 1: Some attempt to describe the effect of changing the flyers on Heyshore Sports Ltd.'s sales but with little analysis of why the changes are likely to have this effect. ***[1 to 2 marks]***
Level 2: A number of effects of changing the flyers on Heyshore Sports Ltd.'s sales have been described, with some analysis of why the changes are likely to have these effects. ***[3 to 4 marks]***
Level 3: There is a detailed description of the effects that changing the flyers are likely to have on Heyshore Sports Ltd.'s sales, and a clear analysis of why the changes are likely to have these effects. ***[5 to 6 marks]***

Here are some points your answer may include:
Heyshore Sports Ltd.'s original flyers prioritised showing the appearance of the centre and price of membership.
However, the market research data shows that in 2012, only 5% of respondents said that the appearance of the centre is the most important aspect of a sports centre, and this had dropped to 3% by 2017.
In addition, only 25% of respondents said price was the most important aspect of a sports centre in 2012, and this had dropped to 16% by 2017.
The new flyers prioritise the choice of equipment and classes, by showing an image of the gym room and advertising the activity classes that people can take.
In 2017, the choice of equipment and classes was the most popular response for the most important aspect of a sports centre.
The percentage of respondents who said the choice of equipment and classes was most important increased from 37.5% to 42% between 2012 and 2017.
So by promoting the choice of equipment and classes at the sports centre, Heyshore Sports Ltd. are likely to appeal to more customers than they did before. So more customers are likely to sign up for membership and their sales are likely to increase.

e) How to grade your answer:
Level 0: Nothing worthy of credit. ***[No marks]***
Level 1: There is some attempt to recommend which improvement Heyshore Sports Ltd. should make, but with little explanation for why this should be done. ***[1 to 3 marks]***
Level 2: Some of the advantages and disadvantages of the different options for improving the sports centre have been given, along with a recommendation of what Heyshore Sports Ltd. should do. There is some reasoning to the recommendation, but it is lacking in detail or not fully explained. ***[4 to 6 marks]***

Level 3: There is a thorough description of the advantages and disadvantages of the different options for improving the sports centre, with a detailed recommendation of what Heyshore Sports Ltd. should do that has been fully explained. ***[7 to 9 marks]***

Here are some points your answer may include:

Option 1:

Heyshore Sports Ltd.'s customers are likely to be more satisfied if they buy more up-to-date exercise machines, since 42% of them said in the most recent survey that the choice of equipment and classes was the most important aspect to them. This is a greater percentage than those who said that the opening hours were the most important aspect to them (39%), so it may be more beneficial than extending the opening hours.

There has been an increase of 4.5% of customers saying that the choice of equipment and classes is the most important aspect to them since 2012, suggesting that the choice of equipment and classes has become more important to customers. Therefore buying more up-to-date exercise machines may also attract new customers.

However, the choice of equipment and classes may depend on other things, such as having a greater variety of machines, or more exercise classes. So buying up-to-date exercise machines may not have a big impact on the choice of equipment and classes that customers have.

It may also be costly for Heyshore Sports Ltd. to buy the up-to-date exercise machines, and they may have to provide training to staff and customers on how to use them safely.

Option 2:

In 2017, 39% of customers said that the opening hours were the most important aspect to them, so extending the opening hours may lead to more satisfied customers.

There has been an increase of 6.5% of customers saying that the opening hours are the most important aspect for them, since 2012. This is a greater increase than for the choice of equipment and classes, so the opening hours have become more important by a greater degree than the choice of equipment and classes. Therefore it may be more beneficial for Heyshore Sports Ltd. to extend the opening hours.

However, extending the opening hours may affect the running of the sports centre, since they will have to employ enough staff to cover the extra operating times.

It may also increase the costs, as they will have to pay for things such as wages and electricity for the extra hours the sports centre is open.

You need to finish your answer with a conclusion recommending which option you think would be better — make sure you've looked thoroughly at all the information given. E.g. 'Heyshore Sports Ltd. should buy up-to-date exercise machines. Although this may be costly, they are likely to have more satisfied customers and it won't affect the running of the sports centre.'

f) total profit of investment = 74 000 + 87 000 + 82 000 + 68 000 + 48 000 + 30 000 + 22 000 – 250 000 = £161 000
average annual profit = 161 000 ÷ 7 = £23 000
average rate of return = (average annual profit ÷ initial investment) × 100
average rate of return = (23 000 ÷ 250 000) × 100 = **9.2%**
[4 marks for correct answer, otherwise 1 mark for correct total profit of investment, 1 mark for correct average annual profit and 1 mark for using the correct equation to calculate the average rate of return]

g) How to grade your answer:

Level 0: Nothing worthy of credit. ***[No marks]***

Level 1: Some attempt has been made to recommend which option Heyshore Sports Ltd. should choose, but with little justification for why this is the better option. ***[1 to 3 marks]***

Level 2: Some of the advantages and disadvantages to stakeholders of each option have been given, along with a recommendation of which option Heyshore Sports Ltd. should choose. There is some reasoning to the recommendation, but it is lacking in detail or not fully justified. ***[4 to 6 marks]***

Level 3: There is a detailed explanation of the advantages and disadvantages to stakeholders of each option, with a well-reasoned and fully justified recommendation of what Heyshore Sports Ltd. should do. ***[7 to 9 marks]***

Here are some points your answer may include:

Option 1

The site is directly behind the sports centre, meaning it will be easy for the sports centre's customers to get to. This may increase customer satisfaction and help to attract new customers. Having all the facilities on one site may also make life easier for the employees and managers, so they will be happy.

The building work at the site is expected to be cheaper than the second option. Lower costs may mean that the expansion is more profitable. The potential to be more profitable is likely to please the business owners, as it may mean they get higher dividends. It is also likely to please employees and managers as it offers them greater job security and may lead to further pay rises for them.

However, Option 1 uses land which is currently a popular picnic spot. The local community may be unhappy with Heyshore Sports Ltd. if they use the land for sports facilities. Also, the local environmental group will be unhappy with Heyshore Sports Ltd. because using the meadowland would probably have a negative impact on the wildlife in the area. The environmental group may persuade other members of the community that Heyshore Sports Ltd. has made a bad decision, which may result in a loss of custom and revenue for the firm, which could lead to lower profits.

Option 2

The site is currently occupied by a derelict factory. Clearing the old factory and using the land for sports facilities might please the local community as it will be more visually appealing.

Using this site might also please the local environmental group as it's unlikely to cause as much harm to the wildlife in the area as using the area of meadowland would.

The site is twice the size of the first option, meaning it may be able to have more facilities and attract more customers. This could increase the revenue it generates, which may lead to higher profits. Higher profits are likely to lead to higher dividends for the owners, and greater job security and possible pay rises for employees and managers.

However, building work at the site is likely to be more expensive than on the meadowland. Heyshore Sports Ltd. may need to increase its membership fees to cover these greater costs, meaning customers may be unhappy. It may also need to use more profit to fund the expansion, meaning the owners will be unhappy as they may receive lower dividends.

The new facilities would be further away from the current sports centre than if Heyshore Sports Ltd. used the meadowland. This may mean that customers would be less willing to use the new facilities, and so Heyshore Sports Ltd. may not see a big increase in revenue as a result of the new facilities.

You need to finish your answer with a conclusion recommending which option you think would be better — make sure you've looked thoroughly at all the information given. E.g. 'Heyshore Sports Ltd. should build their new sports facilities on the meadowland behind the sports centre. Having all the sports facilities near to each other is likely to be more convenient for customers, which may increase customer satisfaction and may help to attract new customers when the new facilities are built, both of which could lead to increased profit for the business. Increased profits would please lots of Heyshore Sports Ltd.'s stakeholders, including the business owners, employees and managers.'

3 a) E.g. to increase market share *[1 mark]*, and to increase sales *[1 mark]*.

b) Working in a way that doesn't damage the Earth for future generations *[1 mark]*.

c) E.g. by promoting itself as a sustainable company, L'Oréal may be able to attract customers who are interested in protecting the environment *[1 mark]*, which may increase sales *[1 mark]*.

d) How to grade your answer:

Level 0: Nothing worthy of credit. ***[No marks]***

Level 1: There is some attempt to describe the impact that the factory could have on L'Oréal's costs, but with little explanation of how the factory may cause this impact. ***[1 to 2 marks]***

Level 2: There is a good description of the impact that the factory could have on L'Oréal's costs, with some explanation of how the factory may have caused this impact. ***[3 to 4 marks]***

Level 3: There is a detailed description of the impact that the factory could have on L'Oréal's costs, and a clear explanation of how the factory may have caused this impact. ***[5 to 6 marks]***

Here are some points your answer may include:

L'Oréal would have had initial costs of building the factory, as well as recruiting and training staff, so they may have seen their costs increase when they first set up the factory.

However, L'Oréal have set up a factory that is close to the market that they're targetting. This should have helped them to reduce transport costs related to getting the products from the factory to shops in India, as they won't have to travel as far.

L'Oréal use local suppliers for many of their raw materials, so their transport costs for getting these materials should be low.

By manufacturing products in India, L'Oréal may not have to pay tariffs to import products produced in other countries, so their costs will be decreased.

e) How to grade your answer:

Level 0: Nothing worthy of credit. ***[No marks]***

Level 1: There is a basic description of how L'Oréal might have invested in the design, but with little explanation of why they might have done this. ***[1 to 2 marks]***

Level 2: There is a detailed description of how L'Oréal might have invested in the design, with a detailed explanation of why they might have done this. ***[3 to 4 marks]***

Here is an answer you could have written:

L'Oréal may have invested in design to make sure the sachets had low manufacturing costs. This would mean L'Oréal could make more profit per product sold / could sell the sachets at a lower price, which would lead to increased sales.

Instead of writing about manufacturing costs, you could also have talked about other elements of the design mix. For example, L'Oréal may have invested in the changing the appearance of the product, or giving it a new function in order to appeal to a new market. Whatever you write about, make sure you explain the impact that the shampoo sachet design is likely to have on the business.

f) How to grade your answer:

Level 0: Nothing worthy of credit. ***[No marks]***

Level 1: Some impacts of the marketing strategy in India on L'Oréal have been stated, but with little explanation of whether L'Oréal will benefit overall. ***[1 to 3 marks]***

Level 2: There is a basic explanation of some of the impacts that the marketing strategy in India is likely to have on L'Oréal. There is some attempt to conclude whether L'Oréal will benefit from this strategy overall, but with little or no explanation to justify the conclusion. ***[4 to 6 marks]***

Level 3: There is an explanation of the impacts that the marketing strategy in India is likely to have on L'Oréal. There is a conclusion as to whether L'Oréal are likely to benefit from the strategy, but the justification is lacking in detail. ***[7 to 9 marks]***

Level 4: There is a detailed and thorough analysis of how the marketing strategy in India is likely to affect L'Oréal. A conclusion has been made as to whether L'Oréal are likely to benefit from the strategy, which has been fully justified using evidence. ***[10 to 12 marks]***

Here are some points your answer may include:

The marketing mix includes product, price, promotion and place.

L'Oréal have adjusted the products they sell in India in response to market research about customer needs in the country.

For example, L'Oréal sell shampoo in a larger range of sizes than they do in other countries, including in sachets for a single use, as market research showed these sachets sell well.

However, developing these products may be expensive, so may have increased L'Oréal's costs.

Manufacturing a larger range of products could increase L'Oréal's manufacturing costs, as they may have to invest in different machines that are capable of making all the products.

So increasing their product range could lead to lower profit per item sold.

These sachets allow L'Oréal to sell shampoo at low prices that people in less affluent areas can afford.

This means that customers in less affluent areas are more likely to buy L'Oréal's products.

This will increase L'Oréal's sales in India.

L'Oréal have used a price skimming strategy by pricing its products slightly above its competitors.

This should help to make L'Oréal seem like a luxury brand, and make it more desirable. This should help to increase demand.

By keeping the price in the same range as its competitors, L'Oréal shouldn't lose too much demand from people who would rather buy cheaper products.

L'Oréal have chosen to distribute their products through small, independent retailers, as well as larger chain stores.

As market research has shown that the majority of consumers in India use small retailers, this should mean that L'Oréal's products reach a large proportion of people in the country.

This means that more people are likely to buy their products, which should help to increase sales.

However, L'Oréal will have to organise delivery to a large number of small, individual stores. This could increase costs for L'Oréal.

L'Oréal are using e-commerce to target more rural areas of India. As people in these areas may be further from traditional retail outlets, it could open up a new market for L'Oréal, which will increase sales.

However, setting up e-commerce may be expensive, as it may require L'Oréal to recruit specialist website or app developers. It also means they will have to arrange delivery to individual customers all over the country, which is likely to be expensive. So using e-commerce is likely to increase costs.

You need to finish your answer with a conclusion about whether or not L'Oréal will have benefitted from its marketing strategy in India — make sure you've looked thoroughly at all the information given. E.g. 'Although adapting the marketing strategy is likely to increase costs for L'Oréal, for example by developing new products, L'Oréal have been able to target their strategy to respond to market research in India. This should mean that L'Oréal are likely to appeal more to consumers in the country. This should benefit L'Oréal by leading to increased sales, and increased profits overall.'

Glossary

advertising	Any message that a firm pays for, which promotes the firm or its products.
aim	An overall goal that a business is trying to achieve.
apprenticeship	A method of training where someone works and learns about their trade at the same time, and is awarded a qualification once they have gained a certain level of skill.
ARR	The average rate of return on an investment.
asset	A valuable item owned by a business, or money owed to the business.
authority	Power that people in an organisational structure have over the people in the layers below.
automation	When a machine works by itself, with little or no human involvement.
autonomy	Where a worker is given the freedom to make their own decisions in their job.
average unit cost	How much each product costs to make (calculated by dividing total costs by output).
award scheme	A method of motivation where employees are given recognition for hard work.
bar gate stock graph	A graph that is used to manage a business's stock levels.
batch production	A method of production in which a firm makes one batch of identical items at a time.
bonus	A lump sum added to an employee's pay, usually once a year.
Boston Matrix	A method used to analyse a business's product portfolio. Products are plotted according to their market share and how fast the market they are in is growing.
brand image	The impression that customers have of a company or the products it sells.
break-even level of output	The level of output at which a company's total revenue equals its total costs.
business plan	An outline of what a business will do and how it aims to do it.
capital	A company's wealth in the form of money or other assets.
capital employed	The total amount of money put into a business.
cash	The money a business can spend immediately.
cash flow	The flow of all money into and out of a business.
cash inflow	Money that flows into a business.
cash outflow	Money that flows out of a business.
census	An official survey of a country's population.
centralised organisation	An organisation with a structure in which all major decisions are made by one person or a few senior managers at the top of the organisational structure.
chain of command	The chain connecting directors to operatives in an organisational structure.
channel of distribution	The way that products get from a manufacturer to a consumer.
commission	Money paid to sales staff for every item they sell on top of their basic salary.
competitive pricing	A pricing strategy in which a firm charges similar prices to other firms.
competitor	A business which sells the same products in the same market as another business.
consumer	The person who uses a good or service.
contract of employment	A legal agreement between an employee and their employer about a job.
cost	An expense paid out to run a business.

cost-plus pricing	A pricing strategy in which the cost of making the product is increased by a certain percentage to work out the price the product will be sold for.
credit	An agreement that a customer will pay for something at a later date.
credit terms	The terms of a credit agreement that tell a customer how long they have to pay.
crowd funding	When a large number of people each contribute money towards funding a new business or a business idea.
current asset	An asset that doesn't last very long (e.g. cash).
current liability	A debt that a business has to pay off soon.
customer service	Any interaction a business has with its customers.
CV (curriculum vitae)	A summary of a person's personal details, skills, qualifications and interests.
decentralised organisation	An organisation with a structure in which the authority to make most decisions is shared between people at different layers of the organisational structure.
delayering	Removing layers of management from an organisation.
delegation	Passing tasks or responsibilities onto another person.
demand	How much of a product or service people will be willing to buy at a given price.
depreciation	The amount of value that assets have lost over time due to wear and tear.
design mix	The different elements of design needed to make a product successful, including its function, cost and aesthetics (appearance).
differentiation	Making products or services distinctive in the market.
diseconomy of scale	When growth leads to an increase in average unit cost.
diversification (business growth)	When two unrelated firms join together, allowing them to move into new markets.
dividend	A payment that a shareholder gets if the company makes a profit.
e-commerce	Buying and selling products on the internet.
e-tailer	A company that sells products online.
economy of scale	A reduction in average unit cost that comes from producing on a large scale.
enterprise	The process of identifying new business opportunities, and then taking advantage of them.
entrepreneur	Someone who takes on the risks of enterprise activity.
exchange rate	A value that tells you how much one unit of a currency costs in a different currency.
extension strategy	An action intended to extend the life of a product.
external expansion	When a company grows by merging with or taking over another firm (also called inorganic growth).
external recruitment	Where a business recruits new people from outside the business.
factor of production	A limited resource used to provide a good or service — e.g. land, labour, capital or enterprise.
fixed asset	An asset that a business keeps long-term or uses repeatedly — e.g. property, equipment, land, computers.
fixed cost	A cost that doesn't vary with output.
flat organisational structure	An organisational structure with very few layers.
flexible working	When working hours and patterns are adapted to suit the employee.
flow production	A method of production in which all products are identical and are made as quickly as possible.
formal training	A method of training which has a set plan with learning objectives and a schedule.

franchise	Where a company lets another firm sell its products or use its trademarks in return for a fee or a percentage of the profits.
freelance contract	When a self-employed person is recruited by a company on a temporary basis, usually to work on a specific project.
fringe benefit	Any reward for an employee that is not part of their regular income.
full-time staff	Employees that generally work 35-40 hours a week.
gap in the market	A customer need that isn't being met.
globalisation	The process by which businesses and countries around the world become more interconnected.
government grant	A sum of money which is given by the government and does not have to be repaid.
gross profit	The profit left over once the cost of sales has been taken away from the total revenue.
gross profit margin	The fraction of every pound spent by customers that doesn't go towards making the product.
hierarchical structure	An organisational structure with lots of layers.
hire purchase	When a firm purchases something by first paying a deposit and then paying the rest in instalments over a period of time, while they have use of the product.
human resources	The people needed to run a business, or the department that organises people in a firm.
income statement	A financial statement that shows how the income of a business has changed over a time period.
incorporated	A business that has its own legal identity.
induction training	A training program that introduces new employees to a workplace.
inflation	An increase in the price of goods and services.
informal training	A method of training which has no strict plan and is usually given by other workers.
insolvency	When a firm is unable to pay its debts.
interest rate	A value which shows the cost of borrowing money or the reward given for saving money.
internal expansion	When a company grows by expanding its own activities (also called organic growth).
internal recruitment	Where existing employees are recruited into new roles within a business.
investment	Money which is put into a business to make improvements in order to make the business more profitable.
job analysis	A process in which every little detail of a job is thought about.
job description	A written description of what a job involves.
job enrichment	Where a worker is given greater responsibility in their job.
job production	A method of production in which each product has a unique design based on the customer's specification.
job rotation	Where a worker is occasionally moved from one job to another.
job share	Where the work and pay of one full-time job is shared between two people.
just-in-case (JIC)	A method used in stock management in which buffer stocks of items are kept at every stage of the production process.
just-in-time (JIT)	A method used in production or stock management in which stock levels are kept at a bare minimum — products are made just in time for delivery to customers.
lean production	A production strategy that aims to use as few resources as possible and to have as little waste as possible.
limited liability	Where the owners of a business are not legally responsible for all the debts a business has.
liquidity	How easily an asset can be converted into money.

loan	A long-term source of money that must be paid back to the lender.
logistics	Getting goods or services from one part of the supply chain to another.
long-term liability	A debt that a business has to pay off over a long period of time.
loss	Where the total costs for a company over a period of time are greater than its revenue.
loss leader pricing	A pricing strategy in which the price of a product is set below cost.
m-commerce	When goods and services are bought on the internet using a wireless mobile device, such as a smartphone or tablet.
margin of safety	The gap between current level of output and the break-even level of output.
market	A place where goods are traded between customers and suppliers, trade in a particular type of product or the potential customers for a product.
market map	A diagram showing some of the features of a market.
market research	When a business investigates different aspects of a market, e.g. demand for a product, the competition and the target market.
market share	The proportion of total sales within a market that is controlled by a business.
market size	The number of individuals (including companies) within a market that are potential buyers and sellers of products, or the total value of products in the market.
marketing mix	The four elements that must be considered for good marketing: product, price, promotion and place.
mass market	A large group of potential customers for a product.
merger	When two companies join together to form a new, larger firm.
mortgage	A loan used to finance buying property.
multinational	A single business that operates in more than one country.
net profit	The profit left over when all costs are taken into account.
net profit margin	The fraction of every pound spent by customers that the company gets to keep.
niche market	A small and specialised group of potential customers for a product.
objective	A measurable step that a business will set in order to work towards an aim.
obsolete	When a product is no longer used, usually because it has become out-dated and has been replaced by something else.
off-the-job training	A method of training in which an employee learns away from their workplace.
on-the-job training	A method of training in which an employee is shown how to do their job by another employee and then given the opportunity to practise.
operating profit	The money left over after paying all the costs of running the business.
opportunity cost	The value of something that's given up in order to do something else.
organic growth	When a company grows by expanding its own activities (also called internal expansion).
outsourcing	When a business pays another firm to carry out tasks it could do itself.
overdraft	When more money is taken out of a bank account than has been paid into it.
part-time staff	Employees that generally work 10-30 hours a week.
partnership	A business ownership structure in which a small number of people (usually between 2 and 20) own an unincorporated company.
performance review	A system for assessing an employee's progress and helping them to develop.
permanent contract	A contract of employment that has no end date.

person specification	A list of the qualifications, experience, skills and attitudes a person needs for a particular job.
pressure group	An organisation that tries to influence what people think about a certain subject.
price penetration	A pricing strategy in which a firm charges a very low price for a product when it is new.
price skimming	A pricing strategy in which a firm charges a high price for a product to begin with.
primary research	Market research that involves getting information from customers or potential customers.
private limited company	A business ownership structure that is incorporated and has shares, but the shares can only be sold with the agreement of all the shareholders.
procurement	The act of finding and buying things that a business needs from outside of the business.
product life cycle	The different stages that a product goes through over time.
product portfolio	The range of different products that a business sells.
productivity	How many products are made in a certain amount of time or for a certain amount of money.
profit	The difference between revenue and costs over a period of time.
promotion	When an employee is given a higher status or position within a firm.
promotional mix	The combination of different promotional methods a firm uses to promote a product.
promotional pricing	When products are put on offer so that their average unit price is reduced for a limited period of time.
public limited company	A business ownership structure that is incorporated and has shares that can be bought and sold by anyone.
public relations (PR)	Business activities which involve communicating with the media in an attempt to promote a firm or its products to the public.
purchasing economy of scale	A reduction in average unit cost that comes from a firm being offered a lower unit cost from suppliers when it buys its supplies in bulk.
qualitative information	Information that involves people's feelings or opinions.
quality assurance	A way of maintaining quality by checking that quality standards are being met throughout each process involved in making a product.
quality control	A way of maintaining quality by checking products for faults at certain stages during the production process.
quantitative information	Information that can be measured or reduced to a number.
remote working	When an employee works in a location away from their employer's offices, e.g. at home.
remuneration	Payment to an employee for the work they have done for an employer.
retailer	A business that sells products to consumers.
retained profit	Profit that is put back into the business.
revenue	The income earned by a business in a given time period.
salary	A fixed payment that is made to employees every month.
sales process	A series of steps for finding and selling to customers, as well as providing customer service.
sales promotion	A short-term method used to boost a firm's sales, e.g. 2 for 1 offers.
secondary research	Market research that involves looking at data from outside the business, e.g. market reports.
segmentation	When people within a market are divided into different groups.
self-employed	When someone owns their own business, and takes their income from the profits of the firm.
self-learning	Where an employee seeks out their own training and development.
share	A unit of ownership in a company. Owners of shares can share in the profits of the company.

share capital	Money gained through issuing shares in the company.
sole trader	A business ownership structure where one person owns an unincorporated company.
span of control	The number of workers who report to one manager in a hierarchy.
sponsorship	A method of promotion in which a business gives money to an organisation or event. In return the organisation or event displays the business's name.
staff retention	When a business keeps its staff.
stakeholder	Any individual or group of people that is affected by a business.
start-up capital	The money or assets needed to set up a business.
statement of financial position	A financial statement that records a business's assets and liabilities at a particular moment in time.
stock market	A market where shares of public limited companies can be bought and sold.
subordinate	Someone below another person in an organisational structure.
supply chain	The group of firms that are involved in all the various processes required to make a finished product or service available to the customer.
sustainability	Working in a way that doesn't damage the Earth for future generations.
takeover	When an existing business expands by buying more than half the shares in another firm.
tall organisational structure	An organisational hierarchy with lots of layers.
tariff	A tax on goods that are being imported or exported.
technical economy of scale	A reduction in average unit cost that comes from a firm being able to afford more advanced machinery or use larger premises than a smaller firm.
telesales	Selling products to consumers via phone.
temporary contract	A contract of employment that is only for a fixed period of time.
total cost	The fixed and variable costs for a business added together.
total quality management (TQM)	A strategy that aims to make quality the responsibility of every employee in an organisation.
trade bloc	A group of countries that has few or no trade barriers between them.
trade credit	When a businesses give firms time to pay for certain purchases.
unincorporated	A business that doesn't have its own legal identity.
unique selling point (USP)	This is some feature that makes a product different from its competitors.
unlimited liability	Where the owners of a business are legally responsible for all the debts a business has.
variable cost	A cost that increases as a firm expands output.
venture capital	Money raised through selling shares to individuals or businesses who specialise in giving finance to new or expanding small firms.
viral advertising	When adverts are shared and viewed many (perhaps millions of) times in a short time period, often via social media.
vocational qualification	A qualification that is specific to a certain job.
wage	Payment that is usually made to employees weekly or monthly.
wholesaler	A business that buys products in bulk and stores them in a warehouse.
working capital	The money available for the day-to-day operating of the business.
zero hour contract	A contract of employment which means the employer doesn't have to offer the employee any work at all and the employee doesn't have to accept any work that is offered to them.

Index

Index

Index